# Russian Antisemitism, Pamyat, and the Demonology of Zionism

## Studies in Antisemitism
*Series Editor* Yehuda Bauer
Chairman, Vidal Sassoon International Center for the Study of Antisemitism
The Hebrew University of Jerusalem

**Studies in Antisemitism** brings together in one series major worldwide research on this complex phenomenon from which the student and decision-maker as well as the general public may learn. The studies cover antisemitism, ancient and modern, from a broad range of perspectives: historical, religious, political, cultural, social, psychological and economic.

**Volume 1**
The Catholic Church and Antisemitism
Poland, 1933–1939
*Ronald Modras*

**Volume 2**
Russian Antisemitism, Pamyat, and the Demonology of Zionism
*William Korey*

This book is part of a series. The publisher will accept continuation orders which may be cancelled at any time, and which provide for automatic billing and shipping of each title in the series upon publication. Please write for details.

William Korey

# Russian Antisemitism, Pamyat, and the Demonology of Zionism

Published for the
Vidal Sassoon International Center
for the Study of Antisemitism (SICSA)
The Hebrew University of Jerusalem

by

**harwood academic publishers**
Australia•Austria•Belgium•China•France•Germany•India
Japan•Luxembourg•Malaysia•Netherlands•Russia•Singapore
Switzerland•Thailand•United Kingdom•United States

COPYRIGHT © 1995 BY
  Harwood Academic Publishers GmbH
  All rights reserved.

HARWOOD ACADEMIC PUBLISHERS
Poststrasse 22
7000 Chur
Switzerland

BRITISH LIBRARY CATALOGUING IN PUBLICATION DATA
Korey, William
  Russian Antisemitism, Pamyat, and the
  Demonology of Zionism. - (Studies in
  Antisemitism, ISSN 1023-6163; Vol.2)
  I. Title II. Series
  305.8924047

ISBN 3-7186-5740-6 (hardcover)
ISBN 3-7186-5742-2 (softcover)


COVER DESIGN BY
  Louise Burston

EDITING AND COMPOSITION
  Alifa Saadya








No part of this book may be reproduced or utilized in any form or by any means, electronic or mechanical, including photocopying and recording, or by any information storage or retrieval system, without permission in writing from the publisher. Printed in Singapore.

Dedicated to

Rachel and Benjamin

## Contents

| | | |
|---|---|---|
| Preface | | ix |
| 1. | Historical Background | 1 |
| 2. | Emergence of the Demonology of Zionism | 13 |
| 3. | Demonology of Zionism: International Dimension | 30 |
| 4. | Zionism–"The Greatest Evil on Earth" | 46 |
| 5. | The Freemason Component | 60 |
| 6. | Demonology: A Concern to the Kremlin? | 74 |
| 7. | Legitimation through the Jewish Anti-Zionist Committee | 86 |
| 8. | Glasnost and the Demonology of Zionism | 115 |
| 9. | Political Uses of the Demonology of Zionism | 147 |
| 10. | Resisting the Demonology | 166 |
| 11. | The Malady Lingers On... and On | 189 |
| Epilogue | | 219 |
| Index | | 231 |

# Preface

The emergence in Russia of the chauvinist antisemitic movement, Pamyat in 1987 has startled Western society even as it has stirred deep fears and anxiety among Jews and democratic forces within Russia. How could a supposedly Communist society whose founder, V. I. Lenin, had railed against racism and bigotry, give birth to a proto-fascist ideology and organization?

This study seeks to respond to the understandable, if provocative, query. The roots of Pamyat's ideology are traced to the tsarist Black Hundreds in the early part of the twentieth century, to certain aspects of later Stalinism and, most especially, to a virulent official Judeophobic propaganda campaign, masquerading as anti-Zionism, from 1967 to 1986.

What emerged in this centrally-directed campaign which saturated the public media was the demonization of Zionism, ascribing to the historic and modern Jewish drive for self-identity an evil and corrupting essence. Zionism was equated on an official level with every form of moral outrage and, at the same time, was applied in a rather unsubtle manner to Jews and Jewishness.

Analysis would demonstrate that the notorious tsarist forgery, the *Protocols of the Elders of Zion,* shielded only by a Leninist linguistic gloss, stood at the core of the propaganda drive. That drive was extended in every direction—internationally, to intimidate the West—and, internally, to Jews themselves in order to silence any aspiration for self-identity.

Although the antisemitic campaign was finally halted at the state level by Mikhail Gorbachev, the social ground had already been fertilized for a populist and chauvinist Pamyat movement, emerging in 1987, which could exploit the much freer atmosphere of glasnost to pursue a program of hate. The earlier ideological roots could now flourish openly. Zionism, perceived as the embodiment of satanism, was to become Pamyat's principal target.

How the new and publicly blatant antisemitism functioned and, more importantly, how it was bolstered by the entrenched nationalist and communist apparatus in political and literary life throughout the glasnost era and beyond constitute the heart of this inquiry. To the extent that these nationalist and chauvinist forces remain throbbing, vital elements in contemporary Russian society, they inevitably invite a profound sense of concern among Jews and in the civilized community generally. Documentation provided here, hopefully, can serve to reinforce that concern.

The Vidal Sassoon International Center for the Study of Antisemitism at the Hebrew University of Jerusalem has contributed significantly to making this work possible. Important additional assistance has been provided by the Sonya Staff Foundation. Valuable support was extended by the Joyce Mertz-Gilmore Foundation. In making travel possible to complete research findings, the Memorial Foundation for Jewish Culture was especially helpful.

The author is deeply appreciative for the constant encouragement of his wife, Esther. He is also deeply indebted to Seymour Reich, former president of B'nai B'rith, and to James Rapp for various types of support. Gerald Baumgarten of the Anti-Defamation League was a continuous source of needed documentation. Excellent secretarial and typing services were rendered by Eva Owen. Finally, I am very much indebted to Alifa Saadya for her extensive technical assistance in the production of this book.

# Chapter 1

# Historical Background

Contemporary Pamyat proudly traces its lineage and heritage to the Union of Russian People, founded in November 1905. Thus, at a meeting in Moscow on June 6, 1990 of a Pamyat group called the "People's Russian Orthodox Movement," the speaker, Aleksandr Kulakov, told seven hundred participants that "we consider ourselves the spiritual successors of the Union of Russian People."[1] Analysis of the Union and its aims, scarcely discussed in western circles, aside from specialists on tsarist history, can serve as a useful point of departure for an inquiry into Pamyat.

Like the latter, the Union emerged into public view during a grave political and economic crisis in the Russian Empire which had weakened the power and authority of tsarism in the wake of defeat during the 1904–05 Russo-Japanese War. Its primary purpose, as perceived by its leaders, was to resist the unleashed wave of reform and revolution and preserve intact the institutions of the monarchy, Russian Orthodoxy, and the empire.

The Union's internal character and tactics were quite distinctive, indeed unique. Until then, tsarism had largely preserved itself along with its handmaidens—the Church and an empire of subjugated nations—by the force of imperial arms and armies. But a defeated Russian army, virtually

---

[1] Notes were made available by an activist in the Moscow Jewish community who prefers to remain anonymous. Aleksandr Shmukler, later a leader of VAAD, vouched for the report's accuracy. For a revealing interview with Kulakov conducted by Leonid Kelbert, see "The Protocols of Pamyat," *Hadassah Magazine,* 72, no. 6 (February 1991): 17–21.

in self-dissolution, made this technique uncertain. In the absence of other available means, populism—marked by a profound, xenophobic chauvinism, constituted the essence of the means by which the Union of Russian People attempted to support law and order, Throne and Altar.

What had been brought onto the historical scene, for both Russia and Europe generally, was a new style of right wing politics involving mass activity.[2] It was perhaps quite appropriate to dub the Union's role, as a prominent European history work would note, as "Europe's first fascist organization."[3] One of the Union's reactionary leaders, V. M. Purishkevich, was referred to by his Soviet biographer as a "fascist" who had set an authentic style for a movement that would blossom forth in Europe a decade later.[4] Some historians have suggested that the Union exerted a "tangible and substantial impact" upon German National Socialism through Baltic and Russian emigrés who found themselves in Germany after World War I.[5]

Attributes of the fascism of the twenties and thirties were not uncommon for the Union, including street violence, paramilitary formations wearing special dress (for example, the "Yellow Shirts" in Odessa), personal assaults upon enemies (even murders), distribution of literature designed to stir envy and hate, marches and demonstrations. At its ideological core stood a vicious antisemitism. Jews were seen as dominating the press, banking and, through the Masonic societies, all key spheres of Russian life and influencing prominent liberal government ministers. Count Sergei Witte was especially singled out as a dupe of Jews and Masons. The Union denounced him as a traitor for "extorting" the democratic October Manifesto from Tsar Nicholas II, and for imposing upon the country a "Judeo-Masonic Constitution."[6]

Equality of ethnic rights, as elaborated by the Constitution of 1905,

---

[2] Hans Rogger, *Jewish Policies and Right-Wing Politics in Imperial Russia* (Berkeley: University of California, 1986), 188–242.

[3] G. Bruun and V. S. Mamatey, *The World in the 20th Century* (Boston: D. C. Heath, 1962), 891.

[4] S. B. Liubosh, *Russkii Fashist Vladimir Purishkevich* (Leningrad: Byloe Publishing House, 1925), 29.

[5] Walter Z. Laqueur, *Russia and Germany* (London: Weidenfeld and Nicholson, 1965), 50–53.

[6] Rogger, *Jewish Policies,* 219, 214.

was regarded as anathema. Instead, what was sought was the severest restriction upon Jews and their total elimination from the capitalist economy. Governmental legislation, economic boycott and, if necessary, expulsion to Palestine was proposed in order to achieve this. Not surprisingly, the Union was a major backer of the notorious blood libel trial of Mendel Beiliss.[7]

Targets of the Union extended to Masons, liberals, capitalists, foreigners, and westerners. They were seen as alien to Russian nationality and its tradition. But all these "cosmopolitan" elements were understood as only instruments of Jews. Antisemitism was the cornerstone of the systemic beliefs of the Union of Russian People. Its followers, along with the members of other small groups of rightist antisemites were dubbed the "Black Hundreds." Not accidentally, when *Pravda* finally acknowledged the existence of antisemitism in the Soviet Union—which didn't occur until July 1990—it referred to Pamyat and other antisemites by the then almost forgotten phrase, "Black Hundreds."[8]

While the Union's chairman was a physician, Dr. A. I. Dubrovin, and his two deputies were a nobleman-landowner (Purishkevich), and an engineer, the majority of the membership ranged from petty-bourgeois elements to unemployed workers, peasants, skilled proletarians, and professionals. Never before had the reactionary right in Russia taken on such an all-class character. Estimates place its size in Moscow alone as 40,000, while overall membership figures—given by the Union—range from 600,000 to 3 million, although a hostile source estimated the membership as only 10–20,000.[9] Even that low figure was significant for the times.

The Union had received financial assistance from officials within the Ministry of Interior. It also had access to the printing presses of the police department, which enabled it to conduct large-scale propaganda campaigns against liberals, democrats and, especially Jews. At the Union's disposal was an underground fighting organization composed of minor police agents, governmental employees, and criminal elements. They often stirred up armed attacks on Jews, while the Union's links to

---

[7] Ibid., 220; and Maurice Samuel, *Blood Accusation: The Strange History of the Beiliss Case* (New York: Alfred A. Knopf, 1966), 19–20.

[8] *Pravda*, 22 July 1990.

[9] Rogger, *Jewish Policies,* 216, 266, fn. 46.

high officials, particularly in the Ministry of Interior, enabled them to acquire a secure immunity.

Interwoven into the Union's belief system was a set of ideas that found expression in the historic forgery, the *Protocols of the Elders of Zion,* which was first published in 1903 by the reactionary tsarist publicist, Pavel Krushevan. Fabricated by a tsarist police agent in Paris who drew upon an obscure work written in the France of Louis Napoleon and totally unrelated to Jews, the *Protocols* took on a life of its own.[10] They were alleged to be the secret decisions taken by the "Elders of Zion," at the first Zionist Congress held in Basel in 1897.

Five major themes predominate in the notorious forgery: 1) international Jewry, or Zionism, through the "Chosen People" concept, aspires to world domination; 2) that aspiration is to be achieved through guile, cunning and conspiratorial devices which will deceive the "goyim cattle" (the language of the *Protocols*) who are easily manipulated; 3) an especially powerful mechanism for achieving world domination is Jewish control over the world banking system whereby "all the goyim" will begin "to pay us the tribute of subjects"; 4) equally crucial as a mechanism of control is the ownership of the press, the seizure of which by Jews or Zionists will enable them to acquire "the power to influence while remaining...in the shade"; and 5) the deception is maximized by infiltration and manipulation of Masonic lodges which will "throw dust in the eyes of their fellows."[11]

Only fifteen years later did the *Protocols* exert a powerful popular impact. It was used extensively during the Civil War in 1918–20 in the Ukraine, when 30,000 Jews were massacred and twenty-eight percent of Jewish homes were destroyed.[12] This was the largest pogrom in Russian

---

[10] For an authoritative analysis, see Norman Cohn, *Warrant for Genocide* (New York: Harper and Row, 1967); John S. Curtiss, *An Appraisal of the Protocols of Zion* (New York: AMS Press, 1942). It is summarized in Senate, Senator Harley M. Kilgore, "A Cruel and Vicious Forgery," Congressional Record, 1 June 1948, 6788–6971.

[11] An early English translation, published in the United States was called *The Protocols of the Wise Men of Zion* (New York: Beckwith Co., 1920). For a summary of the major elements of the Protocols, see William Korey, "The Kremlin's Anti-Semitism," *Midstream,* 24, no. 8 (October 1978): 8.

[12] Salo W. Baron, *The Russian Jew Under Tsars and Soviets* (New York: Macmillan, 1964), 220–21.

history since the massacre of Jews in the Polish Ukraine during the Bogdan Khmelnitsky uprising in the middle of the seventeenth century. Later, the *Protocols* became the solid basis for Adolf Hitler's *Mein Kampf* and his "Final Solution."[13]

The "Black Hundreds," of course, did not spring full-blown from the revolutionary developments and political uncertainties in Russia in the first decade of the twentieth century. The powerful and omnipresent Russian Orthodox Church which had been intimately linked to the tsarist state, had long identified the Jews as "enemies of Christ." When Tsarina Elizaveta in the mid-eighteenth century was asked to invite Jews into the Empire in order to develop greater commerce, she refused saying, "from the enemies of Christ, I wish neither gain nor profit."[14] Only in consequence of the three partitions of Poland in which Tsarina Catherine the Great joined Prussia and Austria, did vast numbers of Jews become part of the Empire. The bulk were forced to live in the Pale of Settlement, prevented from owning land, subjected to a *numerus clausus* in higher education and a host of discriminatory barriers.

Periodic pogroms (the noun is derived from the Russian verb *pogromit,* which means "to destroy" or "to ruin") constituted a signal tsarist contribution to international discourse. Elizavetgrad, a Ukrainian town of 32,000 was the starting point on April 15, 1881.[15] Prompted by emissaries from the St. Petersburg aristocracy calling for the "people's wrath" to "be vented on the Jews," the peasants unleashed violence against the Jews in the small city. A wave of killings, rape, and pillage spread quickly to hundreds of other towns and then to the large cities of Berdichev and Kiev. By the end of the year it reached Warsaw, an outpost of

---

[12] Salo W. Baron, *The Russian Jew Under Tsars and Soviets* (New York: Macmillan, 1964), 220–21.

[13] Lucy S. Dawidowicz, *The War Against the Jews, 1933–1945* (New York: Holt, Rinehart and Winston, 1975), 16, 20.

[14] Zvi Gitelman, *A Century of Ambivalence, the Jews of Russia and the Soviet Union* (New York: Schocken, 1988), xiv.

[15] For background, see Stephen M. Berk, *Year of Crisis, Year of Hope: Russian Jewry and the Pogroms of 1881–82* (Westport: Greenwood Press, 1985); and Irwin M. Aronson, *Troubled Waters, the Origins of the 1881 Anti-Jewish Pogroms in Russia* (Pittsburgh: University of Pittsburgh, 1990).

100,000 were ruined economically and Jewish property valued at $80 million was destroyed. A contemporary Russian writer described the trauma as "unending torture."[16] It triggered the mass emigration of Jews to the West.

Like many other oppressors before and after them, the tsarist authorities blamed the victims for the violence. The Minister of Interior, Count Nikolai P. Ignatyev, in a memorandum to Tsar Alexander III on August 22, 1881, blamed the pogroms upon "the Jews' injurious activities" directed against the peasantry.[17] Hostility toward Jews was not restricted to the tsarist aristocracy and the peasantry. The radical populist intellectuals comprising the Narodnaia Volia urged on the pogromists on grounds that the "kikes...rob and cheat" the peasant and "drink his blood."[18]

The depth of popular anti-Jewish sentiment, while broadly surmised, cannot be known with precision. Negative perceptions about Jews were integral to Russian society. A tsarist Commission, comprised of moderates, after five years of lengthy interviews and in-depth study of the Jewish problem, concluded in 1888 that Jews have a tendency to "shirk state obligations" and to avoid "physical manual labor."[19]

According to the fairly liberal Commission: "The passion for acquisition and money-grubbing is inherent in the Jew from the day of his birth; it is characteristic of the Semitic race, manifest from almost the first pages of the Bible."[20]

Such popular views provided the fertile soil for nourishing the ideas in the *Protocols of the Elders of Zion*. Popular antisemitism in tsarist Russia made possible the extraordinary blood libel trial, the Beiliss Case, in Kiev in 1911–12.[21] Clearly, pogromist ideology was part of the baggage the Russians carried with them into the twentieth century.

---

[16] William Korey, "From Russia with Hate, A Bitter Centennial," *Moment*, September 1982, 43.
[17] Ibid.
[18] Lucy S. Dawidowicz, ed., *The Golden Tradition: Jewish Life and Thought in Eastern Europe* (New York: Holt, Rinehart and Winston, 1967), 406.
[19] Jesse D. Clarkson, *A History of Russia* (New York: Random House, 1961), 333–35.
[20] Ibid., 333.
[21] Samuel, *Blood Accusation*, 15–246.

Vladimir Ilyich Lenin, vigorously fought pogromist attitudes. While seeking to make antisemitism and pogroms a capital offense, he publicly denounced Judeophobia. "Shame on those who foment hatred toward the Jews," he cried.[22] The vicious stereotyping of Jews persisted even as the Bolshevik leadership in the 1920s tried to eradicate it. The populist Kronstadt uprising against Soviet power in 1921 was based in part upon peasant attitudes toward the "cursed domination" of Jews.[23] In November 1926, the Chairman of the Central Committee of the Soviet regime acknowledged that Soviet white collar workers were "more anti-Semitic today than...under Tsarism."[24] An official survey of antisemitism among trade union members conducted in February 1929 in Moscow found that "anti-Semitic feeling among workers is spreading chiefly in the backward sections of the working class that have close ties with the peasantry...."[25] At the heart of the prejudice, as it had been in the 1880s and afterwards, was "talk of Jewish domination."[26]

The 1950–51 Harvard Project on the Soviet Social System was based on interviews with Soviet refugees in the United States, people who had defected or had been captured during World War II or who had fled during 1946–50.[27] The interviews reflected tremendous hostility towards Jews across the board, though the antisemitism of the Ukrainian refugee population was especially severe.[28] Most of those surveyed agreed that Jews occupied a "privileged and favored position" in Soviet society; that they were "business-and-money-minded;" that they were "clannish," "aggressive" and "pushy;" that they don't like to work hard and refuse to serve in the front lines of the armed forces.[29] Despite two to three decades of Bolshevik rule, attitudes of the 1880s had remained

---

[22] Vladimir I. Lenin, *Collected Works,* 4th ed. (Moscow: State Publishers, 1965) (English), vol. 29, 253.
[23] Paul Avrich, *Kronstadt 1921* (Princeton: Princeton University, 1970), 178–80.
[24] William Korey, *The Soviet Cage: Anti-Semitism in Russia* (New York: Viking, 1973), 13.
[25] *Pravda,* 19 February 1929.
[26] Ibid.
[27] Raymond A. Bauer, Alex Inkeles, and Clyde Kluckhohn, *How the Soviet System Works* (Cambridge: Harvard University, 1956).
[28] Korey, *Soviet Cage,* 4–11.
[29] Ibid., 5.

unchanged.

Prejudice reached especially intense levels during the "anti-cosmopolitan" campaign of 1949–53, climaxed by the notorious "Doctors' Plot." Ilya Ehrenburg, otherwise an apologist for Stalin's rule, was so shocked by the "ugly survival" of antisemitism that he was convinced "that to cleanse minds of age-old prejudices is going to take a very long time."[30] Had Stalin not died on March 5, 1953, there was certain to be "only one sequel: a nation-wide pogrom," according to Isaac Deutscher, his distinguished British biographer.[31]

Poet Yevgeny Yevtushenko raised the issue in a major way with his "Babi Yar" in 1961.[32] He bemoaned how "the Russian people were blemished" by antisemitism and how the Communist song, *Internationale*, can "thunder forth" only when Jew-hatred is "buried for good." When Nikita Khrushchev objected to Yevtushenko raising the shameful issue, the poet would not be silenced. The popular hate must be faced, he said, for "we cannot go forward to communism with such a heavy load as Judeophobia."[33]

"Judeophobia" had already become part of official policy by the end of the 1930s. According to Hitler, Stalin told Nazi Foreign Minister Joachim von Ribbentrop in the fall of 1939 that he would oust Soviet Jews from leading positions the moment he had a sufficient number of qualified non-Jews with whom to replace them.[34] Stalin's promise was more than a mere diplomatic gesture to placate his new racist ally. In 1942, one year after the Nazi invasion of Russia, the Soviet authorities handed down a secret order establishing quotas for Jews in particularly prominent posts.[35]

According to Milovan Djilas, Stalin in 1946 boasted to him that "in our

---

[30] Ilya Ehrenburg, *Post-War Years, 1945–54* (Cleveland: World Publishing Co., 1967), 131, 298.

[31] Isaac Deutscher, *Stalin,* 2nd ed., (New York: Oxford University Press, 1967), 627.

[32] William Korey, "A Soviet Poet as Rebel," *The New Republic,* 8 January 1962.

[33] "Russian Art and Anti-Semitism: Two Documents," *Commentary,* December 1963, 434.

[34] Henry Picker, *Hitlers Gespräche in Führerhaupt-quartier, 1941–42,* 2nd ed. (Stuttgart: Seewald, 1976), 472.

[35] John Armstrong, *The Politics of Totalitarianism* (New York: Random House, 1961), 154.

*Historical Background* 9

Central Committee there are no Jews!"[36] Stalin's daughter revealed that after the war, "in the enrollment at the university and in all types of employment, preference was given to Russians. For the Jews, a percentage quota, (as had been the case during the tsarist era) was, in essence, reinstated.[37]

The government's policy of discrimination against Jews as individuals was largely a function of two internal developments in the Soviet Union at the time: deepening Russian nationalism (bordering on xenophobia) and the formation of a totalitarian structure.[38] The new Russian nationalism was a dominant characteristic of the struggle against the Old Guard's "internationalism." Suspicion fell equally upon those suspected of harboring sympathies with various non-Russian nationalities of the USSR and those linked, in one way or another, with the West.

"Cosmopolitanism" became the Aesopian term used extensively beginning in 1948, to mark postwar antisemitism.[39] The media drive was directed against "cosmopolitans"—those without genuine roots in Russian soil, those without spiritual "passports," those not really "indigenous." Marxism was turned on its head. If initially "internationalism"—not national narrowness—was perceived as valuable for a socialist future, now it or its twin, cosmopolitanism, was denigrated and repudiated.

Antisemitism went hand in hand with official Russian national chauvinism, as it had during the tsarist era, at least since the reign of Nicholas I. Certainly, it was not accidental that official antisemitism made its first, if then only momentary, appearance at the time, in 1926, when Stalinist forces were attempting to inculcate a national pride in the doctrine of "socialism in one country."[40] Chauvinism catered to and fed upon popular prejudices. The World War II years were replete with examples of an unleashed bigotry linked to nationalist fervor. Many of the partisan

---

[36] Milovan Djilas, *Conversations with Stalin* (New York: Harcourt, Brace and World, 1962), 154.

[37] Svetlana Alliluyeva, *Only One Year* (New York: Harper and Row, 1969), 153.

[38] Korey, *Soviet Cage*, 68–70.

[39] Yehoshua Gilboa, *The Black Years of Soviet Jewry, 1939–1953* (Boston: Little, Brown, 1971), 146–225.

[40] Isaac Deutscher, *The Prophet Unarmed: Trotsky, 1921–29* (London: Oxford University Press, 1959), 257–58.

units for example, were riddled with antisemitism.[41]

That the Jews were particularly suspect in a totalitarian structure impregnated with a distinct chauvinist character is not surprising, for they indeed were a minority with an international tradition and a worldwide religion. Jews everywhere had cultural, emotional and even family ties that transcended national boundaries.

Furthermore, Hannah Arendt has noted that totalitarianism requires an "objective enemy" who, like the "carrier of a disease," is the "carrier" of subversive "tendencies."[42]

This aspect of totalitarianism had a distinctive impact on the state's relationship to the Jews. The very nature of a system which claims both a monopoly on truth and the control of the "commanding heights" by which the preordained may be reached precludes human error or inadequacy. Only plots and conspiracies by hidden forces could interrupt, hinder or defeat "scientifically" planned programs. Stalin even considered his daughter's marriage to a Jew a "Zionist plot."[43] Other Soviet leaders may not necessarily have perceived the Jew as a "plotter," but, cynically, accepted the functional usefulness of such a perception. The cynicism enabled the Jew to be cast in the role of a scapegoat, to be blamed for failures or difficulties in the regime's internal and foreign policies.

If both chauvinism and totalitarianism lent themselves to the absorption of popular antisemitism at high levels, the background of the Party leadership since the late 1930s helps explain the transmission and persistence of folk imagery about the Jew.[44] With the influx of this group into the leadership, the wide cultural and intellectual horizons which characterized the pre-Purge Party leaders gave way to horizons that were provincial and cramped.

On both national and regional levels, almost half of the top Party executives in the early 1960s had peasant fathers. Only six percent had white collar origins, while a little more than a quarter came from the

---

[41] Korey, *Soviet Cage,* 69.

[42] Hannah Arendt, *The Origins of Totalitarianism,* 2nd ed. (New York: Harcourt, Brace and World, 1962), 423–24.

[43] Alliluyeva, *Only One Year,* 152.

[44] On the new Party leaders' features, see, George Fischer, *The Soviet System and Modern Society* (New York: Atheneum, 1968), 65–117.

proletariat. Most likely, many of them learned negative Jewish stereotypes in their own homes, their own neighborhoods, their own towns.

The "thaw" following the death of Stalin was not marked by any effort be reduce the pervasive negative stereotyping of Jews. The broad discriminatory pattern against Jews sometimes totally, sometimes through tokenism, continued.[45] Jews were excluded from leadership positions in the Party, the Soviets, the state apparatus, the security organs, the diplomatic corps, the foreign trade organs, and the defense establishment. Quota systems in higher education abetted the patterns. Such patterns ineluctably reinforced hostile perceptions of Jews. An interview by a visiting French parliamentary delegation with Nikita Khrushchev in May 1956 highlighted the attitude. Khrushchev was asked about anti-Jewish discrimination. He answered:

> This is a complicated problem because of the position of the Jews and their relations with other peoples. At the outset of the Revolution, we had many Jews in the leadership of the Party and State. They were more educated, maybe more revolutionary than the average Russian. In due course we have created new cadres.
>
> Should the Jews want to occupy the foremost position in our republics now, it would naturally be taken amiss by the indigenous inhabitants. The latter would ill-receive these pretensions, especially as they do not consider themselves less intelligent nor less capable than the Jews. Or, for instance, when a Jew in the Ukraine is appointed to an important post and he surrounds himself with Jewish collaborators, it is understandable that this should create jealousy and hostility toward Jews.[46]

Hostility to Jewry was strengthened when Khrushchev launched in 1959 his campaign against religion generally. The propaganda drive against Judaism ineluctably, unlike the propaganda drive against other religions, took on an antisemitic dimension. Hardly unusual in the campaign was Trofim Kichko's *Judaism without Embellishment,* a book published in 1963 by the Ukrainian Academy of Sciences in Kiev which carried the typical set of canards about Jews: "What is the secular God [of the Jews]? Money. Money. Money, that is the jealous God of Israel."[47]

---

[45] Gilboa, *Black Years,* 244–56.
[46] *Réalités,* 136 (May 1957): 104.
[47] Trofim Kichko, *Iudaizm bez prikras* (Kiev: Ukrainian Academy of Sciences, 1963).

Judaism was linked with Zionism, Jewish bankers, and Western capitalists in a great conspiracy. A distinguishing feature of the work was the incorporation into it of a series of illustrative cartoons showing Jews with hooked noses, and similar vulgar stereotypes. It reminded one of Julius Streicher's *Der Stürmer* in the halcyon days of Hitler. After a worldwide outcry, the Soviet Party's Ideological Commission finally acknowledged in April 1964 that the book "might be interpreted in the spirit of antisemitism."[48]

What complicated the problem was the fact that no efforts were made to reverse the traditional attitudes about Jews that reached back deep into Russian history. References to Jewish history in Soviet textbooks were virtually non-existent. Little mention was made in textbooks or in newspapers of the heroic role played by Jews in the Red Army. Almost nothing was said about the enormous tragedy of the Holocaust or of the Jewish resistance to Nazism.[49] Counteraction to antisemitism was rare. Earlier perceptions about Jews that could be traced back to tsarist epochs, in consequence, were hardly unusual.

Yet, this residue of bigotry from the past was not of a character that would explain the ferocity and virulence of Judeophobia that emerged with glasnost. One of the Soviet Union's most prominent scientists, Professor Yuri Osipiyan, who also served in President Mikhail Gorbachev's inner cabinet, the so-called Presidential Council, stated in the spring of 1990 that "ordinary, everyday antisemitism exists in the Soviet Union, probably to a greater extent than elsewhere in Europe."[50] The past is of course prologue to the present. Can the early twentieth century developments—the Union of Russian People and the *Protocols*—by themselves explain the distinctive Judeophobia of the present?

---

[48] *Pravda,* 4 April 1964.

[49] William Korey, "In History's 'Memory Hole': The Soviet Treatment of the Holocaust" in Randolph L. Braham, ed., *Contemporary Views of the Holocaust* (Boston: Kluwer-Nijhoff, 1983), 145–56.

[50] "The Long Shadow: New Fears of Anti-Semitism in Eastern Europe and the Soviet Union," *Newsweek,* 7 May 1990, 36.

## Chapter 2

## Emergence of the Demonology of Zionism

Of far greater significance in determining attitudes toward Jews during the glasnost era was the massive, extraordinary and intensely-orchestrated propaganda campaign against Zionism during the two decades that immediately predated Gorbachev. If the seeds of hate were sown earlier, it was during the period 1967–86 that the emergent and flourishing plants of bigotry were provided extensive nourishment. Pamyat's favorite writers and lecturers got their start during that period. They appeared then in the leading state journals, or on principal party platforms and were read and heard by millions. An entire generation was nurtured on their outlook.

What was created during 1967–86 was a new official demonology, and it is this demonology which, with dangerous ramifications, persisted into the nineties. The enemy was not the Jew per se; the enemy was Zionism. Launched in the first week of August 1967, the campaign began with the simultaneous appearance in the leading Soviet provincial organs of an article entitled "What is Zionism?" Its opening paragraph struck the dominant note of the campaign: "A wide network of Zionist organizations with a common center, a common program, and funds exceeding by far the funds of the Mafia 'Costra Nostra' is active behind the scenes of the international theater."

Stereotypic images of the Jew abounded in the paranoid portrait sketched by the author. The global "Zionist Corporation" was composed of "smart dealers in politics and finance, religion and trade" whose "well camouflaged aim" is the enrichment by any means of the "international Zionist network." Exercising control over more than a thousand newspapers and magazines in very many countries around the world with an "unlimited budget," the world Zionist "machine" services the vast monopolies of the West in their attempt "to establish control over the world."[1]

If the campaign had its psychological roots in the dark phantasmagoric past, which had been nourished in the climate of Stalin's last years, it also served a pragmatic political purpose. The Soviet Union's client Arab states had suffered a major debacle in the Six-Day War, and the Communist regime itself was badly thwarted in its diplomatic endeavor at the United Nations to compel an Israeli withdrawal from occupied territory; thus a convenient scapegoat was needed to rationalize these severe setbacks.[2] Tiny Israel and public opinion were surely not the causes of these failures. The enemy must rather be presented as a hidden, all-powerful, and perfidious international force, linked somehow with Israel. "World Zionism" was the ideological cloth that could be cut to fit the designated adversary. During the months following the Six-Day War, the citizenry of Communist states as well as those of the Arab and Afro-Asian world were literally saturated with this theme. Foreign radio broadcasts from Moscow chattered away endlessly about Zionism as if this mysterious ghost would take on flesh with repeated incantation.[3]

In the subsequent months and years, especially after 1971 and most notably after 1974, the entire Soviet media was harnessed to the propaganda drive—newspapers, journals, publishing houses, radio, television and lecture halls. The vast and endless outpouring of vitriol directed at Zionism was extraordinary. It was equated with every conceivable evil—racism, imperialism, capitalist exploitation, colonialism, militarism, crime, murder, espionage, terrorism, prostitution, even Hitlerism. No ideology, no "enemy" had received as much attention or been subjected to so much abuse.

What was striking about the Kremlin's perception of Zionism, as re-

---

[1] Yuri Ivanov, "What is Zionism?" *Sovetskaia Latviia,* 5 August 1967. Ivanov was identified by an independent source as a KGB operative on the Party Central Committee serving as its "only specialist on Israel." See *Khronika* (New York), 31 August 1969, samizdat. It is questionable how much of a specialist on Israel Ivanov was; prior to his assignment he had worked in the Central Committee on African problems but was transferred after a reprimand for drunkenness. Copies of the articles from various provincial organs are in the author's possession.

[2] William Korey, *The Soviet Cage,* (New York: Viking, 1973), 125–31.

[3] Summaries of the Russian-language broadcasts are in "Soviet Anti-Zionism or Anti-Semitism," *Jews in Eastern Europe* (London), 3, no. 6 (March 1968), 17–23.

flected in the propaganda, was the enormity of the power and evil with which it was endowed. Diabolical, and displaying transcendent conspiratorial and perfidious talents, Zionism was presented as striving for domination. Poised to resists that aspiration was the great Soviet power. The world was perceived in Manichean terms: the forces of darkness, representing Zionism, were locked in final struggle with the forces of light, as represented by the Soviet state.

Close content analysis of the media outpouring reveal that the inspiration for it came from the *Protocols of the Elders of Zion*. The five major themes outlined in the previous chapter found a precise echo in the post-1967 propaganda campaign. A major analyst of the *Protocols* called them "rank and pernicious forgeries."[4] In a historic Swiss trial in the thirties which focused upon the authenticity of the *Protocols,* the presiding judge wrote: "I hope that one day there will come a time when no one will any longer comprehend how in the year 1935 almost a dozen fully sensible and reasonable men could for fourteen days torment their brains before a court of Berne over the authenticity...of these so-called *Protocols* [which] are nothing but ridiculous nonsense."[5] The jurist's hope appeared to be near fulfillment thirty years later, in 1965, when Norman Cohn completed *Warrant for Genocide,* the authoritative work on the *Protocols*. He observed that at that time it was "quite rare" to find anyone under the age of forty who had ever heard of the "strange ideas" incorporated in the *Protocols*.[6]

Ridiculous nonsense these strange ideas may have been but they enjoyed a stunning renaissance not in some primitive Third World nation, but in the USSR, a superpower and leading industrial country. Moreover, the founder of the Soviet state, Lenin, had expressed total contempt for the Tsarist antisemitic ideology that spawned the *Protocols*. Neither he nor any other Bolshevik leader in the early twentieth century ever published a single article against Zionism. What few references were made on the subject by Lenin were incidental and part of a bitter polemical struggle against the Bund, the Jewish Social-Democratic movement in Tsarist Russia. In Lenin's complete works, numbering forty large volumes in the fourth edition, the word "Zionism" is mentioned but

---

[4] Norman Cohn, *Warrant for Genocide* (New York: Harper, 1969), 16–17, 268.
[5] Cited in Korey, "The Kremlin's Anti-Semitism," 8.
[6] Cohn, *Warrant for Genocide,* 17.

fifteen times.[7] Only once, in Lenin's writing did it merit more than a passing reference. In an article written by him in 1903 and entitled "On the Position of the Bund in the Party," he devoted a few sentences to sharp critical observations about Zionism.[8]

Only once in the fifty-year history of Soviet power before 1967 had Zionism been subject to the kind of media treatment which later characterized Soviet propaganda during 1967–86. This occurred during the last two months of Stalin's life (January 13–March 5, 1953). The notorious "Doctors' Plot" had been conjured up and presented in the Soviet media as an elaborate conspiracy of international Zionism which planned the destruction of the Soviet state by murdering its leaders. The principal agent of the Zionist plot was identified as the American Jewish Joint Distribution Committee (the "Joint"), a Jewish social relief and rehabilitation agency.[9] Several months before the "Doctors' Plot" was unveiled to the Soviet public, a rehearsal of the conspiracy theme was held in Prague under instructions of the Soviet secret police. Rudolf Slansky, the Czech Party Secretary-General and his associates were charged with being agents of the Joint and part of the world Zionist underground.[10]

After Stalin's death, the Doctors' Plot would be officially declared an aberration, a product of the old dictator's paranoia. That aberration became the distinguishing feature of Soviet propaganda in 1967. Tsarist fantasies about Jews, dressed up somewhat in contemporary verbiage, became Soviet fantasies.

Sampling of the media campaign illuminates its character. The flight from reality reached its nadir in the USSR in the fall and winter of 1967. In October 1967, *Komsomolskaia pravda,* the mass-circulation newspaper of the Young Communist League, offered its readers a surrealistic description of the Zionist enemy: "an invisible but huge and mighty empire of financiers and industrialists," Zionism was the lackey "at the beck and

---

[7] Vladimir I. Lenin, *Sochineniia,* 4th ed., 40 vols. (Moscow: State Publishing House, 1950).

[8] For an analytic review of the subject, see Shmuel Ettinger, "Anti-Zionism and Anti-Semitism," *Insight: Soviet Jews* (London) May 1976: 1.

[9] For details, see Yakov Rapoport, *The Doctors' Plot of 1953* (Cambridge MA: Harvard University, 1991). Also see Louis Rapoport, *Stalin's War Against the Jews: 'The Doctors' Plot and the Soviet Solution* (New York: Free Press, 1990), 145–208.

[10] Louis Rapoport, *Stalin's War,* 128–44.

call of the rich master whose nationality is exploitation and whose God is the dollar." With overwhelming economic and political power at its disposal, Zionism was able to exert "effective moral and psychological influence upon the sentiments and minds of people...in many countries." About a dozen countries were specifically mentioned but the author noted that the giant octopus commanded "wide possibilities" in almost seventy countries of the globe.[11]

Most notably subject to Zionist influence was the United States. To document his thesis, the author rattled off unusual data: the number of Zionists in America totalled twenty to twenty-five million (there were but six million Jews in the United States); seventy percent of American lawyers were Zionists; sixty-nine percent of physicists, "including those engaged in secret work on the preparation of weapons for mass destruction"; and forty-three percent of American industrialists. Especially strong was Zionist influence in the mass media, where its adherents allegedly owned eighty percent of the big publishing houses.

So extraordinarily precise were the Soviet published data that observers speculated about their source. Even a fantasy world draws upon elements of reality. Exhaustive research finally unearthed the basis of the author's figure. It was an obscure, eighty-one page pamphlet entitled *America—A Zionist Colony,* published in Cairo in 1957. The writer was a certain Saleh Dasuki, who, besides specifying the percentages noted above, explained that "Jews, whether they have preserved their religion or whether they have adopted other religions, are known in the United States under the collective name of Zionists."[12] Specialists in the field of hate propaganda recalled that in 1957 Cairo had set up a veritable factory for the production of antisemitic literature. It operated under the direction of Johannes von Leers, a former employee of Joseph Paul Goebbels' Nazi Propaganda Ministry, who had adopted the Arabic name, Omar Amin.

Communist stalwarts were given further insights in an article published in December by a key Party organ, *Agitator,* which instructed activists in

---

[11] Yevgeni Yevseev, "Lackeys at Beck and Call," *Komsomolskaia pravda,* 4 October 1967 (Russian).
[12] For background on Dasuki's work, see *Jews in Eastern Europe* (London), 3, no. 8 (March 1968), especially the essay by Shmuel Ettinger, "Soviet Anti-Zionism or Anti-Semitism?"

basic tactical guidelines. The author, Yuri Konstantinov, found the "World Zionist Organization" to be a "political, economic and military concern" with broad interests ranging from "religion to intelligence" and having at its disposal "extremely large funds" obtained from "Zionist multi-millionaires." The influence of the Zionist operation, he claimed, was demonstrated by its alleged ownership or control of 1,036 newspapers and magazines published throughout the world. If this failed to stretch the credulity of the reader, the author retreated to the more conspiratorial warning: Zionists worked hard to deliberately shield their influence from public view. *Agitator* advised Party activists that anti-Zionist propaganda would be accused of being antisemitic, but this was a mere ploy, for the Zionist is the major purveyor of antisemitism.[13]

A disturbing if not surprising feature of the propaganda campaign was the rehabilitation of the Soviet Union's leading purveyor of antisemitic bigotry, Trofim K. Kichko. His 1963 book, *Judaism Without Embellishment,* was so vulgar and noxious in its language and illustrations that Communist parties everywhere joined a world-wide chorus of criticism demanding the withdrawal of the Soviet publication.[14]

But now Kichko reappeared with an article in a Ukrainian Party youth organ which described a plot of "international Zionist bankers," including the Rockefellers, to transform the Middle East into "a strategic launching pad aimed against the socialist world, against the international workers' and liberation movements."[15] Curiously, the Rockefellers appeared in the writings of Kichko and his colleagues as the archetype of the Jewish banker, just as they had in Nazi mythology (they were, of course, Presbyterian Christians). In January 1968, Kichko was awarded the highly prized "certificate of honor" by the Supreme Soviet Presidium of the Ukraine.[16]

Having been duly honored, the Ukrainian "authority" on Judaism proceeded to write a new book, *Judaism and Zionism,* published in 1968 in

---

[13] Yuri Konstantinov, in *Agitator,* December 1967. A summary of the article is in *Jews in Eastern Europe* (London) 3, no. 6 (March 1968): 24–25.

[14] Korey, *Soviet Cage,* 80–81.

[15] Trofim K. Kichko, "Zionism—A Tool of Imperialism," *Komsomolskoye znamia,* 4 October 1967.

[16] *Pravda Ukrainy,* 20 January 1968.

Kiev.[17] The edition was unusually large—sixty thousand copies—and designed "for a wide circle of readers." Kichko's virulent bigotry was again made evident with his description of Judaism as a doctrine which teaches "thievery, betrayal and perfidy" as well as a "poisonous hatred for all peoples." The ultimate objective of Judaism, he claimed, is the fulfillment of God's promise that "the whole world belongs to the Jews." This doctrine, he argued, has been pressed into the service of Zionism in order to help it create a "World Jewish Power" in Palestine and to fulfill "the territorial-colonialist ambitions" of the "imperialist allies and admirers" of Zionism. Zionism, Kichko found, is the reverse side of the coin of "cosmopolitanism," an ideology preaching that "the Fatherland of every person is not the country in which he is born, but the entire world." The forger of the *Protocols* could not have found a more apt spiritual descendant than Kichko.

In the early summer of 1968, the theme of the world Zionist plot began to be employed in a new direction. The focus of Soviet concern was no longer only the Middle East, where a scapegoat was needed to explain the failures of Soviet policy. The basic fear of the Communist leadership in 1968 centered on Czechoslovakia, where the humanizing and democratic tendencies of Alexander Dubcek's government threatened to burst the integument of Soviet totalitarianism. World Zionism would now be depicted as the spearhead of international capitalism engaged in an effort to subvert Communist states and harm relationships between them.

A June 1968 article in the authoritative foreign policy journal, *Mezhdunarodnaia zhizn* signalled the change in emphasis. Entitled "Israel, Zionism and International Imperialism," the article by K. Ivanov recapitulated the international conspiracy thesis linking Zionism, Jewish capitalism, Israel, American imperialism, and West German revanchism in a gigantic plot to overthrow Communist rule. Since Western imperialism was unable to destroy the East European Communist states by military means, he argued, it has been forced to rely upon ideological subversion. This role was played by world Zionists, who "are trying to instill into the minds of Jews in various countries, including the socialist countries, that they have 'dual citizenship'—one a secondary one in the country of actual domicile, and the other, the basic, spiritual and religious

---

[17] Trofim K. Kichko, *Iudaizm i sionizm* (Kiev: Znania, 1968).

one, in Israel."[18]

In August, just a few days before the Soviet invasion of Czechoslovakia, leading Soviet organs, including the important Defense Ministry newspaper, *Krasnaia zvezda,* as well as *Komsomolskaia pravda* dealt at length with mysterious "saboteurs" who threaten to undermine the socialist commonwealth.[19] Judaism was singled out for condemnation as prescribing "racial exclusivism" and as justifying "crimes against Gentiles!" Woven into this warped fabric of thought were such characteristic threads as the sinister role of the Joint, the danger of the dual citizen concept, the challenge of the international Zionist conspiracy.

An early climatic summary of the Kremlin perspective was to be found in a book published in 1969 (in 75,000 copies), *Beware: Zionism!* by Yuri Ivanov, a Party Central Committee specialist on Zionism.[20] In 173 pages it wove together the various strands of the anti-Zionist theme spun over the course of the previous three years. Zionism is presented as a giant international "Concern" of world Jewry. With "one of the largest amalgamations of capital" available to it, the Concern maintains an extensive "international intelligence center" and a "well organized service for misinformation and propaganda." The objective of all the Concern's various "departments," allegedly operated under a "single management," is "profit and enrichment" aimed at "safeguarding" its powers. Details of international Zionism's influence on the policy of Israel, which it considered its own "property," as well as its cunning efforts aimed at subverting both the socialist and new national states, were spelled out. Elaborated too, was the supposed ramified network of Zionist propaganda organs, buttressed by the major mass media, which was said to have been

---

[18] K. Ivanov, "Izrail, sionizm i mezhdunarodnyi imperializm," *Mezhdunarodnaia zhizn,* June 1968. "K. Ivanov" was a pseudonym for V. Semenov, Soviet Deputy Foreign Minister. See *Khronika,* 9 (31 August 1969).

[19] *Komsomolskaia pravda,* 13 August 1968; *Krasnaia zvezda,* 17 August 1968.

[20] Yuri Ivanov, *Ostorozhno: sionizm!* (Beware: Zionism!)(Moscow: Political Literature Publishing House, 1969), 4–7, 71–108, 143. For perceptive analyses of the overall anti-Zionist campaign that extended into the eighties, see Theodore Friedgut, *Soviet Anti-Zionism and Anti-Semitism: Another Cycle* (Jerusalem: Soviet and East European Research Center, Hebrew University of Jerusalem; 1984), Research paper no. 54, mimeograph; and Jonathan Frankel, *The Soviet Regime and Anti-Zionism: An Analysis* (Jerusalem: Soviet and East European Research Center, Hebrew University of Jerusalem, 1984), Research paper no. 55, mimeograph.

*Emergence of the Demonology of Zionism*

"penetrated" by "sympathizing elements."

The significance of this obsessive work might ordinarily be minimized as an isolated literary phenomenon were it not that its publication was accompanied by a synchronized campaign of laudatory reviews in almost all major Soviet newspapers and magazines, and in broadcasts by TASS in numerous foreign languages. The voice of the official Soviet authority was not disguised. It spoke clearly through *Pravda:* "From the pages of Yuri Ivanov's book emerges the true evil image of Zionism and this constitutes the undoubted importance of the book."[21]

Even belles-lettres were infected by the anti-Zionist venom coursing through the body politic. The publication in 1970 of two vicious antisemitic novels by Ivan Shevtsov, a retired naval officer who had acquired a reputation as a hard-line Russian chauvinist and antisemite, was an example. Publication of the two books was his first venture into the literary world.[22] The first novel, *In the Name of the Father and the Son,* published by one of the principal state publishing houses, Moskovskii Rabochii, appeared on March 23 in an edition of sixty-five thousand copies which sold out in two days. The second, *Love and Hate,* appeared in April in an extraordinary edition of two hundred thousand copies. What made the publication even more impressive—and ominous—was the fact that its publisher was none other than the Ministry of Defense, an institution that was the very incarnation of official patriotism. With such strong patronage, Shevtsov's second work was also sold out in only a few days.

*In the Name of the Father and the Son* recalled the propaganda of *Der Stürmer* in the Nazi era. "Zionism," a character in the novel stated, "moves under cover, secretly infiltrating all the life cells of the countries of the entire world, undermining from within all that is strong, healthy and patriotic...grasping all the importance administrative, economic, and spiritual life of a given country." Echoes of the *Protocols* reverberate throughout this and similar passages in its 399 pages: Zionism, according to Shevtsov, even sent its agents into the international Communist workers movement, penetrating into the leadership of the Russian Com-

---

[21] *Pravda,* 9 March 1969.

[22] Ivan Shevtsov, *In the Name of the Father and the Son* (Moscow: Moscovskii Rabochii, 1970); idem., *Liubov i nenavist* (Moscow: Military Publishing House, 1970). Additional background information on Shevtsov is in Reuben Ainsztein, "The End of Marxism-Leninism," *New Statesman* (London), 15 December 1978, 94–98.

munist Party itself. Thus, "Judas Trotsky (Bronshtein), a typical agent of Zionism," entered into the Party leadership and became "international provocateur Number One."

The techniques of putting Trotsky's original name in parenthesis to emphasize his Jewish origin recalled methods used by Stalin's editors during the "anti-cosmopolitan" campaign to identify Jews for the Soviet public. Needless to say, the reference to Trotsky as a Zionist was without foundation, but the author clearly intended, in this way, to associate Zionism with the archetype of villainy (in Soviet mythology) and Jewry to boot. Trotsky would after this appear regularly in Soviet publications as the embodiment of Zionism.

The theme of the *Protocols* was made explicit in the author's description of the relationship between Zionism and "American imperialism." Soviet propaganda had mainly depicted Zionism as a mere instrument of "American imperialism," but here Shevtsov reversed the relationship, in the voice of one of his major characters: "You think no doubt that international Zionism is in the service of American imperialism. For my part, I am convinced that it is the other way around. American imperialism constitutes the economic and military base of Zionism. It serves the aims of Zionism."

A lengthy and definitive article by Vladimir Bolshakov in *Pravda* in February 1971 set the tone for an intensification of the campaign and provided it with a greater ideological sanction. Zionism was labelled "an enemy of the Soviet people." For the first time a phrase was used which harked back to the Great Purges of the late thirties. A more threatening reminder to Soviet Jewry could not be envisaged. Bolshakov put it bluntly: "a person who turns to the Zionist belief automatically becomes an agent of the international Zionist concern and, hence, an enemy of the Soviet people."[23]

The *Pravda* article recapitulated charges that had appeared in the summer of 1967: Zionism was the spearhead of imperialism's campaign against the USSR; its main content "was bellicose chauvinism, anti-

---

[23] Vladimir Bolshakov, "Anti-sovetizm—professiia sionistov" (Anti-Sovietism—the profession of Zionists) *Pravda,* 18 February 1971. The author became a "specialist" on Zionism and wrote a crucial brochure on the subject. See his *Sionizm na sluzhbe antikommunizma* (Zionism in the service of anti-communism) (Moscow: Novosti, 1972), 46–89.

Communism and anti-Sovietism;" at one and the same time, it was "one of the major associations of financial capital, an international espionage center, and a smoothly functioning service for misinformation and slander." Zionism conjoined major monopoly and banking interests—such as Lazard Frères, Rockefeller, Morgan, Kuhn-Loeb, and the Rothschilds—not only in a vast effort to weaken Arab countries but to recover investments these interests had lost in Russia as a result of the October Revolution. Thus, Zionism is principally engaged in "subversive operations... against the Soviet Union and other socialist countries."

The entire history of Zionism was portrayed by Bolshakov as given over to destroying Soviet power: it allegedly collaborated with all the counterrevolutionary forces during the civil war of 1918–20; it presumably entered into a "dirty alliance" with the Hitlerites during World War II (even to the extent of collaborating with the Nazis in the massacre of Jews at Babi Yar!); and, finally, after the war, placed itself wholly at the disposal of U.S. monopoly capital in its thrust to destroy socialism.

In the fall of 1974, the anti-Zionist media campaign assumed a monumental character—broader in scope, more frequent, and more vulgar. An unprecedented high-level Party Central Committee decision was taken which provided for a seven-point "Plan of Measures to Strengthen Anti-Zionist Propaganda and Improve Patriotic and National Education of the Workers and Youth."[24] The plan was not published in the press but sent secretly to every district committee of the Party with instructions for an "intensification of the struggle against the anti-Soviet activity of Zionism." Specifically requested in the Central Committee directive was the creation of a special group of lecturers from the Znanie Society—an official body frequently promoting atheism—"to give lectures on Zionist themes."

The number of articles in newspapers and journals escalated. Hostile Judeophobic anti-Zionist pieces increased 600 percent from 1967.[25] From one-half to two-thirds of articles about Jewish subjects were devoted to assaults upon Zionism. The number of books carrying an anti-

---

[24] The text circulated in samizdat, n.d. See *Yevrei v SSSR*, 8 (April 1976); and *Khronika tekushchikh sobytiy*, 37:77–78, samizdat.
[25] World Conference on Soviet Jewry, *The Position of Soviet Jewry, 1977–1980: Report on the Implementation of the Helsinki Final Act Since the Belgrade Follow-Up Conference* (London: Institute of Jewish Affairs, 1980), 53.

Zionist theme published during the late sixties and seventies totalled 112.[26] A vast industry servicing antisemitism, although masquerading as anti-Zionism, had been created.

The newly-authorized lectures on the Zionist evil by trained specialists from Znanie constituted a crucial dimension of the campaign. Lectures gave the subject a directness and immediateness which made the "enemy" far more palpably threatening than newspaper articles. The Party had always placed great emphasis upon agitation—which, in part, meant lectures and, not surprisingly, the official journal instructing the lecturer and propagandist, *Agitator,* gave prominent attention to anti-Zionism. In 1972, the number of Party lectures was twenty million while their audience totalled some one billion persons, according to figures in a key Party journal.[27]

With Znanie instructed by the 1974 Central Committee directive to play a leading part in the stepped-up campaign, it is pertinent to take note of one its prominent lecturers, Valery Yemelyanov, who also taught Middle East languages at the Maurice Thorez Institute in Moscow.[28] How many lectures Yemelyanov gave is not known but the character of his oral presentation, as revealed in two samizdat documents, is instructive. On February 7, 1973 at a Znanie auditorium in Moscow, he told his audience: "The Jews will go over the heads of other nations to dominate the world. It is well known that the Zionists are planning to seize power over the world by the year 2000." He anticipated that the Soviet struggle against Zionism will be extremely bloody. Recalling that Hitler allegedly "commanded 20 percent of the world's economy" and that the battle against him "cost our people 20 million lives," he concluded that, since "world Zionism currently controls 80 percent of the world economy,"

---

[26] Ibid.; also see, *Anti-Semitism in the Soviet Union: Its Roots and Consequences,* vol. 1 (Jerusalem: Hebrew University, Centre for Research and Documentation of East European Jewry, 1979).

[27] *Partiinaia zhizn,* 12 (June 1972), 14. The report to the Party organ was given by I. Artobolevsky, Znanie Board Chairman. The total number of Party lectures devoted to anti-Zionism is unknown, but it must have been sizeable in view of the fall 1974 secret Party directive. Also see World Conference on Soviet Jewry, *Position of Soviet Jewry,* 54.

[28] For background, see William Korey, "Anti-Zionism in the USSR," *Problems of Communism,* 27 (November–December 1978), 66.

therefore, one can "imagine how much the fight against it will cost us."[29]

In a second lecture delivered at the Scientific Research Institute on February 19, 1974, Yemelyanov was more elaborate in presenting Zionism as a cosmic power. It represented, he said, "the most powerful interstate monopoly," "controlling up to 80 percent of the economy of the capitalist world" and 90–95 percent of the mass media. With this power, Zionism was determined to achieve "world mastery towards the year 2000."[30]

What explained Zionist expansionism, Yemelyanov stated, was Judaism itself. The holiest book of Judaism, the Torah, was described as "the blackest book created in the space of the entire history of mankind." It taught that Jews were the "chosen people" and this, he argued, legitimized the seizure of "other peoples' territories" even as it claimed that "the Jew is the superior race and the others are inferior."

Yemelyanov, like other traditional antisemites, delighted in using the term, "goy," (non-Jew) in a virulent fashion; he claimed that Judaism justified swindling or killing the "goy," as well as performing medical experiments upon him with new drugs. The ultimate aim of Zionism was to conquer and subordinate the multi-billion "goyim" through "the fifth column of Judaism—Free Masonry," which was created among "goyim" as a "daughter enterprise" to inform upon and destroy other "goyim." Yemelyanov saw the Masonic enemy everywhere. Examples were Aleksandr Kerensky, Aleksandr Solzhenitsyn, Alexander Dubcek—all enemies of Soviet power. Toward the end of his lecture, Yemelyanov's remarks took on a dangerously incitatory character. "We have no room for the Masonic trash. I cannot give you recipes, but you are an educated people."

Later, in early 1977, Yemelyanov elaborated upon the Masonic-Zionist theme in a 10,000-word analysis of the new Carter administration.[31] Distributed to the Communist Party leadership, the analysis contended

---

[29] Reports on these lectures were published in samizdat in Moscow. It first appeared in *Yevrei v SSSR,* February 1973.
[30] A detailed summary of this lecture appeared in *Nasha strana* (Tel Aviv) 28 May 1976.
[31] Memorandum to the Communist Party Central Committee, 10 January 1977, samizdat. A brief summary of the Yemelyanov memorandum is in Insight: Soviet Jews, 4, no. 12 (December 1978), 5–6; see also Reuben Ainsztein, "End of Marxism-Leninism."

that the resignation of President Richard Nixon was "forced" by the "Supreme" Zionist-Masonic Lodge, B'nai B'rith. The Carter administration was presented as made up largely of either Masons or Zionists, and, therefore, controlled by B'nai B'rith. To enforce the control, B'nai B'rith used the Anti-Defamation League, whose vice-chairman, the late Senator Jacob Javits, saw to it that domination was maintained through the "Zionist-Masonic Mafia of the US Congress."

Yemlyanov did not restrict himself to a Soviet audience; he also provided advice to the Palestine Liberation Organization journal in Beirut. In an interview published in March 1976, he said: "We must intensify our...ideological activities, together with you, the Arabs, in order to bring a striking blow on Zionism...."[32] Advice to the uninformed was also provided in his book *Dezionization* which asserted that a "conspiracy of Zionists and Masons was thought up 3000 years ago by King Solomon with the aim of seizing power over the world by the year 2000 [A.D.]" Apparently the book was considered bizarre even by the Party propaganda authority, for he was not given approval to publish it in the USSR. Instead, it was published in Paris.[33] Yemelyanov's oddness found expression in other ways. In early 1980, he murdered his wife in a fit of anger, chopped up her body, and set it on fire. In April, he was sentenced to confinement in a hospital for the criminally insane, but was released several years later. Once released, he quickly assumed a prominent role in Pamyat.[34]

Especially important in enabling the Zionist demonology to become firmly rooted in the Russian consciousness was the publication of major books on the subject in massive editions. One estimate calculated that fifty volumes on the demonology of Zionism were published in editions totalling nine million copies.[35] Three volumes, in addition to the Ivanov work discussed previously, merit special attention because of the size of the editions, the powerful endorsement they won in the principal Party and state organs and, most pertinently, because their authors would serve later as advisers and leaders of Pamyat. These books, together with their

---

[32] *Falastin al Thawra,* 21 March 1976.

[33] Valery Yemelyanov, *Desionizatsiia* (Paris: n.p., 1978). On Yemelyanov's strange personality, see World Conference on Soviet Jewry, *Position of Soviet Jewry,* 54.

[34] Institute of Jewish Affairs, *Research Report* (London), 5 (1989), 7–8.

[35] Semyon Reznik, "The Rifle on the Wall," *National Interest,* Fall 1989, 90.

authors, were bridges between the official antisemitism of the Brezhnev era and the "street" antisemitism of the glasnost era of Gorbachev.

*Fascism Under the Blue Star,* by Yevgenii Yevseev, appeared in 1972.[36] The author was a prominent researcher in the prestigious Institute of Philosophy of the Soviet Academy of Sciences, who enjoyed considerable Party prestige as a specialist on Zionism and whose articles appeared in numerous party journals and newspapers. The number of copies printed of *Fascism Under the Blue Star* (the "Blue Star" referred to Zionism) was 75,000—thereby testifying to the support he enjoyed in high Party circles.

Indeed, *Pravda* in February hailed the book for disclosing "the true face of Zionism" and the "chauvinist, racist dogma of the 'Chosen People.'"[37] The essence of the work was to be found in Yevseev's assertion that Judaism had "zealously drummed into the heads of the young generation" ideas of genocide and "criminal methods of attaining power." The title of the book indicated a policy line which he later would strongly advocate in internal debates at the Academy of Sciences—that Zionism and fascism were the same.[38]

The second and third volumes were written by a prominent hatemonger from Minsk, Vladimir Begun, a senior writer and researcher at the Byelorussian Academy of Sciences who often contributed to Byelorussian newspapers. In 1974, in keeping with the new Central Committee directive on Zionism, he published *The Creeping Counter-revolution* in an edition of 25,000 copies.[39] The "counter-revolution" was, of course, Zionism, but the principal source of the latter was presented as Judaism which, he said, was racist and "extremely reactionary." As described by Begun, Judaism divided mankind "into two unequal parts: the Jews 'chosen by God' and the non-Jews 'despised by God'...." The Torah was described as "an unsurpassed textbook of blood-thirstiness, hypocrisy, treason, perfidy and mere degeneracy—all the lowest human qualities." The Jewish religious ethic, with respect to the non-Jew, was a compound

---

[36] Yevgenii Yevseev, *Fashizm pod goluboi zvezdoi* (Moscow: Young Guard, 1971).

[37] *Pravda,* 3 February 1972.

[38] Samizdat reports on the internal debates is in *Yevrei v SSSR,* (Moscow) 14 (January 1977).

[39] Vladimir Begun, *Polzuchaia kontrrevoliutsiia*(Minsk: Belarus, 1974), especially 48–60, 81–82.

of "shamelessness and cynicism" which played "an exceptionally harmful role in the long history of the Jews."

Begun traced "Zionist gangsterism" to the teachings of the Torah and the Talmud. He perceived the Judaic tradition as one sanctioning the conquest and enslavement of all non-Jews. And it was precisely such religious belief that had brought "calamity on the adherents of Judaism." He found the Purim story particularly instructive as a means which "serves to teach treachery...bloodthirstiness and criminal methods of conquest of power." Those persons who professed Judaism were "excellent material for the Zionists," while the synagogue provided "a potential basis for subversive activity."

In three important respects, Begun's work added new dimensions to Soviet antisemitic literature. First, if others saw in Zionism a tool of an external factor, of Western capitalist imperialism, for the domination of the world, Begun would eliminate the external factor altogether. In his view, Zionists, representing the Jewish big bourgeoisie, have drawn up "delirious plans of world domination and enslavement of nations." This presumed aspiration was depicted as an outgrowth of the teachings of the Torah which supposedly required all nations to be transformed into "slaves of the Jews." Begun found a "unity" in the Judaic world outlook with "the ideology and strategy of the present-day servants of Zion." As part of their "strategy," Begun asserted, the Zionists sought to win control in 1968 of the governments of Poland and Czechoslovakia.

Second, the modern striving for political domination by Zionism was not to be understood as merely a contemporary phenomenon. Even during the late Tsarist period, Begun argued, Zionists were intent upon achieving domination of Russia. A certain Aron Simanovich, Begun found, "dominated" Rasputin who, in turn, "dominated" the Tsar and the Tsarina. Begun's "research" had led him to believe that Simanovich, a court jeweler, was Rasputin's private secretary and the Court's *éminence grise*. Needless to say, the belief corresponded in no way with historical truth. Participating in the alleged "domination of Russia," according to Begun, were "the biggest Jewish capitalists and businessmen" of the time.

Third—and most incendiary—overt, antisemitic outbreaks were justified as part of the class struggle of the oppressed against oppressors. This appeared to be the first time that such a rationale for hatemongering could be found in Marxist or Soviet literature. Begun, after taking note of the pogroms in Tsarist Russia in the late nineteenth century, argued that "anti-Semitism can occur as the spontaneous reaction of the oppressed strata of the toiling population to their barbarous exploitation by the Jewish bourgeoisie." An extraordinary passage then followed: "We do not grieve today if our fathers, grandfathers and great grandfathers in their distress and want, treated their oppressors disrespectfully, regardless of whether they were native or alien by blood." To make this argument, Begun was required to perform a monumental distortion: the oppressed Jewish community of Tsarist Russia, subject to a host of discriminatory restrictions, suddenly was transformed into oppressors. Begun found no difficulty in doing so. He wrote that "the real power of the Jewish bourgeoisie was incomparably higher than its formal civil rights."

The hate-pandering of Begun soon received national attention in a major national literary publication.[40] Begun was quick to exploit his newly-acquired national renown. He wrote a second work in 1977, *Invasion Without Arms,* published not in Minsk but in the Soviet capital, in an edition of 150,000 copies, which then was reissued in a second edition of 50,000 additional copies.[41] His thesis was that "Jewish bankers" were striving to take "control of national governments" even as Zionists aspired to take "into their hands the most powerful propaganda apparatus—the mass information media." The *Protocols* theme is here writ large. It was given additional emphasis with his comments upon Judaism. "The ideological sources of Zionist gangsterism," Begun wrote, "originated in the scrolls of the Torah." And, the Torah, he commented, was "a textbook unsurpassed for bloodthirstiness, hypocrisy, betrayal and moral dissoluteness...."[42]

---

[40] *Moskva,* 3 (March 1977). The reviewer was Dmitri Zhukov, an ardent anti-Zionist.
[41] Vladimir Begun, *Vtorzheniye bez oruzhiia* (Moscow: Political Literature Publishing House, 1977).
[42] Ibid.

## Chapter 3

## The Demonology of Zionism: International Dimension

Zionist demonology, especially as it masked a pronounced antisemitism, could hardly attract favorable attention in a world where perceptions of the Holocaust remained vivid. Nor could it attract domestic support from those who were sensitive to the effects of the Holocaust. Besides, it was hardly consonant with Bolshevik tradition. External circumstances in the fall of 1975 offered a unique opportunity to provide the demonology an international dimension and sanction.

A resolution defining Zionism as "a form of racism and racial discrimination" had been introduced into the Third Committee of the UN General Assembly.[1] In terms of the discourse of the international organization, nothing personified evil incarnate and, therefore, was anathema and unacceptable to civilized society so much as "racism." That the proposed definition was Orwellian in nature, a distortion of meaning, was clear to anyone familiar with Zionism and its history. But the USSR was in need of such a crude definition and stood in the forefront of the struggle for its adoption.

As the notorious "Zionism equals racism" resolution was about to come to a vote in the Third Committee of the General Assembly on October 17, 1975, some observers felt a heavy atmosphere of Judeophobia weighing upon the UN chamber. The prominent British critic, Goronwy Rees, later recorded his impressions in an article in *Encounter:*

---

[1] For a discussion of the subject, see Daniel Patrick Moynihan, *A Dangerous Place* (Boston: Little, Brown; 1978).

There were ghosts haunting the Third Committee that day; the ghosts of Hitler and Goebbels and Julius Streicher, grinning with delight, to hear not only Israel, but Jews as such denounced in language which would have provoked hysterical applause at any Nuremberg rally....[2]

The perception was crucial. To many in the West, the resolution was primarily seen as the legitimization of antisemitism. Andrei D. Sakharov succinctly summed up the essence of this perspective: "If this resolution is adopted, it can only contribute to antisemitic tendencies in many countries by giving them the appearance of international legality."[3] But others, with their attention drawn largely to Middle East politics, saw the UN resolution as performing a different function: the de-legitimization of Israel.

The distinction is of vital importance in determining the differing motivations of the main actors in the drama that unfolded. On the one hand, the PLO and the Arab states, in pursuit of their major objective of ousting Israel from the international community, sought to depict Israel as the embodiment of evil by presenting its ideology and philosophy as rooted in international immorality and criminality; that is, racism. On the other hand, the USSR was not seriously interested in this aim. Israel's presence in the Middle East and in the international community was not subject to fundamental challenge by the Kremlin.[4]

Yet Moscow played a strikingly important role in the final adoption by the UN in the General Assembly plenary on November 10 of the infamous equation of Zionism and racism. That role could be noted on several levels. First, the USSR was a sponsor of the resolution and directly contributed a minimum of ten votes to its passage and to the defeat of efforts for its tabling. Second, several of the Soviet dependents and proxies performed leading parts in sponsoring the resolution, serving as its primary advocates and rounding up the necessary votes. The foremost spokesman of the sponsoring group was Somalia which, at the time, was heavily dependent on Soviet military assistance in its conflict with Ethiopia over the Ogaden area. Cuba was a vital link to the non-aligned, Third World countries, and its representatives were everywhere lobbying

---

[2] Goronwy Rees, "Zionism," *Encounter,* 46 (January 1976), 29–31.

[3] Cited in Moynihan, *Dangerous Place,* 191.

[4] William Korey, "The Kremlin and the UN 'Zionism Equals Racism' Resolution," *Israel Yearbook on Human Rights,* Vol. 17 (Dordrecht: Kluwer Nijhoff, 1988), 133–48.

for the resolution's approval. Dahomey (Benin), whose ideology at the time was oriented to the USSR, was especially active in rounding up support in the crucial area of Africa.[5]

Equally important was the fact that the Kremlin had provided a precedent for the resolution in the UN forum a decade earlier. Proposals about the "Zionist evil" had already entered, via Moscow's initiative, the lexicon of the international organization. In 1964, when the UN Commission on Human Rights (20th Session) was debating Article 3 of the draft International Convention on the Elimination of All Forms of Racial Discrimination—which would condemn "racial segregation and apartheid"—the U.S. representative, Mrs. Marietta Tree, intervened.[6] She initially proposed adding "antisemitism" to Article 3 and then modified the idea by recommending a separate article condemning antisemitism. At first the Soviet response was not altogether negative. Its delegate simply asked that, in addition to antisemitism, the new article should also condemn "Nazism, including all its new manifestations (neo-Nazism), genocide... and other manifestations of atrocious racist ideas and practices."[7]

In 1965, the debate on the draft Convention on Racial Discrimination passed to the General Assembly. The United States, along with Brazil, formally proposed an additional article stating that "States Parties condemn antisemitism and shall take action as appropriate for its speedy eradication in the territories subject to their jurisdiction."[8] Historical experience, especially that of the Nazi racist doctrines, testified to the meaning and significance of antisemitism. The U.S. representative to the Third Committee, William P. Rogers, explained that the proposed article "would appropriately highlight the application of the Convention to antisemitism."[9]

The Kremlin, clearly fearing that the draft article could be utilized to focus world attention on internal Soviet practices toward its Jewish community, presented an amendment that it must have known would kill the

---

[5] Ibid.

[6] United Nations Commission on Human Rights, *Report on the 20th Session* (February 11–March 18, 1964), 36.

[7] Ibid. The original amendment appeared in UN document E/CN.4/L.701. The Soviet amendment is in E/CN.4/L.710.

[8] United Nations General Assembly, Third Committee, A/C.3/L1211 (8 October 1965).

[9] Moynihan, *Dangerous Place,* 174.

U.S. proposal. The Soviet amendment read: "States Parties condemn anti-Semitism, Zionism, Nazism, neo-Nazism and all other forms of the policy and ideology of colonialism, national and race hatred and exclusiveness and shall take action as appropriate for the speedy eradication of those inhuman ideas and practices in the territories subject to their jurisdiction."[10]

It was the first time in UN annals that Zionism was formally linked to racism along with Nazism. The linkage with antisemitism was both absurd and amusing, but prefigured a policy line of Leonid Brezhnev in 1981. Most importantly, what was set forth in the Soviet amendment was the core of an idea that ten years later became a formal decision of the United Nations itself. In 1965, the amendment effectively succeeded in wrecking the U.S. proposal to underscore the danger of antisemitism as a form of racism. To avoid harsh and vehement rhetoric and probable defeat, the proponents of the special article on antisemitism retreated. Finally, a decision was taken not to give priority to any "specific forms of racial discrimination," whether antisemitism or Zionism.[11]

The Kremlin had effectively laid the ideological groundwork for transforming Zionism into the *bête noire* of the international community. Six years later, in 1971, the USSR chose to give emphasis to the thesis of Zionism as evil incarnate. The notion of Zionism as racism was fleshed out in a major speech in the Security Council given in September by Soviet Ambassador Yakov Malik. So stunning is it in terms of the then emerging Soviet ideology as well as in unabashed bigotry that it merits quoting in full:

> Mr. Tekoah [Israeli ambassador to the UN] was indignant at our parallel between Zionism and Fascism. But why not? It is all very simple: both are racist ideologies. The Fascists advocated the superiority of the Aryan race as the highest among all the races and peoples in the world. The Fascists considered that the ideal was the Aryan with his blue eyes and blond hair. I do not know what are the external signs with the Zionists; but their racist theory is the same. The Fascist advocated hatred toward all peoples and the

---

[10] United Nations General Assembly, Third Committee A/C.3/1.1231 and Corr. 1 (13 October 1965).

[11] United Nations General Assembly, Third Committee, A/C.3/L.1244 (20 October 1956). Also see the *20th Session General Assembly Official Records,* A/C.3/SR1312 (20 October 1965), 115–18.

Zionist does the same. The chosen people: is that not racism? What is the difference between Zionism and Fascism, if the essence of the ideology is racism, hatred toward other peoples? The chosen people. The people elected by God. Where in the second half of the twentieth century does one hear anyone advocating this criminal absurd theory of the superiority of the one race and one people over others? Try to justify that from the rostrum of the United Nations. Try to prove that you are the chosen people and the others are nobodies."[12]

Presenting the Judaic religious concept of the "chosen people" as "racial superiority" is straight out of the *Protocols of the Elders of Zion.* Antisemitic writings of the twentieth century have drawn continuously upon this source and endlessly repeated the "chosen people" canard.

The Malik speech was a rare and extraordinary departure for Soviet representatives at the UN. Not that Malik was a closet antisemite who hid his bigotry. Malik's colleagues at the UN knew him to spout off-color stories about Jews. One that he especially liked to tell was about a Soviet Minister of Commerce who, while visiting Birobidzhan (the Jewish Autonomous Republic), commented on the poverty of the people. He was informed that, since the place had been reserved for Jews, there were no Russians to cheat.[13] Nonetheless, there is a difference between tales told among colleagues and broadcasting crude anti-Jewish remarks from the UN platform. Malik's willingness to do so—which must have received prior policy approval from the Politburo—testified to a new, clear Soviet "line."

If the USSR had contributed in a substantial measure to the adoption of the "Zionism equals racism" resolution, the key question revolved around the motivation factor. What prompted the Kremlin in 1975 to press at the UN for a resolution that sanctioned antisemitic propaganda in the guise of anti-Zionism? Close analysis of Soviet propaganda in newspapers, journals and books during 1975 and afterwards illuminates the Kremlin's keen interest in the "Zionism equals racism" theme, particularly when it became a formal UN resolution. Probably nowhere else

---

[12] United Nations Security Council, *Provisional Verbatim Record*, A/PV.1582 (25 September 1971), 128–30. Malik repeated the slander in the General Assembly on October 21, 1971: United Nations General Assembly, *Provisional Verbation Record,* A/PV. 1972 (21 October 1971), 52.

[13] Moynihan, *Dangerous Place,* 170.

did that General Assembly resolution receive the massive attention and endorsement it acquired in the USSR.

Analysis indicates that what had been missing from the domestic anti-Zionist campaign was the kind of moral sanction that could provide an ideological legitimacy to the drive, with its clear antisemitic overtones.[14] There was discouragingly little on the subject of Zionism in the sacred writings of Bolshevism's founding fathers, to offer as a justification for the media drive. Indeed, the inherent bigotry in the propaganda campaign, as some sensitive foreign Communists noted, did violence to classical Marxism and especially to Lenin. It was for this reason that the Kremlin could and did seize upon the UN "Zionism equals racism" resolution when it was initially mooted at the General Assembly in the fall of 1975, with the Soviet Union becoming its greatest champion. Such a resolution could offer an ideological rationalization for virulent anti-Zionism, as the sanction carried an international character and sprang from the single most prominent global institution.

Several months prior to the 1975 UN debate on the resolution, a nationalist Soviet publication, *Moskva,* set the tone for the stepped up, vehement anti-Zionist drive with a review of Vladimir Begun's hate book. The reviewer was Dmitri Zhukov, another party specialist on Zionist issues. The significant Zhukov review began: "The Zionists and their underlings...have gathered into their hands the press, radio and television in many countries...have agents in almost all corners of the world [and] are trying to put to sleep the vigilance of the peoples...." Zhukov then went on to endorse the main thesis of the Begun book, that "the chief strategic aim of Zionism" is to transform the "Jewish bourgeoisie into the ruling caste of capitalist society." The process was purportedly initiated in the late nineteenth century during the era of imperialism when the Jewish bourgeoisie "decided to establish Zionist organizations," the members of which would then secretly "penetrate into all government institutions and public movements and operate within them."[15]

---

[14] Citations from Karl Marx would not be appropriate as he belonged to a pre-Zionist era; Lenin's comments were largely related to the Bund, and referred neither to the "chosen people" concept nor to the imagined world power of the Zionists; Stalin, after 1956, was too discredited.

[15] *Moskva,* 3 (March 1977).

Aside from the theme of domination, Zhukov focused upon another characteristic: Jewish clannishness or exclusivity. It was the exclusivity theme, transformed into the "racist" thesis, which was at the core of the UN resolution. According to Zhukov, the Zionists, after seizing control of the press and of government institutions in a number of capitalist countries, place other Jews in key positions and keep out "talented people of non-Jewish origin." Citing a like-minded publicist of Poland, Jerzy Urban, who "spent some time in the midst of Zionists," Zhukov observed that even scientific discoveries were differentiated "in their importance" by Zionists in terms of whether they were made by someone "among whose ancestors it was possible to find a Semitic grandmother."

Clannishness was viewed as a product of Zionist ideology, which allegedly divided the world into two groups: "superior" Jews and "inferior" non-Jews. Such "nationalistic raving" can in turn be traced, according to Zhukov (citing Begun), to "the dogmas of the Jewish religion," especially the "chosen people" concept. Various archaic passages from ancient Jewish religious works were quoted to demonstrate that "the best of the goyim deserves being killed" and that the property of the non-Jew can be legitimately seized by the Jew.

The capstone of Judaic "monstrous thinking" was held to be the "particularly repellent" notion of "mastery of the world," presumably "formulated" in the "Holy Writings of Judaism" and "reflected in prayer." The Zionists, drawing upon the traditions of "exclusivity" and "racial purity," began "dreaming of mastery of the world." Zhukov proceeded to the extraordinary conclusion that Hitler "borrowed his own racist concepts directly from the Zionists." From this perspective, further shocking assertions could no longer be excluded. Zhukov found that Zionism and Fascism shared "mutual ties" in their basic "approach to the racial problem" and in "their hatred for the Soviet Union."

The aim of the Zionists was still to be realized, Zhukov stated, for "the Jewish bankers are not yet in power everywhere." In consequence, quoting Begun, the critic concluded that "the most important task of the Zionist brain center" was to seize "key positions in the economy and in the administrative and ideological apparatus of the States in the Diaspora."

In the ideological sphere, Zhukov said, the Zionists strive to destroy national cultures, presumably acting out what had earlier been called their cosmopolitan and alien propensities. They strike at prevailing socialist ideologies with the objective of "ethical decomposition" through the vilest means. They "sow poison and corruption" by sly and hypocritical means. Czechoslovakia, under Dubcek, was a testing ground for the Zionist technique. Having seized control in Prague of the creative arts and the press, they allegedly required every performer, artist and writer who wished one or another favor to "dance" to their "tune." The Zionists in Czechoslovakia, according to Zhukov, constituted—together with their brethren abroad—an "international clan, which not only speculated in culture, but, what is worse, carried out a genuine ideological subversion." Similar striving by Zionists in Poland were "unanimously stopped by the Polish people."

Zhukov concluded his review with unqualified encomiums. Begun's book is distinguished "by a deeply scientific approach," by "a wealth of material" and by a "principled attitude and argumentation." If Zionism was "like Fascism," it was "better concealed" and was "more ramified." Begun's contribution was to disclose its strategy and reveal its roots and branches. The "perfidious scheme" of the "enslaver" who operated "under the blue star of David," Zhukov believed, was now clearly revealed, while Zionism itself was "doomed to perish." For standing in its path was the "camp of socialist countries" which was the "chief obstacle" to the realization of the "mad plans for world mastery and the enslavement of peoples...."

In addition to writing the *Moskva* review, Zhukov joined two others in 1975–76 in preparing a full-length documentary film entitled *The Secret and the Overt (The Aims and Actions of Zionists).* To judge from a report on the film in the Soviet movie journal, *Kino,* it is of a piece with Zhukov's review of the Begun book. According to the film article, "The entire shameful road of Zionism is the road of insolent deception, dark intrigues, treason, treachery and bloody violence.... The Zionists are racists." The leaders of Zionism, the journal asserted, had operated in collusion with the Nazis and, indeed, provided Hitler with financial capital. Even though the Nazis burned in gas ovens hundreds of thousands of Jewish "workers" and the Jewish "poor," the Zionists continued to the bitter end their collaboration with Fascism.[16]

That film was later be shown to selective audiences and on Soviet military bases. As reported by one Jewish broadcaster who had seen the film, it opened with the crack of a pistol shot and the commentator's voice

---

[16] *Kino,* August 1975.

saying: "That was how the Jewess, Fanya Kaplan, tried to kill Lenin."[17]

The strong endorsement of the Begun book signalled a vastly stepped-up campaign. Zionism was definitively linked with fascism and racism. A massive outpouring of vitriolic propaganda about Zionism filled the press and the other media, beginning especially in the summer of 1975. Guidelines for the campaign were provided by the journal, *Agitator*, which is designed to instruct professional agitators and propagandists on the correct Party line to be pursued on basic policy issues. In June, *Agitator* carried one of its rare pieces on the subject, entitled "The Zionist Feedbag of the Aggressor," by no less an authority than the well-known specialist on Zionism, Yevgeny Yevseev.[18]

In an inquiry designed to uncover the source of Israel's "adventurous course" that presumably fires the tensions of the Middle East, Yevseev stressed the "wide support" for Israel "among the leading circles of international Zionism, among the manufacturers and sellers of arms in the various countries of Europe and America." Singled out were the World Zionist Organization with branches in seventy countries, and the World Jewish Congress with centers in no less than eighty states of the globe. The two organizations were said to "have enmeshed almost the entire capitalist world as if by a net." Besides recruiting "cannon fodder" for the Israeli army, they conduct "espionage and subversion" on behalf of anti-Soviet groups.

At the center of the Zionist operation, according to Yevseev, were some five hundred of the "most influential and most mighty bankers and businessmen from dozens of small and large capitalist countries of all the continents." It is these "golden feedbags" of capitalism who "personify the true master of Israel" and "determine its political course." If earlier they had hidden their influence, according to Yevseev, now they have shed former restraints and display their role openly, at least in the United States. Thus, when American General George Brown had dared to criticize them, the "entire mechanism" of Zionism swung into operation, forcing him to "retract his words officially." The power of the "mechanism" resulted from the supposed "fact" that 80 percent of the local and international information agencies "belong to the Zionists." And in the world

---

[17] Ruvim Vygodsky's article in the *Jerusalem Post* is cited in detail in *Insight: Soviet Jews,* 3, no. 11 (November 1977): 7.

[18] Yevgeny Yevseev, "The Zionist Feedbag as the Aggressor," *Agitator,* June 1975.

of capital, Yevseev observed, "he who pays the piper, calls the tune."

Trofim Kichko, another prominent propagandist who had not appeared in print for more than a year, now returned to the intensified propaganda battle. Writing in *Dnipro,* published in Kiev, he and a colleague, D. Koretskoy, drew special attention to the attempts of Zionists to attract youth. They have done "all they can to turn young people into unthinking executors of mad plans." Even Communist youth were not excluded: "particularly perfidious" was their role in penetrating radical youth movements in order to "disarm them ideologically" through the Zionists' control of the "ramified system of mass propaganda, information, and art...."[19]

Even serious publications of the USSR were harnessed to the anti-Zionist campaign. *Voprosy istorii* (in July), the Soviet journal of the historical profession, featured a voluminous article on "Social-Democracy, Zionism and the Middle East Question" by L. Dadiani.[20] Couched in language of sobriety and equipped with extensive footnotes, the article nonetheless made the necessary obeisance to the propagandist: "As is known, Zionism had been and remains a reactionary and absolutely nationalist ideology...of the big Jewish bourgeoisie...." Dadiani also borrowed a leaf from Kichko. He stated that a principal task of the Zionist labor movement was "to brainwash Jewish youth in various countries." But the main burden of his research was directed to demonstrating the alleged penetration of international Social-Democracy by Zionism and the "intimate" links of their relationship. Vulgarity and open bigotry were eschewed, but at the same time, the article served the purpose of justifying the all-out propaganda campaign.

A leading Soviet literary periodical, *Literaturnaia Rossiia,* in September reviewed a new collection of documents, prepared by the Institute of Oriental Studies of the USSR Academy of Sciences and entitled *Against Zionism and Israeli Aggression.*[21] According to the review, the "scholarly" volume, containing 274 pages of material taken from the Communist press of Israel and other countries, provided an "exposure" of the "class essence" and "imperialist character" of Zionism. The reason for the new and serious academic stress upon Zionism was made clear in

---

[19] *Dnipro,* 7 (July 1975).

[20] L. Dadiani, "Sotsial-Demokratiia, sionizm, i blizhnevostochnyi vopros," *Voprosy istorii,* 7 (July 1975).

[21] *Literaturnaia Rossiia,* 37 (12 September 1975).

the opening paragraph of the review. In the contemporary "historical struggle of two world systems—the capitalist and the socialist," which was marked by "considerable intensification," international Zionism constituted one of the main "shock troops" of "imperialist reaction."

An important Soviet international affairs periodical, *Mezhdunarodnaia zhizn,* joined the chorus of anti-Zionist abuse with an article, "The Victims of Zionist Deception," by V. Vladimirsky. The emphasis was upon Soviet Jews who had been "lured" to Israel by the "lying propaganda" and "subversive activity of world Zionism." Israel's economic difficulties were highlighted to illustrate the nature of the "deception." The result, the author asserted, was the growth of emigration from Israel and the collapse of the "mythical" concept of a "Biblical Homeland."[22]

It was precisely at the moment when the Soviet mass media campaign against Zionism was mounting that the draft resolution equating Zionism with racism was introduced into the Third Committee of the General Assembly. The reaction in the USSR, not surprisingly, was enthusiastic. What the USSR had been incessantly preaching was now acquiring an international sanction. As if by signal, the Soviet press launched a monumental effort both to laud the UN resolution and to interpret its meaning and significance. The new and clearly orchestrated antisemitic campaign, masquerading as anti-Zionism, exceeded previous efforts in scope and magnitude.

While the campaign did not swing into high gear until final action by the Assembly, *Pravda,* as early as mid-October, began orienting the Soviet public to the significance of the UN resolution. Two days after a vote in the Third Committee of the General Assembly, the Soviet Party organ called the resolution "authoritative."[23] It went on to hail the UN "condemnation" of "Zionist ideology" on grounds that the ideology was linked "with the most reactionary forces of imperialism."

Following the final plenary vote, 72 to 35 on November 10, the floodgates of the Soviet propaganda machine opened wide. *Trud,* the official trade union organ, summarized the UN decision as well as previous actions in international forums where Zionism had been condemned as

---

[22] V. Vladimirsky, "Zhertvy sionista obmana," *Mezhdunarodnaia zhizn,* 9 (September 1975).

[23] *Pravda,* 19 October 1975. The vote was taken at the UN in the Third Committee on October 17.

a "form of racism."[24] *Moskovskaia pravda,* the city Party newspaper, printed a long article with the headline, "Zionism in the Pillory." Commenting upon the UN decision, the writer stated that "the world forum of the peoples of our planet has nailed Zionism to the pillory of history as a political ideology of imperialism and racism." The article's final statement was particularly provocative. For the Soviet reading public, the author interpreted the UN action as meaning that "the great majority of the peoples of the world... resolutely demanded the eradication of that [Zionism] from our planet."[25]

*Sovetskaia Rossiia* was equally shrill on the same day with a headline, "Zionism—This Is Racism." the author of the lengthy piece concluded that the "genuine racism" practiced "daily" by Zionism was "the same as is today practiced in South Africa and Rhodesia" and as had been practiced "in the recent past in Hitler's Germany."[26]

Yevgeny Yevseev, widely known for his strong anti-Zionist views, entered the list of commentators on the UN vote, with a special article for the Soviet farm periodical *Selskaia zhizn.* His language was, not unexpectedly, venomous. Defining Zionism as an ideology having a "man-hating and Fascist character," he welcomed its "authoritative condemnation" by the UN. He saw in the vote the first major setback for mankind's great enemy:

> For the first time in many years, the Zionists did not succeed in using effectively hidden methods for silencing the voices of condemnation and criticism directed against the aggressors and rapists who operate under the six-cornered Star of David.[27]

Yevseev, no doubt anticipating a free rein to express his feverish propaganda, concluded that the UN vote carried "great political significance."

In mid-November, both *Izvestiia* and *Pravda Ukrainy* carried articles with the same headline, "Zionism—A Form of Racism." The authors, however, were not the same. *Izvestiia* treated the "important event" of the UN vote in a prosaic, matter-of-fact way, though of course with the usual

---

[24] *Trud,* 12 November 1975.
[25] *Moskovskaia pravda,* 13 November 1975.
[26] *Sovetskaia Rossiia,* 13 November 1975.
[27] *Selskaia zhizn,* 14 November 1975.

governmental anti-Zionist bias.[28] The Ukrainian party newspaper was characteristically more vehement. In describing Zionism, the author stressed that its theory and practice "is founded on the racist fabrications about the 'God-chosenness' of the Jewish people."[29]

The most vitriolic of the commentaries on the UN resolution was written for *Komsomolskaia pravda* by Yuri Ivanov, the author of the initial and authoritative *Beware: Zionism!* His name had not figured in the Soviet national press for several years. His return, following the UN decision, was obviously of considerable significance. The overt bigotry associated with his name was now being given clear signals of official encouragement.

Ivanov, true to his earlier form, did not cloak his personal dislikes. The opponents of the resolution were "the typical bearers of hatred of man—the Zionist magnates and their toadies who nestle everywhere where the Dollar, Gulden and the Rand rule." However, even if they suffered defeat, what is important to them is not what the "goyim" say. (Ivanov cited here a quote from a five-year-old Paris newspaper article and then defined goyim as non-Jews.) The Zionist "magnates" still exerted a powerful influence in "the world of imperialism."[30]

To illustrate Zionist influence, Ivanov reached far into the past for a quote from auto magnate Henry Ford in the *New York Times* of March 8, 1925 as purportedly saying that if the "50 Jewish financiers who are richer than I am" and "who create war for their own profits" were subject to public control, then "wars will be eliminated." Ivanov added: "In the United States of today, just as in the majority of other capitalist countries, such an exposure of the Zionist Mafia is like death for any businessman, no matter how rich he is."

It is fascinating and instructive that the Soviet author of an anti-Zionist classic would seek documentation from the observations of Henry Ford, whose well-known bias against Jews had found its ultimate expression in the publication of the *Protocols of the Elders of Zion* in his *Dearborn Independent*. An examination of *The New York Times* of March 8, 1925, indeed, revealed Ivanov's special interest in the *Protocols*. The Ford quotation appeared on the front page of the book review section where

---

[28] *Izvestiia*, 15 November 1975.
[29] *Pravda Ukrainy*, 15 November 1975.
[30] *Komsomolskaia pravda*, 19 November 1975.

the book under review was *Secret Societies and Subversive Movements* by Hesta H. Webster. The reviewer, Silas Bent, observed that Mrs. Webster accepted the *Protocols* as valid. It is not unlikely that Ivanov steeped himself in Mrs. Webster's antisemitic work. But what was even more striking was the fact that Ivanov had tampered with the Ford quote. The *Times* citation attributed to Ford did not carry the words "who are richer than I am" after "50 Jewish financiers." Evidently, even Ford was not sufficiently antisemitic for Ivanov; he obviously felt the necessity of forging additional words to give emphasis to Ford's and his own antisemitism.[31]

Commentary on the UN vote in the Soviet mass media continued until the end of November. *Za rubezhom* which focused on foreign developments offered one of the most elaborate and lengthy discussions of the UN debate under the headline, "Zionism in the Pillory," in which the penultimate paragraph equated Zionists with "Nazis who have lost all feeling of morality and humanity."[32] Another lengthy and more tendentious treatment appeared in *Sovetskaia kultura,* a key Party ideological organ. The author, S. Astakhov, a frequent anti-Zionist propagandist, called the UN resolution a "truly historic document" and proceeded to explain why it has aroused rage among Zionists. Again, the theme of the chosen people concept—appropriately distorted—was emphasized, with the elements of "racial superiority" and "exclusivity" thrown in.[33]

The principal ideological journal of the USSR, *Kommunist,* summed up the campaign in a long article in its December 1975 issue. Zionism was declared to be "from the very beginning a reactionary, bourgeois-nationality ideology" which became "a tool of imperialist policy and...a defender of the interests of the monopolistic bourgeoisie." The racist character of Zionism was recapitulated with the usual references both to the UN decision and to Israeli practices. Within Israel, the "racist" essence of Zionism "has been raised to the level of state policy,"

---

[31] *New York Times,* 8 March 1925; Sid Resnick, "Henry Ford's Anti-Semitic Views Revived by Yuri Ivanov," *Freiheit,* 23 January 1977. On the role of Ford's *Dearborn Independent* in promoting the Protocols, see Norman Cohn, *Warrant for Genocide,* .

[32] *Za rubezhom,* 21–27 November 1975.

[33] *Sovetskaia kultura,* 25 November 1975.

according to the author.[34]

From 1975 until the eighties, the UN resolution became the point of departure for a number of Soviet books dealing with Zionism, which were also replete with anti-Jewish hatemongering. Several score of such volumes have been published. Most significant was the volume written by a member of the Soviet Academy of Sciences, Lydia Modzhorian, a specialist on international jurisprudence. Her book was appropriately entitled *Zionism as a Form of Racial Discrimination,* the precise language of the UN resolution itself.[35]

The Modzhorian book became a standard Soviet work on the subject of Zionism. In it, the UN resolution was shown as providing the legitimization of the struggle against Zionism conducted in the USSR and elsewhere. That the book was unusually tendentious was immediately apparent. Illustrative were her comments about the notorious pogroms during the Tsarist epoch. She justified them on grounds that they were "a reaction to the exploitation to which the broad masses were subjected in capitalist enterprises." In her view, the pogroms were "artificially exaggerated and widely used by Jewish entrepreneurs and rabbis."

For the Kremlin, the UN resolution had become the single most important sanction for a domestic propaganda campaign that made Zionism the embodiment of the Soviet Union's "enemy" and the epitome of world evil. Zionism, via the Judaic concept of the "chosen people"—appropriately distorted, of course—would be presented as racism, the striving for racial domination over the non-Jew. So conventional had the thesis become that Leonid Brezhnev at the 26th Party Congress in February 1981 ironically equated Zionism with antisemitism.[36] Soon afterwards, his principal aide, Konstantin Chernenko, in an authoritative Soviet book on human rights, reiterated the extraordinary equation, a stunning inversion of history and of language itself.[37]

Not surprisingly, the Kremlin stood in the forefront of efforts at the UN and at UN-sponsored conferences to repeat the 1975 formula and, if pos-

---

[34] *Kommunist,* December 1975.

[35] Lydia Modzhorian, *Sionizm: Form rassovoi diskriminatsii* (Moscow: International Relations, 1980).

[36] *Pravda,* 26 February 1981.

[37] Konstantin U. Chernenko, *Human Rights in Soviet Society* (New York: International Publishers, 1981), 50.

sible, to extend it. In the fall of 1984, Soviet delegates in the UN Economic and Social Council pressed for a special reference to the "Zionism equals racism" formula. It was to be incorporated in a draft resolution by Ethiopia formally establishing a Second UN Decade to Combat Racism and Racial Discrimination.[38] Resistance by the United States and the West, supported by moderate Third World African countries, killed the Soviet effort. What emerged was a consensus agreement on the draft resolution which omitted any reference to "Zionism equals racism."[39]

More significant was the application of Soviet pressures at the UN conference concluding the Decade for Women held in Nairobi, Kenya in July 1985.[40] The USSR lobbied intensely for language to be incorporated in the final conference document that would equate Zionism with racism and apartheid. Adamant opposition by the U.S. delegation, including the threat of a walkout, supported again by the West and moderate African countries halted the Soviet drive.

Ambassador Alan L. Keyes, the leading U.S. State Department official in the delegation, summed up the American and Western view: "We reject the obscene notion that Zionism is a cause of racism, and we believe, no matter how often that slanderous lie is repeated, no amount of reiteration shall ever lend any truth to this whatsoever."[41] Moscow clearly perceived the issue differently. The "slanderous lie" would not quickly be reversed.

---

[38] Details were provided the author by Dr. Harris O. Schoenberg, Director of the B'nai B'rith UN Office.

[39] Elaine Sciolino, "UN Women's Conference Drops Reference to Zionism as Racism," *New York Times*, 27 July 1985.

[40] *Report of the Commission on the Status of Women, Acting as the Preparatory Body for the World Conference to Review and Appraise the Achievements of the United Nations Decade for Women, Resumed Third Session*, A/Conf.116/PC/25 Add.2, 16 May 1985.

[41] *New York Times*, 27 July 1985.

## Chapter 4

## Zionism—"The Greatest Evil on Earth"

The climactic official statement on the demonology of Zionism appeared in December 1976 in a major and extensive article in *Izvestiia,* the principal government organ. Zionism was singled out among all the "enemies" of the Soviet Union, including the "imperialists and imperialist reaction" as "particularly loud" and "particularly hysterical."[1] It was described as the "most reactionary movement" which "as far back as the beginning of the century had already declared socialism as its mortal enemy." Two unknown documents alleged to be located in the state archives of the October Revolution were cited as declaring socialism to be the "mortal enemy" of Zionism. One was presumably dated 1898; the other was said to have been written shortly after October 1917. No specific identification of either of the documents was given, and neither citation conforms with what is generally known about the Zionist movement in Russia.

An uninterrupted flow of invective distinguished the bulk of the *Izvestiia* essay. Zionism had a "particularly malicious character" in its "subversive activity" directed against the USSR. It engaged in an "inciting and provocatory" strategy which "does not disdain any means." It spread "slanderous" and "coarse anti-Soviet lies." It both opposed and exploited detente through "insolent interference" into the internal affairs of other states. It indulged in a "crude violation of the norms of international law" and, as the General Assembly indicated, it exemplified racism and racial discrimination.

---

[1] *Izvestiia,* 24 December 1976.

Especially emphasized in the article was the theme of Jewish "identity" and consciousness. The striving of Jews for identity and for the preservation of their own historic heritage and culture was nothing short of a plot to undermine the Soviet Union. The desire of Jews to study Hebrew or to relate themselves spiritually to the "God-chosen country" of Israel or to establish connections with Jewish religious communities in the USSR were merely an expression of "racism."

The *Izvestiia* article served as a backdrop to spark more potent media virulence. The propaganda took on such a uniquely incendiary character that a prominent Soviet Jewish activist, Anatoly Shcharansky said he detected the "smell of pogrom" in the atmosphere.[2] The year 1977 would constitute the apotheosis of the decade-old antisemitic campaign both in the quantity and (intensively vitriolic) quality of hate propaganda. Of even greater significance was the appearance, as part of the campaign, of a work carrying the imprimatur of the prestigious Soviet Academy of Sciences, which for the first time provided a "scientific" and ideological rationale for the extraordinary propaganda drive against Jewry.

The particularly potent medium of television became the means for launching the significantly stepped-up drive. On January 22 in prime time (7 p.m.), Soviet television carried a newly-produced, one-hour-long documentary, "Traders of Souls."[3] It was replete with juxtaposed visual images of Jews and Israelis that had the clear design of evoking suspicion and hatred of Jews. World Jewry was personified by a grossly corpulent personage with an unusually ugly face who was shown passing five-pound sterling notes to demonstrators in London protesting Soviet treatment of Jews. An American Jewish tourist at Moscow airport was shown confessing, during an interview, that he attempted to smuggle anti-Soviet material into the USSR, and that he acted on instructions of Zionist organizations which may have maintained "clandestine ties with the CIA and [which] do its bidding."

The image of the Jew as money-changer ran throughout the documen-

---

[2] Martin Gilbert, *Shcharanskii, Hero of Our Time* (New York: Viking, 1986), 166.

[3] The documentary, *Skupshchiki dush*, is summarized in *Soviet Jewry and the Implementation of the Helsinki Final Act, Report* (London: Institute of Jewish Affairs, 1977), 48. A detailed review and analysis of the film is in Gilbert, *Shcharanskii,* 161–65. After the film was shown, seventy-eight Jewish activists from nine cities joined in a statement condemning the "pogrom atmosphere" created by the film, ibid., 166.

tary. He is the "trader of souls" who not only "bought" demonstrators in London but funded Soviet Jewish activists or provided "prisoners of conscience" with money orders. Photos of such checks were shown on the television screen with the impression left that the activists and prisoners were mere speculators in foreign currency. The "prisoners" were also depicted as hooligans and drunks.

Television footage on Israel portrayed scenes of battlefields strewn with hideously misshapen corpses or showed screeching jets followed by closeup shots of bandaged Arab children. The narrator's voice commented: "Israeli jets bomb peaceful Arab villagers. This is what Israel has brought to the Arab world." Soviet Jewish activists, such as Vladimir Slepak, were shown embracing Israeli athletes while the commentator asked: "How can it be that Zionist cadres were allowed to form inside the USSR?" The names and addresses of various activists were flashed on the screen with the background voice declaring: "These people are all soldiers of Zionism within the Soviet Union and it is here that they carry out their subversive activities."

The specific reference to names and addresses inevitably brought alarm to the activists who saw it as endangering the personal safety of the people mentioned. But of equal concern was the impact the program would have on public attitudes toward Jews. It was seen by Soviet Jewish activists as appealing to the "basic instincts of the most ignorant elements in the population" which could trigger pogroms were the local police to relax their vigilance.[4]

"Traders of Souls" offered the basis for extensive and enthusiastic commentary in newspapers and journals. TASS gave emphasis to it on the day of its transmission[5] while Novosti a week later highlighted a summary of the film for both the internal and external audiences.[6] It was lauded by *Vechernaia Moskva*,[7] and by Yevgenii Yevseev, in *Sovetskaia kultura*.[8] The weekly supplement to *Izvestiia*—*Nedelia*—was particularly effusive. The film, it said, clearly revealed the "ugly...activities of the Zionist center and their bosses" which engaged in "crude interventions,"

---

[4] Gilbert, *Shcharanskii*, 163.
[5] TASS, 22 January 1977.
[6] Novosti, 7 February 1977.
[7] *Vechernaia Moskva*, 28 January 1977.
[8] *Sovetskaia kultura*, 1 February 1977.

## Zionism—"The Greatest Evil on Earth"  49

in "all possible provocations" and in "the fabrication of forgeries." The "traders of souls" were accused of using the "cover" of philanthropic and religious organizations, such as B'nai B'rith, in "many Western capitals" to pursue their aims.[9] An orchestrated campaign of applause followed in virtually every provincial organ.

*Sovetskaia kultura,* whether consciously or not, provided evidence of the antisemitic purpose of the organized one-sided public dialogue. Referring to the traditional Jewish emblem, the Star of David, it commented that "it is not by accident" that the Zionists strove to "send their six-cornered figure" into other countries, both legally and illegally, for the emblem was designed to reveal the "symbol" of their "influence."[10] Virtually all of this particular issue of the Party ideological journal was turned over to various individual commentators on the film each of whom bestowed lavish praise upon it.

Appropriately, the authorities arranged, on grounds of "popular demand," for a reshowing of "Traders of Souls" on March 11.[11] The impact of the film and the various public commentaries upon it was not unexpected. The power of negative visual imagery, especially when so calculatingly endorsed by the principal media sources, prompted "everyone in busses and subways"—as a perceptive observer noted—to engage in open discussions of the film. The result, he added, was "a very much higher level" of popular antisemitism. Another observer found that even Soviet children were calling Jewish youngsters by the slur word *zhidi* (kikes).[12]

The weekly *Ogonek,* with a circulation of two million, could be expected to champion and sustain the new antisemitic onslaught. On January 29, a week after the first television showing of "Traders of Souls," the journal charged that "Zionist agents" have succeeded in the "direct penetration of foreign secret services" with the aim of exercising "influence" over the intelligence operations of a "whole number of states," including the United States and England. The title of the article, "The Espionage Octopus of Zionism" was self-explanatory. The conspira-

---

[9] *Nedelia,* 7–13 February 1975.

[10] *Sovetskaia kultura,* 15 February 1977.

[11] *Soviet Jewry and the Implementation of the Helsinki Final Act,* 48.

[12] These comments were made by various refuseniks to Robert Toth, the Moscow correspondent of the *Los Angeles Times.* See Gilbert, *Shcharanskii,* 166.

torial power of Zionism was seen as so potent that "any state that refuses to carry out the will of the ringleaders of Zionism, who operate on a world scale, like a sort of Mafia, immediately becomes the object of [its] espionage and subversive activity...."[13]

The author of the *Ogonek* article was Lev Korneyev, who had more recently joined the ranks of the leading professional peddlers of hate—Kichko, Begun, Ivanov, Yevseev, Bolshakov. A week later, he applied his vitriolic pen in the journal, *Sotsialisticheskaia industriia,* to a new charge. Zionism was responsible for dumping arms into the world market in order to foil detente and foster racism. He stressed especially Israel's trade with South Africa thereby demonstrating "the similarity between Zionism and apartheid." In his view, "any racist or profascist regime immediately becomes a customer of Israel."[14]

In early February, *Ogonek* returned to an analysis of the television program "Traders of Souls." The article, "Bought Souls," contended that the Zionist organizations of the West "are a state within a state." To document the accusation, it alleged that in the US, Zionists "control half of all the magazines published there, half of the radio stations, three quarters of the correspondents' agencies of American newspapers, magazines and press agencies abroad...."[15]

Stress upon the supposed martial character of Zionism was repeated in the official atheist organ, *Nauka i religiia,* during the same month. Zionism, it charged, interpreted the Book of Joshua as a kind of Hitler's *Mein Kampf,* a call for aggression and war. Like the latter, Zionism implanted a religiosity "bordering on fanaticism" with the intention of advancing its goal of conquest, even to the extent of using the atom bomb.[16]

Korneyev articulated a similar theme in *Moskovskaia pravda* in mid-February. He declared that, in the USA, the military-industrial monopolies were "to a considerable degree controlled or belong to the big pro-Zionist bourgeoisie." "Many" of the oil companies, which were included in the one hundred largest suppliers of the Pentagon, were "directly controlled by pro-Zionist capital." In consequence, Zionism "has become one

---

[13] Lev Korneyev, "Shpionazhii vosminog sionizma," *Ogonek,* 19 January 1977.

[14] *Sotsialisticheskaia industriia,* 2 February 1977.

[15] *Ogonek,* 5 February 1977.

[16] *Nauka i religiia,* February 1977.

of the shock troops of imperialism in the struggle against peace...."[17]

In addition to its alleged propensity to war, international Zionism was charged by Korneyev with being allied to "the organized world of crime in the USA...." The next month, he developed this new theme, in a long article in the important military-ideological journal, *Communist of the Armed Forces*. Contending that Meyer Lansky was the "chief bookkeeper" of the Mafia, and noting that he was a "generous donor" to Zionist organizations, Korneyev reached the conclusion that "there is no doubt" that from the coffers of "organized crime in the USA" a "considerable part of the budget of the Israeli secret services is covered...."[18]

The article of Korneyev in the armed forces journal requires special attention because of the audience to which his bigotry was directed. That his views appeared to carry the endorsement of the military could not but powerfully reinforce latent or burgeoning anti-Jewish hostility. The article was entitled "The Secret War of Zionism," and, besides referring to the supposed secret "alliance" of Zionism with organized crime, it repeated his previous views on the military aspirations of Zionism.

More important, still, was the manner in which he handled the subject. The military aspirations of Zionism were said to flow from its "class foundation" which was said to be composed of the big bourgeoisie of Jewish origin. Korneyev no longer blurred the distinction between Zionist and Jew. He stated his words plainly. The big Jewish bourgeoisie, he wrote, was distinguished by "racism, extreme reaction, and a clearly expressed expansionism." Its "fast-growing financial might" was accompanied by a "search for additional spheres of influence" throughout the world. This led "international Zionism" to strive "to get into its hands the military-industrial complex as the most profitable sphere of business." And, this explained why Zionism is a "rabid opponent of the relaxation of tension...."

Korneyev did not limit his thesis of the Zionist "evil" to crime and military aggression. Espionage and subversion also were its hallmarks, he contended, with targets being especially the USSR and the socialist countries of Eastern Europe. To illustrate his theme and prove his point, he wrote the following: "Israeli spies in the USSR for a number of years

---

[17] *Moskovskaia pravda,* 16 February 1977.

[18] Lev Korneyev, "Tainaia voina sionizma," *Kommunist vooruzhennykh sil,* 6 (March 1977).

were engaged in the compiling of a special 'handbook' with addresses and names of Soviet citizens of Jewish nationality: scientists, leading specialists in various spheres of technology, workers in art, literature, journalism, etc." The object of this exercise, Korneyev was convinced, had been to "create a Zionist underground in the USSR and to conduct military and industrial espionage in our country."

The month of March was especially rich in media articles which revealed the extraordinary depth of the hysteria about Zionism which had seized Soviet policy makers. Besides the Korneyev essay in the armed forces publication, two especially vulgar hatemongers—Yevseev and Yemelyanov—reappeared. The former wrote a special piece for *Komsomolskaia pravda* which dealt with the seizure of the B'nai B'rith building in Washington, D.C. by the Hanafi terrorists. If virtually everywhere in the civilized world the violence was deplored, Yevseev found justification for the action. What the gunmen wanted, he held, was merely, the halting of the showing of the film "Muhammed—the Messenger of Allah" which supposedly "offends the religious feelings of the Moslems."[19]

Why did they strike at B'nai B'rith? According to Yevseev, it was "one of the chief organizations of the international Zionist system" and its members "are closely connected with American cinema producers and owners of cinema theaters and cinema halls." The fact that the film was funded, produced, and distributed by Arabs went unmentioned by Yevseev. All he saw was the Zionists' "indifference and lofty scorn" to the pleas of the Moslems for stopping the film showing, an indifference that resulted from their "unrestrained thirst for profits." The terrorists seized the building because they hoped "to paralyze the activities of that huge political octopus and affect the cessation of the film showing."[20]

If Yevseev perceived international Zionism at work in offending religious feelings of Moslems, Yemelyanov saw it engaged in suppressing archaeological evidence of the Ebla tablets found in Syria. He delivered a lecture on this subject to the Palestine-Russian Society at the Soviet Academy of Sciences, which was summarized in a Moscow radio broadcast beamed abroad on March 27. The plot of the Zionists, according to the "young scientist, Valery Yemelyanov"—as characterized by Moscow Radio—was the creation of the myth that Jews had settled the Middle

---

[19] *Komsomolskaia pravda,* 16 March 1977.
[20] Ibid.

East area in ancient times, and the destruction of contrary evidence.[21]

Far more provocatory were articles in *Izvestiia*. On March 4, it carried two very long articles covering almost an entire page formally linking Soviet Jewish activists with the Central Intelligence Agency in a plot to "undermine the foundation of Soviet power." Thus, based upon the confession of a single self-acknowledged "spy"—Sanya Lipavsky—the articles strove to smear the entire Jewish movement in the USSR—*Izvestiia* printed photographs purporting to show payoff money given by the CIA to a Soviet Jewish doctor, as well as drawings and photostats of alleged American intelligence instructions to him.[22] (The March 4 publication date was curiously coincidental. It almost marked the twenty-fourth anniversary of Stalin's death—March 5—which had ended the trauma of the Doctors' Plot, but which had also begun with an allegation of Jews being linked with American intelligence.)

The confession of Lipavsky would be repeated several months later at a press conference, published in *Izvestiia* under the headline, "How the CIA Recruited Me."[23] The thrust of the human rights movement in the West and the aspirations of dissenters and Jewish activists in the USSR were presented by Lipavsky as only a cover for stirring up anti-Soviet activity and for the accumulation of espionage information. A somewhat similar "confession" would soon be printed in *Vechernaia Moskva*. Foreign Zionist organizations, according to the informant—L. Tsypin—"did not spare money" to encourage Soviet Jews "to fabricate slanderous information" and "to prepare provocative 'actions'" so that an anti-Soviet reaction could be evoked in the West.[24]

The provocatory "disclosures" of March were immediately followed up by the publication of one of the most venomous assaults upon Zionism, a 285-page book entitled *Wild Wormwood* by Tsezar Solodar.[25] The

---

[21] "Archaeology and Israel's Historical Origins," *Radio Moscow* (in Arabic), 27 March 1977 in *BBC Summary of World Broadcasts,* SU/5475/A4/3–41, 29 March 1977.

[22] *Izvestiia,* 4 March 1977.

[23] *Izvestiia,* 8 May 1977.

[24] *Vechernaia Moskva,* 17 May 1977.

[25] Tsezar Solodar, *Dikaia polyn* (Moscow: Sovetskaia Rossiia, 1977). Solodar, although Jewish and apparently versed in Yiddish, was one of the Soviet Union's most strident and vitriolic anti-Zionist propagandists. The publisher of the book was an organ of the Party Central Committee.

book's main theme was that Zionism is akin to Nazism. The author "recalls" as a youngster of twelve in Vinnitsa the speeches of Zionist leaders in 1919. They are alleged to have said:

> The Jewish nation has been chosen by God; we are the first among all peoples. And everyone who belongs to our world nation, which is now dispersed throughout the entire world, must be ready to raise his sword, under the white and blue banner.... This struggle must start today, no matter in what country the Jew lives and no matter what he does....

Solodar, in his recollection, is as imaginative (and malevolent) as the authors of the *Protocols* had been. The dominant theme of the two works with respect to the "chosen people" concept was precisely the same. After recalling the purported example of "rabid chauvinism" illustrative of "racist ideology" to be found in the "inhuman theory of Zionism," Solodar went on to relate that he had heard an exact "echo" of the Zionist when in 1941 he had attended the interrogation of four captive SS men. One of them was supposed to have declared: "We, the Germans, are the chosen nation. We are called upon to destroy all those who prevent the purification and the flourishing of the most exclusive, the purest of all races—the Aryan!" The "cult of the Semitic race," as practiced by the Zionists, Solodar contended, was the same as "the cult of the Aryan race" as practiced by the Nazis. Much of the rest of the book was devoted to charges about the presumed collaboration of Nazism and Zionism.

Solodar's revelations were perceived by Soviet authorities as especially important in the struggle "against international Zionism, one of the main detachments of anti-communist forces"—as noted in the flyleaf of the book. The number of printed copies of the volume was extraordinary— 200,000. In addition, major Soviet journals extended it prominent and laudatory attention: *Ogonek* ("Zionism Without a Mask")[26]; *Literaturnaia gazeta,* ("Zionism Accused")[27]; *Komsomolskaia pravda* ("Bitter is the Bread of the Promised Land")[28] and in *Sovetskaia kultura* ("Ordinary Zionism"). A paragraph in the latter, which incidentally focused upon "the gallery of Jewish exploiters" presented by Solodar, summed up the official Soviet opinion as it related to the implication of the book:

---

[26] *Ogonek,* 12 March 1977.
[27] *Literaturnaia gazeta,* 6 April 1977.
[28] *Komsomolskaia pravda,* 2 July 1977.

This is the question about the incessantly growing list of crimes of Zionism, of its unprincipled deals over the course of decades with all the various tools of world reaction—from Petliura to the White Guard emigres, from Hitler to the military-industrial complex of the USA.[29]

The "crimes of Zionism" were to be further delineated in the Soviet media during the following months. Solodar himself spelled out a new "crime," heretofore not attributed by the Soviet propagandists to Zionism. In a two-part series entitled "The Goods" published in *Ogonek* on May 21 and 28, Solodar charged that Zionism was responsible for bringing young immigrant girls to Israel and turning them into prostitutes. "Consistently, methodically, and undeviatingly," he wrote, the "Zionist bosses" have stimulated "the trade in feminine flesh, spiritually corrupting both the sellers and purchasers." The "Zionist bosses," in addition, "protect procuring and brothel-keeping" and thereby "implant immorality and scorn for the norms of morality."[30] The *Protocols*, too, had presented the "Elders of Zion" as responsible for prostitution, as well as alcoholism.

The *Izvestiia* supplement *Nedelia*, in two issues, accused "Zionist doctors" in West Germany of murdering a Soviet Jew who had emigrated to Israel and from there "fled to Germany." The German authorities, "under the pressure of the Zionists" were said to have refused to prosecute the criminals "in white coats" and even rejected any effort to locate his body.[31]

*Mezhdunarodnaia zhizn*, in an article by Astakhov, accused Zionism of "collusion" with apartheid as well as claiming "the superiority of Jews... over all the other races in general."[32] Astakhov, in another diatribe written for *Sovetskaia kultura*, charged "Zionism and Judaism" with "waging a real campaign for the purity of the Jewish race." The campaign, he declared, drew upon the "best models of the Nazis" and was pursued "under the leadership of the rabbis and the help of the Zionist activists...."[33] The crime of subversion, previously elaborated upon, was

---

[29] *Sovetskaia kultura*, 7 June 1977.
[30] Tsezar Solodar, "Tovary," *Ogonek*, 21 May and 28 May 1977.
[31] *Nedelia*, 18–24 July 1977 and 25–31 July 1977.
[32] *Mezhdunarodnaia zhizn*, July 1977.
[33] *Sovetskaia kultura*, 12 July 1977.

again worked over in a long review article in *Novoe vremia*.[34] The book reviewed was *Top Secret* written by four *Izvestiia* staff writers. Presumably it characterized the "Zionist apparatus" as the principal agency of imperialism for subversion against the socialist countries.

The catalogue of "crimes" made Zionism—as a letter quoted in *Vechernaia Moskva* on June 28 put it—"the greatest evil on earth." But what the decade-old campaign against "the greatest evil" had lacked was a Marxist-Leninist ideological underpinning even, if a moral sanction had been found in the UN General Assembly resolution of November 10, 1975 defining Zionism as a "form of racism and racial discrimination." For that reason, the USSR had played a leading role in promoting the resolution and publicizing in both within and outside the country. Still, the UN decision could not offer an ideological sanction. Definitions of Zionism to be found in standard dictionaries could not simply be discarded by means of Orwellian inversion. A hostile economic and historical analysis of Zionism, drawing upon Leninist methodology and ideology, was still missing.

The required ideological legitimization finally came in the summer of 1977 with the publication by the prestigious Academy of Sciences of *International Zionism: History and Politics*.[35] The 176-page work, composed of articles written by "scholars" drawn from various institutes of the Academy, was trumpeted by TASS in a special release and commentary.[36] The book's introduction explained the intent of "the exposure of the ideology of Zionism of its theory and practice." The essential academic gloss to provide a kind of intellectual foundation to the ten-year-old propaganda drive against Zionism had finally been found.

*International Zionism: History and Politics,* to a remarkable degree, echoed the themes of the *Protocols of the Elders of Zion.* The central theme of the latter had been that Jewry aspired to world domination by means of control over the international banking system. The same theme predominated in the new Soviet work. According to its authors, the "Jewish bourgeoisie," using Zionism as a cover, have sought "the expansion of their positions in the economy of the largest capitalist

---

[34] *Novoe vremia*, 22 July 1977.
[35] V. I. Kiselev, et al., eds., *Mezhdunarodnii sionizm: istoriia i politika* (Moscow: State Publishing House, 1977).
[36] TASS, 22 July 1977.

states...and in the economic system of world capitalism as a whole." If, heretofore, Soviet propaganda masked overt antisemitism by meticulously referring to Zionists rather than to Jews, now its ideologues dropped the mask altogether. Several banking firms, in addition to the bugbear of the *Protocols*—the Rothschilds—were listed as "large financial-industrial Jewish monopolies whose sphere of interests spreads over many countries of Europe, America, Asia and Africa."

Singled out in the United States were six Wall Street investment firms: Lazard-Frères, Lehman Brothers, Kuhn-Loeb, Loeb-Rhoades, Bache & Co., and Goldman-Sachs. The last five were said to hold approximately 23 percent of the shares of the "large industrial companies" of America and occupied about 15 percent of the directorial positions in 1000 various corporations. The size and significance of these corporations were not examined. Instead, the writer of the book's principal essay—V. Kiselev—restricted himself to the observation that the "influence of the finance bourgeoisie of Jewish origin now extended to "many spheres of material production" including ore-mining, oil and chemical industry, transport, publishing, advertisement and newspaper business. An oddity was added: "enterprises of culture and information organs."

Especially "noticeable," said the author, was the alleged role of American Jewish finance capital in the "military-industrial complex." Only two examples were offered, the accuracy of which was more than merely questionable. Lehman Brothers was said to have played a key role in creating General Dynamics, Lytton Industries, LTB, and Sperry Rand. Lazard-Frères was declared to be in "control of Lockheed Aircraft." (A similar relationship was said to exist between the English Rothschilds and the "military-industrial Vickers Concern.")

The *Protocols* had propagated the well-known antisemitic canard that Jewish magnates were intimately linked, family-wise, with one another in a giant conspiracy. It was a reflection of the traditional classic notion of clannishness that, in the eyes of the prejudiced, stamped the Jew. The new Soviet study enlarged upon the clannish thesis. "Among the Jewish bourgeoisie," Kiselev contended, "the use of all sorts of extra-market...kinship relations through 'one's own'...has always been practiced in a particularly wide manner." Thus, the Lazard-Frères and Lehman groups were said to have "firm ties" with one another. As with the Rothschild family interconnections, these ties symbolized an "international amalgamation of Jewish finance capital."

The documentation for the supposedly "scientific" study was remarkably sparse, in addition, of course, to being distorted. Reference in the text is made to an unknown work by one I. I. Beglov called *The USA— Property and Power*. Heavy reliance was placed upon the antisemitic writings of Ivanov *(Beware: Zionism!)* and of Bolshakov. A "Supplement" in the last part of the Academy of Sciences book suggested the repositories of much of the source material. The section was, indeed, revealing. In laudatory fashion, it described the operations of two so-called "scientific research centers" which were said to specialize in studying and publishing material on "international Zionism": the Palestine Research Center established in 1965 by the Palestine Liberation Organization in Beirut; and the Scientific Center of Palestinian Research attached to the University of Baghdad. The Supplement also referred to two papers read at an International Conference on the Problems of Israel and Zionism. One of the papers, "The Near East in the Plans of Imperialism and Zionism" was reported to have been written by Yevgeny Yevseev, the antisemitic propagandist, who was described in the Supplement" as a "Soviet scholar."

A related major focus of the *Protocols* which now found reflection in the Soviet book, had been the Judaic concept of the "chosen people." In the former it was perceived as the religious and ideological rationale for world domination. The Soviet authors stressed the same medievalist perception contending that Judaism considered the "goy" (non-Jew) as the "enemy" against whom "violence" was required. They then built upon the theme by adding their own specious interpretation of messianism. The Judaic belief in the messiah was supposedly inculcated so that Jews will aspire to "mastery over all mankind."

As in the *Protocols,* the Zionists were said to strive for the status of a "super-government" with Jews encouraged to become "fifth columns" throughout the world. Israel was characterized as but the "connecting" link in the vast and monumental effort of "the big Jewish bourgeoisie" to achieve "the consolidation of their positions in the world of capital" and for acquiring "superprofits." Through Israel and by means of Zionist influences, the Jewish finance capitalists were said to have acquired "additional possibilities for the expansion" of their sphere of capital investment in Asia, Africa and Latin America. Zionism was thus a "cover" for "neo-colonialism."

That the Academy's book was designed not for a limited academic audience but rather for a broad popular readership was indicated by the number of copies printed: 26,000.[37] The price of 76 kopeks per copy made certain that the distribution would be reasonably wide. The strong endorsement of the work by TASS ensured national public attention to its contents. A "scholarly" imprimatur had now been given to a refurbished *Protocols of the Elders of Zion.*

---

[37] See William Korey, "Legitimizing Anti-Semitism: The Role of the Soviet Academy of Sciences," *Israel Yearbook on Human Rights,* 9 (Tel Aviv: Intersdar Shamir, 1979), 140–59.

## Chapter 5

## The Freemason Component

Absent from the Academy of Sciences study of Zionism was one vital component of the *Protocols*—the role of freemasonry as an instrument of the "Elders of Zion" for domination of the world. The subject, however, was by no means neglected. Indeed it occupied a prominent place in the anti-Zionist media campaign. It, too, had its special demonology, intimately interwoven with the Zionist one. Appropriate historical background would be useful in order to throw light on the demonological origins of both, and of their interconnections.

A striking feature of extreme antisemitic bigotry throughout modern history is the myth of the supposed linkage of Jews (or Zionists) with freemasonry, jointly engaged, presumably, in a secret, conspiratorial activity to overthrow the prevailing social order and attain power or domination. However absurd and unrelated to reality the myth is, it appears to have had an extraordinary vigor. Remarkably, it persisted in the USSR and, at not infrequent intervals, would find expression in books, pamphlets and the media. Clearly, the Kremlin or important segments of the Soviet leadership, found it a useful theme to promote.

The linkage of the myth was distinctly anti-modernist, reactionary and obscurantist. Masonry itself was initially targeted in the eighteenth century by the supporters of the authoritarian, monarchical regimes, backed by the church ("Throne and Altar"), as a direct threat to their survival. Since the Masonic order, in various of its free and secret societies, was a channel for the ideas of the Enlightenment, there was a basis for regarding it as a serious challenge to existing hierarchical forms. How serious the challenge actually was remained quite another question. Perceiving Masonry as the vanguard of the political and social revolution required a stretch of the imagination, but arch-reactionary forces of the eighteenth and nineteenth centuries unleashed a vast pamphlet campaign to do just that—predicting "inevitable revolutions" from the Masonic "houses of political and moral pestilence."[1]

When wedded to Jewry, the belief in a threatening and dangerous Masonry took on a far more potent dimension. The linkage was first made by the Dominican Greinemann from Aachen, in 1778.[2] Speaking from the pulpit, Greinemann traced the Masons back to the time of Christ: "The Jews who crucified the Saviour were freemasons: Pilate and Herod were Masters of Lodges; Judas, before betraying Jesus, went to a lodge and became a mason." It would hardly come as a surprise to find that his preaching led to pogrom-type outrages against Masons.

It was perhaps not accidental that Jews could be linked in some perceptions with Masonry. Freemasonry, as part of the Enlightenment, had helped contribute to the emancipation of Jews, and, indeed, various Masonic lodges had admitted Jews into membership, one of which—the Frankfurt lodge—was comprised predominantly of Jews.[3] The established churches and political counter-revolutionaries were strong opponents of the Enlightenment; Jews were seen as its beneficiaries and, therefore, as instruments of the anti-Christian and revolutionary elements. Thus, a German translation in 1800 of a classic work on the Masonic conspiracy thesis—the Barruel Memoirs—referred to "the Jewishness of the Freemason" or the "Freemasonry of the Jews."[4]

By the last quarter of the nineteenth century, the linked Masonic-Jewish conspiracy myth had made considerable strides in antisemitic and reactionary circles. A major theorist, G. M. Pachtler, who was a prominent Jesuit, declared in his book published in 1876 that freemasonry had provided "Christ-hating Jewry a veritable haven and a highly desirable base for their operations."[5] The notorious French antisemite, Edouard Drumont, in his key work published in 1885, characterized the

---

[1] Johannes Rogalla von Bieberstein, "The Story of the Jewish-Masonic Conspiracy, 1776–1945," *Patterns of Prejudice,* 11, no. 6 (November–December 1977), 2.

[2] Ibid.

[3] Ibid., 3; see also Jacob Katz, *Jews and Freemasons in European History, 1723–1939* (Cambridge: Cambridge University Press, 1970).

[4] Bieberstein, "Jewish-Masonic Conspiracy," 4.

[5] Ibid., 5.

founder of the quasi-Masonic Order of Illumination, Adam Weishaupt, as Jewish.[6] Weishaupt wasn't, but that made little difference to Drumont who considered that Jews were the prime beneficiaries of the Enlightenment and the French Revolution.

Pope Leo XIII, in his encyclical *Humanum genus* of 1884, provided momentum to the Masonic conspiracy theory. He accused the Masons of working for the replacement of the Kingdom of God on earth by a Kingdom of Satan under their own control. Some leading Catholic officials simply extended the conspiracy to the Jews. French Archbishop Leon Meurin wrote a book in 1893, *French Masonry-Synagogue of Satan,* which focused heavily on the "Jewish Lodge" of Frankfurt and concluded that the secret of freemasonry lay in its being an instrument of Jewry.[7] The notion was further developed by the Abbé Bertrand in his pamphlet, *Freemasonry, Jewish Sect,* published in 1901. More elaborate was the argument advanced by Monsignor Anselme Tilloy in his book *The Jewish-Masonic Peril* (1897). Tilloy contended that France was already under the yoke of the Judeo-Masonic sect both politically and economically.

The Dreyfus case had of course mobilized a vast effort by the Right to preserve the orthodox version of the status quo, threatened presumably by republican and secular forces. The Jewish-Masonic conspiracy myth was a convenient device to exploit public stereotypes and fears against Dreyfus and his supporters. Far deadlier than the writings of French antisemites and extremists was the forged document, the *Protocols of the Elders of Zion.*

In the forged *Protocols,* Jews were presented as engaged in a worldwide conspiracy to achieve world domination. To achieve this aspiration, the Jewish or Zionist elders exploited freemasonry for their own purposes, along with liberalism and democracy, to subvert the prevailing monarchical order in Eastern Europe. The thesis of preserving Throne and Altar of the eighteenth century had now been brought up to date with devastating repercussions. The *Protocols,* especially in the hands of tsarist court and military circles, became a weapon for the promotion of antisemitism and pogroms.

From Eastern Europe, the *Protocols* and its Jewish-Masonic conspiracy myth would shortly be transferred to Germany where it would be ab-

---

[6] Ibid.
[7] Ibid.

sorbed into Nazi philosophy and become the "warrant for genocide" against Jews. As early as World War I, it was being argued in Germany that the war was engineered by the freemasons of the Entente in order to subvert the "bulwark of monarchical thinking and guardians of the Christian faith."[8] By 1918, the president of the German Naval Union, Prince Otto von Salm-Horstmar, was publicly contending that all revolutions in modern times had been caused by the Masons who had always been the instruments of the Jews. He considered that the Russian Bolshevik leaders, Lenin and Trotsky, were Jews and Masons.[9]

A key German organization that played a crucial role in transmitting the conspiracy thesis was the Thule Society, formed in 1918.[10] A number of its principal leaders would later become dominant figures in the Nazi Party. The society declared firm opposition to Masonry and war against Jews. Adolf Hitler, while serving in the army intelligence services, made contact with the Thule Society and other ultra-right circles. The principal Nazi ideologist, Alfred Rosenberg, joined the Society at the end of the 1918 and published a German edition of the *Protocols*.[11] By the early twenties, he was turning out pamphlets which distilled the history of the Jewish-Masonic conspiracy thesis.

Rosenberg's views were being echoed in other rightist circles. Franz Haiser, founder of the All-Aryan League, published a book in 1924 which warned that "Jewish democratic Freemasonry" was "undermining... Throne and Altar." Later, in 1927, General Erich Ludendorff declared that "the nations are being enslaved by the Jewish-Masonic catchwords 'Freedom, Equality and Fraternity.'" The propaganda of the extreme right during the Weimar Republic was oriented to demonstrating that the Versailles treaty was an anti-German plot hatched by the "Jewish-Masonic democratic" Entente and as an "act in the spirit of freemasonry."[12]

The groundwork for the Nazi ideology had been laid. Hitler's *Mein Kampf* already had incorporated the *Protocols* myth, especially the Jewish-Masonic conspiracy, as central to his own dogma. It would find

---

[8] Norman Cohn, *Warrant for Genocide* (New York: Harper and Row, 1967); Walter Z. Laqueur, *Germany and Russia* (London: Weidenfeld and Nicholson, 1965).
[9] Bieberstein, "Jewish-Masonic Conspiracy," 6.
[10] Ibid.
[11] Ibid., 7.
[12] Ibid., 8.

detailed expression in Nazi theory and propaganda. Heinrich Himmler, in a special lecture dealing with the nature of the SS in January 1927, defined the "natural opponent" of the Third Reich as "international Bolshevism run by the Jews and Freemasons."[13] Joseph Paul Goebbels, in an article in the *Völkischer Beobachter* in February 1939, targeted "the circles of international Jewry, international Freemasonry and international Marxism" as the enemy of a peace-loving Nazi Germany.[14]

The destruction of the Nazi war machine put a temporary end to the "Jewish-Masonic" myth. Obscure neo-Nazis continued to peddle the theme but the channels which had been used were now so severely restricted that its impact was negligible. Not until 1975, thirty years after the internment of Nazi ideology did the myth suddenly reappear as part of the Kremlin drive against Zionism. Stunningly ironical was the transmutation of the myth from Nazi Germany—where the ultimate target was perceived as Communism—to Communist Russia itself.

A major published work in the Soviet propaganda campaign, particularly in the Ukraine, was the book, *Zionism and Apartheid,* by V. I. Skurlatov.[15] Published in 1975 (appropriately in Kiev, the publishing center of a number of antisemitic books by Trofim Kichko), the new and rather extraordinary work argued that modern racism had naturally unfolded from the Judeo-Christian tradition. At the heart of that tradition, Skurlatov held, was the Judaic concept of "God-chosenness," which was supposedly rooted in notions of superiority and exclusivity—the essence of racism. Freemasonry became the principal means for propagandizing "Jewish racism." As noted by Skurlatov, "the ideas of 'secular Judaism'—freemasonry—became widely disseminated in the upper strata of bourgeois society." Clearly, freemasonry was seen as but the expression of modern, secular Judaism.

The absurdity of the argument may be generally apparent but Soviet propagandists seized upon a superficial resemblance between Masonic

---

[13] Ibid., 1.

[14] Ibid.

[15] Valery Ivanovich Skurlatov, *Sionizm i aparteid* (Zionism and Apartheid)(Kiev: Political Publishers of the Ukraine, 1975). After an uncertain career in the Komsomol, Skurlatov was returned to an official position, this time in the Soviet Academy of Sciences. During the debate in the Academy in February 1976, enlightened scholars denounced the book as being part of "Black Hundred methods of struggle against Zionism."

Lodges and pre-World War II B'nai B'rith Lodges to advance their viewpoint. The latter had been marked by closed meetings and special ceremonials. Such features disappeared in major Jewish population centers during the postwar period, and only persisted until the next generation as vestigial remnants in isolated areas.

Soon after the Skurlatov book appeared, in mid-February 1976, *Nedelia* (the weekly supplement of the Soviet government newspaper, *Izvestiia*), further developed the B'nai B'rith-Masonic connection.[16] In Vadim Raevsky's article, he declared that B'nai B'rith had been "created in accordance with the principle of Masonic lodges." If there was an element of truth in terms of origins, the article went on to extend and distort the superficial resemblances. B'nai B'rith was said to have worldwide links with "CIA organizations" such as the Simon Wiesenthal Documentation Center in Vienna. A cartoon accompanying the article demonstrated the bigoted intent of the author and of his sponsors. It showed a man's arms, with the Star of David imprinted on one hand, embracing the entire globe.

The key Soviet government organ returned to the theme in the following year. In July 1977, *Nedelia* carried an article by Vadim Pigalev, which focussed on the forces of "international reaction" as posing a major threat to socialism.[17] As spelled out in *Nedelia,* the components of "international reaction" were "neo-Fascism, international Zionism and the dregs of the criminal-political world." Central to the article was the assertion that these components "jointly use the old mechanism of Masonic lodges more and more frequently."

A significantly more elaborate presentation of the myth came in *Komsomolskaia pravda,* in September 1978.[18] Addressed to a vast youth audience, a lengthy article, entitled "Insidious Plagiarism" by V. Polezhaev, contended that Freemasons were the centerpiece of the worldwide campaign against the USSR and socialism generally. It was they who developed the "strategy and tactics" of raising human rights issues in Eastern Europe. Western governments simply plagiarized this "strategy."

According to Polezhaev, freemasonry had become so increasingly influ-

---

[16] *Nedelia,* 9–15 February 1976.
[17] *Nedelia,* 4–10 July 1977.
[18] *Komsomolskaia pravda,* 13 September 1978.

ential that it constituted an "invisible form of government." The influence and power of the Masons, he said, had inevitably attracted the "Zionists" who seek to use Masonic political control "in order to secretly manipulate the economy." Zionists were also attracted to the Masons, thought Polezhaev, because they "worship the six-cornered Star of David" and presumably observe other supposed Judaic rituals. Especially singled out for criticism in the article were the Bilderberg Club (presented as a kind of international Masonic power center) and the "Zionist-Masonic Lodge of B'nai B'rith."

Occupying a particularly prominent place in the development of the myth was Valery Yemelyanov, the anti-Zionist propagandist of *Znanie*. In his lectures, Zionists were described as utilizing the manpower of freemasonry as "Judaism's fifth column" for purposes of achieving their aim and purpose.[19] In Yemelyanov's analysis of the Carter Administration, he found that virtually all of its key members were either Masons or Jews.[20] He considered the threat of "Zionist-Masonic" domination so immediate and palpable that he called upon the Kremlin for an all-out educational campaign to "unmask" Zionism.[21]

Yemelyanov exerted considerable propaganda impact in the mid-seventies and his views persisted in various Kremlin opinion-making quarters. Following the 1981 "P2" scandal in Italy which focused upon a Masonic lodge, some of whose prominent members of rightist persuasions secretly engaged in criminally subversive tactics, a leading Soviet journal gave the incident special attention. *Golos rodiny* carried an article by B. Aleksandrovsky (who in 1969 had written a book on freemasonry) which described the "true face, structure and tactics of this mighty and, essentially criminal international association."[22] But, as with Yemelyanov and other hatemongers, Aleksandrovsky found that freemasonry was "extremely closely linked, by threads invisible to mere mortals, with the top bosses of world capital and the highest Zionist

---

[19] See *Chronicle of Current Events*, 37 (30 September 1975), 77–8.

[20] Yemelyanov's analysis of the Carter Administration is in his memorandum to the Central Committee of 1977, which is in the author's possession.

[21] Ibid. For a sketch of Yemelyanov and a detailed presentation of his views, see Howard Spier, "'Zionists and Freemasons': A New Element in the Soviet Propaganda Campaign Against Zionism," *IJA Research Report*, December 1978.

[22] *Golos rodiny*, 47 (1981).

organizations."

*Golos rodiny* was the voice of nationalism and made strong efforts to appeal to Russian patriotism both at home and abroad. Another organ oriented to the promotion of Soviet patriotism and Russian nationalism was *Sovetskii voin*. In March 1982, this military journal presented an article by Vadim Pigalev which interpreted the Solidarity phenomenon in Poland as a Masonic-Zionist plot.[23] Professor Bronislaw Geremek, a leading adviser of Lech Wałęsa, was said to have left the Polish Communist Party after the "Zionist putsch" of 1968 had failed. To suggest that the Polish student revolt of 1968 had been a Zionist putsch was straining the imagination. But Pigalev found it a reasonable concoction, and he went on to assert that Geremek took instructions from a Masonic group in Paris, which he transmitted to Poland.

Pigalev did not limit himself to "exposing" Solidarity. He found that all instances of destabilization and chaos, whether in Turkey, Taiwan, Italy or Poland were the results of the Zionist-Masonic conspiracy. More precisely, it was the consequence of a Zionist plot for, he found, the Freemasons were "overwhelmingly directed by international Zionism." Gentiles might assume high office in freemasonry but they were "in one way or another sifted by the Zionists"; indeed, they merely "function as the active accomplices of this international lobby."

The Soviet Union's most prolific antisemitic researcher and propagandist, Lev Korneyev, at the time an official of the Academy of Sciences' Institute of Oriental Studies, not surprisingly joined the chorus of analysts dealing with the Zionist-Masonic conspiracy. He first developed it in *Neva*, the Leningrad monthly, in May 1982.[24] Six months later, writing under a Jewish pseudonym "Solomon Verbitsky"—a not unusual device of Korneyev—he sought to expose the "criminal links" of Zionists with "the Nazis and neo-Fascists, the Mafia and Freemasons."[25]

That Soviet authorities were planning to develop the Zionist-Masonic conspiracy even further was evidenced by reports about two new books

---

[23] See Vadim Pigalev's essay in *Sovetskii voin*, 3 (March 1982).
[24] See Lev Korneyev's essay in *Neva*, 5 (May 1982).
[25] *Neva*, 1 (January 1983), 202.

which were scheduled for publication in 1984.[26] The first was entitled *Behind the Screen of the Masons* by V. V. Malyshev. The announced press run was quite high—100,000 copies. The second volume, strikingly, was to be by the notorious Jew-baiter, Vladimir Begun of Minsk. His book, entitled *Tales of a "Widow's Children"* with a scheduled press run of 10,000 copies, was described in advance notices as "a critique of Free-Masonry."

A new antisemitic book, published in the Ukraine in 1984, also took note of the Zionist-Masonic conspiracy. Entitled *In the Service of Aggression* and written by V. A. Stefankin (in an edition of 25,000 copies), the volume carried a section on the military-industrial complexes of the West supposedly controlled by Zionists.[27] In it, the author asserted that one such complex is the Honeywell Corporation which was said to be run by a Zionist who, "like many other American magnates, belong to the Zionist-Masonic Lodge."

Ukrainians were not the only target for the propaganda drive against the Masonic-Zionist conspiracy. *Vendetta: American-Style,* written by S. Pavlov and published in 1985 in the Byelorussian capital of Minsk, described how the Masons play "an extremely important role" in the structure of contemporary imperialism.[28] As "a deeply conspiratorial international political mafia," Masonry, according to the reviewer in *Sovetskaia Byelorussia,* is propelled toward American imperialism and Zionism which, in turn, "pursue their racist ideology and imperial policies through secret Masonic channels."[29]

The fact that the publishing houses in the USSR were state-owned highlighted the coordinated and centralized character of the propaganda campaign against Masonry and Zionism. The intent, it was clear, was to provide the ideologist and broad segments of the reading public with a definition and characterization of the deadly hidden and conspiratorial enemy. Even a more sophisticated journal which acted as the mouthpiece

---

[26] See Howard Spier, "Zionist-Masonic Theme Fashionable in Soviet Publications," *Radio Liberty Research,* RL 75/84, 15 February 1984. This instructive article served as a guideline for a part of this chapter.

[27] V. A. Stefankin, *Na sluzhbe agressii* (Kiev: Political Publishers of the Ukraine, 1984).

[28] *Sovetskaia Byelorussiia,* 20 October 1985. The newspaper carried an extensive review of the book.

[29] Ibid.

of the Soviet Foreign Ministry, *New Times,* in October 1986 chose to describe Zionism as a secret conspiracy aimed at establishing domination over, as well as undermining, socialist society.[30] Significantly, it singled out B'nai B'rith, perceived in Masonic terms, as the key organized structure of the Zionists.

Surprisingly, scholarship of a certain type had provided the campaign with a special, if partial, legitimacy. The well-known Soviet historian, Professor Nikolai Yakovlev, who was a section head at the Institute of Social Studies of the USSR Academy of Sciences, had devoted considerable attention to Masonry during World War I. In his best-selling work on the war, *August 1, 1914,* Yakovlev came to the incredible conclusion that a critical factor in the internal crisis faced by the tsar at the time was an anti-patriotic Masonic conspiracy which is attributed to "the ruling circles of the Entente."[31] Indirect evidence suggested that a crucial source for this thesis was the KGB which was known to have offered Yakovlev unique and favorable treatment.[32]

While Yakovlev chose in his writings not to establish the vital link of Masonry to Zionism, he nonetheless could provide the myth with an academic underpinning. If Masonry was presumed to be powerful, conspiratorial and subversive, it required but several pen strokes to link it to that other presumably satanic force of anti-Russian and anti-Soviet persuasion—Zionism. This could be done by a host of official propagandists, no doubt with the encouragement of the KGB, even as Nikolai Yakovlev was provided "research" sustenance by it.

In dredging up the prime symbols of satanic evil as perceived by reactionary obscurantists of the eighteenth and nineteenth centuries, by the fabricators of the *Protocols of the Elders of Zion* and by Hitler's ideologues, the Soviet Union's propagandists and ideologists of the seventies and eighties took their departure from the real world and entered a fantasy universe. Especially archaic and anomalous was the restoration of the significance of freemasonry. The movement may have carried a certain political significance in the eighteenth and early

---

[30] *New Times,* October 1986.
[31] Nikolai Yakovlev, *1 Avgusta 1914* (Moscow: Young Guard, 1974).
[32] See Vladimir Tolz, "Foremost Soviet Historian Nikolai Yakovlev: A Doughty Opponent of the CIA, Dissidents, and Masons," *Radio Liberty Research,* RL 386/83, 17 October 1983, 5–6.

nineteenth centuries. But, over time, this aspect had diminished and virtually disappeared.

In the recent period, freemasonry embraced a broad mass membership filling nearly 10,000 lodges located in over thirty countries.[33] It is given to fraternal and humanitarian purposes in Western society. Freemasonry was forbidden only in Communist countries which, like Nazi Germany and Fascist Spain (extending to the very end of Franco's rule), considered any autonomous structures as a threatening challenge to totalitarian rule. In reality, however, the functions of freemasonry, almost wholly oriented to purposes of benevolence, can scarcely have been perceived as subversive or a challenge to the established order anywhere.

How then explain the persistence of the myth about freemasonry (joined to Zionism) engaging in a massive conspiracy against socialist society? Russian history provides some illumination. Freemasonry in the late eighteenth and nineteenth centuries did exert a considerable influence on the intellectual life of significant segments of the aristocracy.[34] Its very corporate-autonomy posed a challenge to the centralizing authority of tsarism, so it is scarcely surprising that Catherine II and later autocrats were extremely suspicious of it. But, when the autonomous group, in which secrecy was a distinctive feature, became linked to either rationalism or to mystical striving for purity, freemasonry might be seen as a revolutionary challenge to tsarism. The Decembrists, groups of noblemen influenced by the French Revolution who confronted and appeared to threaten tsarist state power in 1825, had sprung from Masonic lodges, as did earlier advocates of liberalism like Radishchev and Novikov.[35]

Thus, freemasonry in Russia did reflect, for some time, a tradition of challenge to state authority, even if it increasingly took on a mystical character and shed its earlier rationalism. Fears of its presumed insurrectionist power were somehow incorporated into the thought patterns of the guardians of autocratic power. Once Communist rule passed from internal revolutionary pursuits and purposes to rigid conservative aims with the preservation of power becoming an obsession

---

[33] *Encyclopaedia Britannica* (Chicago: William Benton, 1966), 9:840–44.

[34] James H. Billington, *The Icon and the Axe: An Interpretative History of Russian Culture* (New York: Alfred A. Knopf, 1966), 242–68.

[35] Ibid., 242–49, 267–68.

of the Kremlin totalitarians, then the myth of the Masonic conspiracy could be drawn upon. It was, after all, well embedded in Russian history.

Pertinently, that tradition also included a Jewish strand. In the latter part of the eighteenth century, a prominent French mystical thinker and advocate of Masonry, Henri de Saint-Martin, had become convinced that Jews and their conversion were critical to salvation.[36] He had been particularly influenced by Martinez de Pasqually, reportedly a Portuguese Jew, who had organized his own secret order of "elected Cohens" (priests). That group (as well as some of the Masonic lodges) frequently invoked Jewish kabbalistic words and symbols.

A certain gifted preacher named Theodosius Levitsky arrived in St. Petersburg in 1823 and began prophesying the imminent end of the world.[37] It was urgent and essential, in his view, to convert the Jews to Christianity before the millennium. His impact was especially strong in White Russia. There and elsewhere, a sect had emerged which rejected traditional forms of Russian Orthodoxy and advocated the unity of Christians and Jews in a new church which would celebrate the Sabbath on Saturday rather than Sunday. As the sect grew to significant numbers, it inevitably incurred the suspicion of the central state (and religious) authority. The tsar's key advisers concluded that a subversive plot against the established order was emerging. Inevitably, there was a crackdown on this group as on similar sectarian movements.

The mechanics by which the myth of the Masonic-Jewish conspiracy was absorbed into the massive anti-Zionist propaganda campaign of the Kremlin, beginning in the nineteen seventies, is by no means clear. The key link would appear to be the *Protocols of the Elders of Zion*. Puzzling is the question of how the *Protocols*, totally discredited in modern society and certainly after the destruction of Nazism, came to be used, if not officially and openly, at least informally, in an "Aesopian" manner, as it were. Two pieces of evidence suggest that key Soviet propagandists were steeped in the *Protocols*, and were anxious to disseminate its basic thesis.

The first piece of evidence is the fascinating article by Yuri Ivanov (a central figure in the early stages of the Kremlin's anti-Zionist drive) published in *Komsomolskaia pravda* on November 19, 1975.[38] His cita-

---

[36] Ibid., 255.
[37] Ibid., 288–89.
[38] *Komsomolskaia pravda,* 19 November 1975.

tion of an obscure *New York Times* review of the Hesta Webster book about the *Protocols,* written a half-century earlier, indicated the curiously profound interest of a well-placed Soviet *apparatchik* in the Party Central Committee in works supportive of that genre. It is not unlikely that Ivanov had mastered the *Protocols* along with every work that was related to it. He certainly could spew out the ideas of the tsarist Okhrana forgery although, in keeping with official ideology, he would make certain that his language variation carried a certain Leninist linguistic veneer.

A second illustration was provided by an article in the authoritative Party ideological newspaper *Sovetskaia kultura* on April 5, 1977. Entitled "A Well-Paid Advertisement," the essay constituted a review of the Broadway play, *Herzl,* written by Amos Elon and Dore Schary. The following striking passage appears in the essay:

> According to Herzl's assertion, he was moved in Paris to write the brochure *The Jewish State*—today proclaimed as "The Bible of Zionism." The idea of the book, he stated, was supposedly inspired from above and, during his writing of it, he had heard the rustling of eagle's wings.... In reality, it all took place in a much more prosaic manner. One day, Herzl happened to take into his hands the book of the French Mason, Maurice Joly...which had been published anonymously in Switzerland thirty years earlier. Herzl thought that the content of the book was interesting and the half-forgotten brochure became the foundation of a shameless literary plagiarism. Herzl stole from Maurice Joly eighteen basic provisions without changing a thing and presenting them as his own "revelations"; in addition, he slightly altered over thirty passages.[39]

The facts about Maurice Joly and about the origin of the *Protocols* are quite different. Joly was a liberal French lawyer who had written and published in Brussels, in 1864, a satirical work sharply critical of Napoleon III.[40] The satire, *Dialogue aux Enfers entre Montesquieu et Machiavel,* took the form of a dialogue between liberalism (Montesquieu) and cynical despotism (Machiavelli) which was designed to expose the manipulative and corrupt methods of the ruler of France's Second Empire. Joly was arrested and sentenced to fifteen months imprisonment and his book banned and confiscated.

---

[39] *Sovetskaia kultura,* 5 April 1977.
[40] Background details are in Cohn, *Warrant for Genocide.*

The work of Maurice Joly, in fact, had nothing to do with either Masons or Jews. But a tsarist intelligence operative in Paris, thirty-five years after the banning of the book, thought it could lend itself to an extraordinary forgery. Joly's *Dialogue* was shamelessly plagiarized and transformed into the *Protocols of the Elders of Zion*. What Joly had put in the mouth of Machiavelli, the forgers of the latter, in large measure, now assigned to the unnamed Elders of Zion. Approximately 160 passages of the *Protocols,* some forty percent of the entire text, were based upon the Joly satire with the same sequence of paragraphs preserved and, frequently, even with the same wording.

Theodor Herzl knew nothing of the Joly work and, of course, could not and did not engage in the alleged plagiarism. But certain Communist ideologues, working for *Sovetskaia kultura,* and inspired by the distinctive tradition of tsarist ideologies concerning Jews, Masons and conspiracies, sought to demonstrate what the *Protocols* forgers wanted the world to believe: that Herzl (and the other Elders of Zion) was the true author of the *Protocols*.

The writer of the Soviet essay was obliged to take account of disclosures by historians concerning the plagiarism from Joly. But he consciously or unconsciously rejected the more fundamental fact uncovered by researchers that the plagiarized *Protocols* was the product of a Tsarist intelligence official and certainly not of any Zionist. In any case, it is instructive that the ideologists at the leading cultural organ of the USSR were clearly extremely well-versed in the literature dealing with the origins of the *Protocols*.

## Chapter 6

## Demonology: A Concern to the Kremlin?

Not until July 1990, did *Pravda* acknowledge that the Soviet anti-Zionist writers of the seventies (and later) had drawn their inspiration from the Black Hundreds and, hence, from the *Protocols*. The remarkable admission read:

> Considerable damage was done by a group of authors who, while pretending to fight Zionism, began to resurrect many notions of the antisemitic propaganda of the Black Hundreds and of fascist origin. Hiding under Marxist phraseology, they came out with coarse attacks on Jewish culture, on Judaism, and on Jews in general.[1]

The reference was obviously to Ivanov, Yevseev, Begun, Yemelyanov, Bolshakov, Kiselev, Korneyev and a host of lesser names who had access to—and were to continue to have access to—major Soviet publications. What Lenin would certainly have disdained with unredeemed contempt had acquired a powerful Kremlin sanction.

If Black Hundred ideology had been resurrected—without, of course, referring specifically to that discredited group—it was with the use of certain Marxist and, especially, Leninist language and concepts (largely drawn from Lenin's work, *Imperialism, the Highest Stage of Capitalism*) and thus given an unofficial sanction. By the early eighties, it had even become appropriate to refer favorably to notorious Black Hundred authorities. Thus, Korneyev, in one of his major writings, published in 1982, warmly cited a book by a leading Black Hundred proponent, Aleksei

---

[1] *Pravda,* 22 July 1990.

*Demonology: A Concern to the Kremlin?* 75

Shmakov. Shmakov, a lawyer, had been a violent Jew-baiter in the post-1905 revolutionary period and served as an important advocate for the prosecution in the Mendel Beilis case.[2] It would have been unheard of for Kremlin editors, after 1917, to permit favorable reference to such a pronounced tsarist antisemite. By 1982, it had obviously become legitimate.

Certainly, in 1977, a climactic point was reached in the incendiary character of the anti-Zionist drive. The books, the articles, the television documentary, together with the arrest of Anatoly Shcharansky on charges of subversion, greatly intensified Jewish fears. For the first time, Soviet Jewish activists began speaking of the possibility of pogroms.[3]

Strikingly, only four years later, on February 23, 1981, President Leonid Brezhnev, in the course of a five-hour policy address to the Twenty-sixth Communist Party Congress, publicly denounced antisemitism in the USSR. At no previous Party congresses had the principal policy address of the Party leader ever referred to antisemitism, although Vladimir Lenin in various public statements did condemn it, as did Josef Stalin on one occasion.[4] After the Stalin era, reference to the subject by leaders had disappeared. It was not until July 18, 1965 that a high Soviet official, Prime Minister Aleksei Kosygin, chose to publicly denounce manifestations of antisemitism in a speech given in Riga which was carried in *Pravda* the next day.[5] Later, on September 5, 1965 *Pravda* vigorously editorialized against antisemitism, citing Lenin's comment that it was a "malicious exaggeration of...national enmity."[6] After that, the subject was dropped, to be replaced in 1967 by the authoritative comment: "there has never been and there is no anti-Semitism in the Soviet Union."[7]

The Brezhnev acknowledgement of the existence of antisemitism in the USSR fourteen years later and his sharp rejection of it came in the course

---

[2] Maurice Samuel, *Blood Accusation: The Strange History of the Beiliss Case* (New York: Alfred A. Knopf, 1966), 159, 179, 166–67, 221–22.
[3] Martin Gilbert, *Shcharansky, Hero of our Time* (New York: Viking, 1986), 166.
[4] Quoted in the *New York Times*, 15 January 1931.
[5] *Pravda*, 19 July 1965.
[6] *Pravda*, 5 September 1965.
[7] *New York Times*, 27 June 1967. The same statement was made by him in Canada and in Denmark, see *Chicago Tribune*, 21 October 1971 and *Jewish Chronicle* (London), 10 December 1971.

of observations on the nationality question of the Soviet Union, which, oddly enough, had nothing to do with the Jewish issue. Brezhnev had taken note of the sizeable movement into various Soviet republics of persons belonging to ethnic groups that were not indigenous to the specific republics.[8] Observing that the indicated ethnic groups had "specific requirements in the spheres of language, culture and everyday life," he strongly suggested that these "requirements" were not being met, with the consequent emergence of bitter interethnic tensions. He asked that the Party leadership on regional levels "penetrate deeply into such issues and propose ways of resolving them in good time."

The recommendation was immediately followed by the usual Party soporific on the nationality question: "the national feelings and national dignity of each person are respected in our country." The next sentence—the key one—was notable for juxtaposing the expected general Party message with a totally unexpected example. It read:

> The CPSU [Communist Party of the Soviet Union] has fought and will always fight resolutely against such phenomena [interethnic tensions] which are alien to the nature of socialism as chauvinism or nationalism, *against any aberration such as, let us say, anti-Semitism or Zionism* [emphasis added]. We are against tendencies aimed at artificial erosion of national characteristics. But to the same extent, we consider impermissible their artificial exaggeration. It is the sacred duty of the Party to educate the working people in the spirit of Soviet patriotism and socialist internationalism, of a proud feeling of belonging to a single great Soviet motherland.[9]

The chosen illustration of "nationalistic aberrations" would appear to be largely irrelevant as Soviet antisemitism was certainly not the primary expression of interethnic tensions in the USSR flowing from internal geographic mobility and migration. Indeed, the reference to antisemitism seemed almost accidental. However, as is known, nothing was accidental in the policy speech of the highest Communist Party authority, which was broadcast over radio, carried in the press, and most importantly, carefully studied for guidance and implementation in all Party organs.

Why, then, the stunning critical reference to antisemitism after a lapse

---

[8] *Pravda*, 23 February 1981. Also see Foreign Broadcast Information Service, FBIS-3, No. 036, Supplement 001 (24 February 1981), 38.
[9] Ibid.

of so many years? Two separate, although complementary, hypotheses can be advanced. The first relates to external considerations, the other, far more critical, to internal factors. That there existed an urgent need to refurbish the Soviet image, by now badly tarnished through public disclosures of the Kremlin's virulent antisemitic propaganda campaign, must have been patently obvious to Kremlin policy makers. The Council of Europe in Strasbourg had officially documented the massive hate drive as had an Australian parliamentary inquiry.[10] The Conference on Security and Cooperation in Europe, meeting in Madrid in November and December 1980, heard an elaboration of the charges of Soviet antisemitism, most notably by the Belgian delegate, René Panis.[11] Indeed, the Belgian's accusation was one of the rare occasions during the Madrid proceedings that prompted an angry and emotional response from the Soviet delegation. That response had taken the form of a vehement denial of the existence of Soviet antisemitism, which evoked laughter from the participants.

The Kremlin leadership may very well have reasoned that an improvement of relations with the West, worsened by the Afghan adventure of Moscow, necessitated the elimination, or at least the diminution, of the more extremist manifestations of antisemitism. Significantly, Brezhnev vigorously emphasized the value of detente several times in his address, in particular observing that "the vital interests of the European peoples" demand following the "path...which was laid in Helsinki." The Helsinki process negotiations in Madrid, he said, should continue "uninterrupted." Acknowledgement and public repudiation of Soviet antisemitism could conceivably help the Helsinki process. Certainly, the Kremlin's image was badly in need of polishing.

Strikingly, a Soviet diplomatic initiative in Washington, D.C., in late February and early March of 1981, which focused upon the American Jewish community, gave emphasis to the Brezhnev speech. Sergei Rogov, a prominent Soviet academic from the Moscow Academy of Sciences' In-

---

[10] Council of Europe, *Parliamentary Assembly Resolution No. 740 (1980) on the Situation of the Jewish Community in the Soviet Union,* Doc. 4580, 3 October 1980. Also see World Conference on Soviet Jewry, *The Position of Soviet Jewry, 1977–1980* (London: Institute of Jewish Affairs, 1980), 53, 83–92.

[11] William Korey, *Human Rights and the Helsinki Accord,* Headline Series (New York: Foreign Policy Association, 1983), 54.

stitute on American and Canadian Studies who was then serving as an envoy in the Soviet embassy in Washington, approached B'nai B'rith and several other Jewish organizations in Washington to call specific attention to the public repudiation of antisemitism. Rogov also emphasized a reference in the Brezhnev speech to ensuring "the security and sovereignty of all the states of this [Middle East] region, including Israel...."[12] It was the same Rogov, incidentally, who in July 1990 published an essay in *Pravda* condemning antisemitism.

Still, the image-building was far less important to Soviet officials than maintaining the power of the reigning Kremlin elite. How did Brezhnev and his close associates assess the burgeoning antisemitic vituperations in the mass media? Was Jew-baiting perceived as a serious challenge confronting Brezhnev's rule? The question was by no means as bizarre as it might seem. Exactly two years before the Brezhnev speech to the Party Congress, on February 23, 1979, a six-page typescript article replete with antisemitic invectives was placed in mailboxes throughout Moscow and distributed in Leningrad.[13] The striking aspect of the article was its open attack upon Brezhnev and seven of his associates on the Politburo as "Kremlin Zionists." They were distinguished from the "faithful sons" of Russia on the Politburo—top ideologist Mikhail Suslov, Leningrad Party chief Grigory Romanov, Party second secretary A. P. Kirilenko, and Prime Minister Kosygin.

The article reflected the rising chauvinist and xenophobic Russian nationalism that had deep roots in the Party and its leadership. Signed by an anonymous "Russian Liberation Organization," the antisemitic essay offered the following physical characteristics as guidelines for recognizing Zionists: "hairy chest and arms," "shifty eyes," and hook-like nose." The hirsute physical reference obviously pointed to Brezhnev whose name was somehow seen as part of an elaborate secret code designed to help "hidden Zionists" recognize one another. He was openly denounced for "blatantly usurping" the presidency of the USSR by ousting Nikolai Podgorny.

The fact that the reproduction and widespread distribution of this hate literature could take place in the monolithic Soviet totalitarian society

---

[12] Ibid.

[13] Dan Fisher, "Anti-zionist Trend Reveals Strains in Soviet Society," *Los Angeles Times*, 23 May 1979.

testified to the serious and growing challenge of Russian extremism. After all, duplication machines were strictly controlled and allocated by the authorities in Soviet society. It was not only from anonymous, subterranean sources that Brezhnev might have perceived threats to his authority. Several months before the Russian Liberation Organization article appeared in Moscow, the Philosophy Institute of the Soviet Academy of Sciences produced an anti-Zionist booklet designed for a very limited and select audience—only five hundred key Party officials.

The booklet, *Zionism in the Chain of Imperialism,* was written by one of the Soviet Union's most prolific propagandists against Zionism, Yevgeny Yevseev.[14] He now charged that Zionism was "more dangerous than German, Italian and Spanish Fascism." In his view, Zionism was "destroying the spiritual and moral health of the working class." The "enemy" was not merely abroad; its agents also could be found within the borders of the USSR. Yevseev criticized Soviet literature, movies, and television because "from time to time, people of Jewish origin appear as positive heroes or as supporting heroes." The challenge went deeper. Prominent Soviet literary officials, including Sergei Narovchatov, the chief editor of the major Soviet journal *Novy Mir,* and philosophy specialists like B. Kedrov and Mark B. Mitin, were declared to be "Zionist supporters" on grounds that they had written that Jews are an ancient people and Zionism appeared historically as a reaction to antisemitism.

Far more significant than the booklet itself was the question of how it was produced. The printing was done not in a publishing house but by a facility housed in the Ministry of Internal Affairs, which supervised Soviet police work.[15] Clearly, authority to produce the booklet had been granted at the very highest state levels.

Those accused of being Zionist supporters bitterly complained, and on March 11, 1979 the issue was formally aired in the Central Committee where Yevseev was reported to have been verbally chastised.[16] Yet, neither he nor the Philosophy Institute, which had sponsored the booklet, were punished. Clearly, chastisement was seen, in some quarters, as un-

---

[14] *Vremia i my,* 4 (August 1979): 134–56.
[15] Ibid. Also see, S. Lukin, "Snova ob sionizma," *Yevrei v SSSR,* 20 (Summer 1979).
[16] *New York Times,* 27 June 1979. Disclosure was made by Craig Whitney, the *Times* Moscow correspondent.

warranted. Two months later, scores of influential people received a mimeographed letter signed with a pseudonym—Vasily Ryazanov—which charged that "a powerful Zionist lobby" existed within the very Central Committee of the Soviet Communist party.[17] How the "lobby" functioned was detailed in the following manner: "They do not allow themselves to be attacked with the excuse that this would bring on accusations of antisemitism, negative reactions in world public opinion and damage to the policy of detente." The extremist and rightist challenge to the Kremlin was rare but nonetheless indicated the possible consequences of a previous unrestrained anti-Jewish propaganda campaign.

High level concern about a growing chauvinist thrust with distinctive antisemitic features became even more pronounced in 1980. This was disclosed in an extraordinary and unprecedented discussion between a Soviet Jewish researcher and a key official in the secretariat of the Party's Central Committee. The discussion was triggered by a two-year research project undertaken by Ruth Okuneva, a refusenik and former historian and researcher at the USSR Academy of Pedagogical Sciences. She assembled in three parallel columns statements concerning the character and culture of Jewry and proposals for solving the "Jewish Question." One column carried the assertions of the reactionary Black Hundreds organization (during the tsarist epoch); the second carried the statements of Nazi Germany's ideologists; and the third carried extracts from recent and current Soviet anti-Zionist books.[18]

The study, entitled "A Few Pages of Analogy," ran to eighty-seven pages. The documentation of antisemitic propaganda that echoed tsarist and Nazi hate was devastating. Okuneva sent the study to Brezhnev, as Party General Secretary, on April 12, 1980 with a covering letter noting that a half-dozen Soviet authors producing the massive anti-Zionist propaganda in articles and books were "violating the ideals of socialist internationalism that form the basis of the Communist Party's national policy." Her summary of the findings was sharp: "their works are full of savage hatred of Jews, not Zionism, and they do not conceal it. They

---

[17] Ibid.; see also the report of the *Washington Post* correspondent in Moscow, Kevin Klose, published in the *Jerusalem Post*, 23 July 1979.

[18] Ruth Okuneva, "Anti-Semitic Notions: Strange Analogies," in *Anti-Semitism in the Soviet Union: Its Roots and Consequences*, vol. 2 (Jerusalem: Hebrew University, 1980).

present the Jews as the enemies of the Soviet state, as counter-revolutionaries, spies, accomplices of Hitlerism."

On June 23, a surprised Okuneva received a postcard from the Central Committee requesting her to call Anatoly Aleksandrovich Sazanov, a committee official. Sazanov met with her on July 4. His queries and comments were cordial. Noting that her documentation was "very thorough," he went on to say that "it will be of use to us." Sazanov's observations were revealing. According to Okuneva, he said: "Don't think, however, that you have invented the bicycle. We are also working on this matter; we are concerned about exaggerations in this literature." Sazanov went on to say that he agreed with Okuneva's "evaluation" of specific Soviet authors, including Yevseev, Vladimir Begun, Valentin Pikul, Lev Korneyev, and Valery Yemelyanov—all literary hate peddlers.[19]

Sazanov's comments, while encouraging in their indication of the depth of concern in some official quarters, also suggested that the issue of the hatemongers' propaganda was far from being resolved. Sazanov told Okuneva that "we are not always able to keep track of all their tricks; these authors often manage to evade our control." Clearly, powerful forces were yet in contention.

Still, it was apparent that Brezhnev's men in the Party apparatus were profoundly concerned with the emergent antisemitism in the media and were determined to confront it head-on. Party officials concerned with internal matters may have believed that the struggle against extremist antisemitism could produce an additional useful bonus. The Party leadership had decided some time earlier to cut back the Jewish emigration rate and, since late 1979, had instituted harassment that reduced the exodus flow at first by approximately two-thirds, and later by three-quarters.[20]

One way to ease emigration pressure was to reduce antisemitism. Marxist dissenter Roy Medvedev, whose contacts with Central Committee officials were never totally severed, had warned for some time that the single most important factor generating Zionist impulses among Jews was

---

[19] Okuneva apprised the author of this development. See William Korey, "Brezhnev and Soviet Anti-Semitism." In Robert Freedman, *Soviet Jewry in the Decisive Decade, 1971–80* (Durham: Duke University, 1984), 33.

[20] World Conference on Soviet Jewry, *The Position of Soviet Jewry: Human Rights and the Helsinki Accords* (London: Institute of Jewish Affairs, 1985), 3–7.

official antisemitism.[21] Significantly, on the eve of the Twenty-sixth Party Congress, 130 prominent Soviet Jewish activists sent a ten-page plea to the delegates, forcefully asserting that the antisemitic media campaign was one of two "principal causes" for the rapid rise in the number of applications for emigration. (The other was the lack of facilities for cultural self-expression.) The Jewish activists appealed for a "change in the Party's attitude to Soviet Jewry," in particular the "virulent anti-Zionist campaign" that had reached "hysterical proportions" and "was coloring" the public's attitude toward Jewry.[22]

Even before the Brezhnev denunciation of antisemitism, close students of Soviet propaganda noticed a quantitative reduction of antisemitism in the media. The number of hate articles in the press during 1980 was certainly less than during 1979. In that sense, Sazanov's assertion to Okuneva that he and at lease some of his Party colleagues were "concerned" and "were working" on the matter is not without substance and significance.

Nonetheless, antisemitic propaganda had by no means ceased, and its qualitative character, echoing the tsarist *Protocols of the Elders of Zion* remained unchanged. The plea of the 130 Jewish activists to the Twenty-sixth Party Congress called attention to crude bigotry in *Pionerskaia pravda,* a tabloid organ of the powerful Komsomol for nine- to fourteen-year-olds. An article in the tabloid's October 10, 1980 issue by Lev Korneyev was not unusual. The following excerpt was characteristic:

> In view of the fact that Zionism is the instrument of the big Jewish bourgeoisie, it is backed by its enormous resources that are being pumped out from the gold, diamond and uranium mines of South Africa, the workshops and industrial plants of Europe, America and Australia. Zionists are trying to infiltrate into all the spheres of public life, into ideology, science, commerce. Even "Levi's" jeans are part of their operation; the profits from selling the pants are used by the firm for helping Zionists. Most of the major monopolies producing arms are controlled by Jewish bankers. The business made on blood brings them enormous profits. Bombs and shells explode in Lebanon—the bankers Lazards and Loebs are counting their profits. Bandits in Afghanistan are poisoning school children by gasses-

---

[21] Roy Medvedev, *Blizhnevostochnyi konflikt i yevreiskii vopros* (Moscow, 1970, mimeographed).

[22] The appeal circulated in samizdat, n.d.; a copy is in the author's possession.

-and stacks of dollars multiply in the safes of the Lehmans and the Guggenheims. It is understandable that for Zionism peace in the world is the main enemy.[23]

Korneyev's other assertions carried similar thrusts. The Jewish concept of the chosen people was said to be a "racist invention" of the Zionists who "instill enmity and hatred towards all non-Jews." Practitioners of subversion and espionage, of racism and racial discrimination, of militarism and imperialism, Zionism was declared to be "the Fascism of today."

The Korneyev article highlighted the basic limitation of the Brezhnev denunciation of antisemitism. The coupling by the Party general secretary of antisemitism with Zionism, to a significant degree, reduced and constrained the struggle against hate propaganda. Zionism, since 1967 and especially since 1971, had become the code word for Jewry, just as "cosmopolitanism" had been the code word during the "Black Years" of Stalin's antisemitism, 1948–53. It was precisely the media drive against Zionism that unleashed and gave sanction to the stereotypes, images, and formulations of vulgar antisemitism.

The inadequacy of the Brezhnev condemnation was glaringly revealed by an instructive article in the principal journal of Byelorussia, *Sovetskaia Byelorossiia,* on March 6, 1981 only two weeks after the Brezhnev address to the Party congress. Written by an especially infamous antisemitic propaganda specialist, Vladimir Begun of Minsk, the article was entitled "Danger: Zionism," but its theme, stripped of Aesopian formulations, was one of the most incendiary to have appeared in several years.[24]

The Begun article was formally designed as an answer to a letter that the newspaper was said to have received from a "war veteran." The letter had posed the following query: "At the beginning of the 1950s, the press carried articles about the Zionist organization, the 'Joint,' and its activities on behalf of the enemies of peace. I am interested in learning whether this organization still exists." The specific reference to the 1950s and the pointed question about the Joint were extraordinary. The early fifties was precisely the period when antisemitism in the USSR reached its most extreme form with the secret trial and execution of Jewish intellectuals and writers (July and August of 1952) and the unveiling of

---

[23] *Pionerskaia pravda,* 10 October 1980.
[24] *Sovetskaia Byelorussiia,* 6 March 1981.

an alleged "Doctor's Plot" (January through March 1953), which generated an especially dangerous pogrom atmosphere in the Soviet Union. The Joint, or more precisely, the American-Jewish Joint Distribution Committee, had been singled out in a massive propaganda campaign as the master instrument of world Zionism in a plot to murder all top Soviet leaders. The agents of the Joint were said to be nine Soviet doctors, mainly Jewish.[25]

Had the Doctors' Plot campaign reached its climax, the mass expulsion of Soviet Jews to Siberia and Central Asia would have followed together with executions of the principal "culprits."[26] Only the death of Stalin on March 5, 1953 brought a halt to the unfolding catastrophe and saved Soviet Jewry. Shortly afterward, the plot was disclosed by Stalin's successors to have been a total fabrication. Nikita Khrushchev would later reveal in his "secret speech" to the Twentieth Party Congress how the plot was concocted by Stalin and how torture was used to extract fraudulent confessions.[27]

The Doctors' Plot was so totally discredited and repudiated in official statements at the time that references to it—and to Joint—disappeared from the media. The indirect resurrection of the affair through the distinctive incendiary focus on the JDC was surprising and a stunning reminder that those seeking a violent resolution to the Jewish problem continued their efforts.

The appearance of the Begun article on the twenty-eighth anniversary of Stalin's death, almost to the exact date, must have triggered powerful—and dangerous—associations. Putting the query in the mouth of a "war veteran" was clearly designed to reinforce patriotic and chauvinistic memories, even as it dredged up the passions of Jew-hatred. The article itself regurgitated myths about the Elders of Zion, about how "powerful Jewish magnates"—Kuhns, Loebs, and Lehmans—manipulate Zionist-Jewish organizations, about how the Joint, acting as the instrument of the World Zionist Organization, engaged in espionage in the socialist countries and subsidized "the Zionist secret service."

---

[25] Yehoshua Gilboa, *The Black Years of Soviet Jewry, 1939–1953* (Boston: Little, Brown; 1971) 293–310.

[26] Ibid., 330–31.

[27] The text obtained by the State Department appeared in the *New York Times,* 5 June 1956.

Clearly, the juxtaposition of Zionism with antisemitism, like the juxtaposition of Zionism with racism, gave emphasis to the demonology of the subject. If the Party, at its highest levels, was concerned that antisemitism might be getting out of hand, they formulated no effective way to cope with it. On the contrary, bracketing antisemitism with Zionism merely underscored the evil of the latter and offered a justification for continuing the bigotry drive with the caveat of avoiding language directly referring to Jews.

Anti-Zionism remained a cardinal feature of Soviet ideology. In an authoritative work on "human rights" by Brezhnev's successor, the aged Konstantin Chernenko simply reiterated the fake and morally obtuse bracketing of Zionism and antisemitism.[28]

---

[28] Konstantin U. Chernenko, *Human Rights in Soviet Society* (New York: International Publishers, 1981), 50.

## Chapter 7

## Legitimation through the Jewish Anti-Zionist Committee

Eight years after Moscow acquired an international sanction for an official domestic anti-Zionist propaganda campaign that had taken on (in 1977) hysterical antisemitic features, the Kremlin nonetheless found that the sanction failed to allay concern, dismay, and anger in the West. Indictment of Soviet bigotry became a major feature of the West's presentations in international forums, such as the Helsinki review conferences. The subject evoked deep responses and hostile commentary in critically important sectors of Western public opinion, most notably among scientists and intellectuals, and even among key Communist parties such as those in Italy and France.

If the UN legitimation of anti-Zionism was effective at all, it was largely, though not exclusively, in Third World circles, especially in Arab countries. At the UN, of course, the resolution equating Zionism with racism unleashed endless diatribes and hindered any movement toward a Middle East dialogue. Beyond the UN itself, some left wing circles and some student groups were provided levers for attacking Israel. But the bulk of the West remained immune and, instead, considered the resolution—as did Sakharov—as an "abomination."

As the crescendo of angry criticism in the West mounted, Moscow sought a new way to cope with the problem. A new kind of legitimacy could be provided for the demonology, one that would appear to have sprung from Soviet Jews themselves. How could the views of these Jews, clearly the ones most directly affected by antisemitism, be challenged or placed into question?

The Soviet Public Anti-Zionist Committee came into existence on April 21, 1983.[1] It was and remained the special voice of the Kremlin on Jewish questions issued through selected persons whose commitment to Jewry was as nonexistent as their obeisance to Soviet ideology and power was palpably evident. The Committee proved to be the handmaiden of Moscow in performing vital state functions. At regular intervals, its voice could be heard through the press or in broadcasts abroad channeling the Kremlin's special propaganda to various public levels, both within the Soviet Union and abroad. Over time, the Committee assumed an increasing number of functions and, played an especially important, if deeply disturbing, role as the apologist and articulator of the Kremlin's propaganda policy on Zionism.

Using prominent Jews as the instrument of the totalitarian state to perform functions of control and propaganda with reference to the Jewish community as a whole was, of course, not new. The Nazis perfected the technique of utilizing existing Jewish councils or creating new ones initially to manipulate and control the Jewish community. The USSR had not been averse to exploiting specially-created Jewish mechanisms. When Stalin, during the era of the Doctors' Plot in early 1953, was planning to evacuate the Jews of the major urban areas of western Russia en masse to Kazakhstan in Central Asia, he arranged for prominent Jewish establishment figures to prepare a large-scale petition signed by them specifically "requesting" the evacuation for alleged humanitarian reasons—to rescue Jewry from public hostility.[2] Curiously, the newly-appointed head of the Anti-Zionist Committee, General David Dragunsky, was reported to have been among the first leading Jewish figures to sign the draft petition in early 1953. This was noted by Paul Novick, the editor of the New York Yiddish newspaper, *Freiheit,* in recalling his conversations with Ilya Ehrenburg.[3]

More nearly similar, particularly in its anti-Zionist focus, had been the

---

[1] TASS, 21 April 1983. Announcement of its formation appeared the same day in Reuters and UPI.

[2] Louis Rapoport, *Stalin's War Against the Jews: The Doctors' Plot and the Soviet Solution* (New York: Free Press, 1990), 176–90. Also see Roy A. Medvedev, *Let History Judge* (New York: Alfred A. Knopf, 1971), 494.

[3] Paul Novick noted the point in an article in *Freiheit* and communicated it orally to the author.

infamous press conference held on March 4, 1970 at the so-called "House of Friendship with the Peoples of Foreign Countries." The conference officially dealt with "questions relating to the situation in the Middle East." A group of prominent "citizens of the USSR of Jewish nationality" (a newly-created designation) was paraded at the conference in order to perform two functions. The first was to denounce Zionism or, more specifically, Israel. "The crimes of the Israeli military," it was said, "revive memories of the barbarism of the Nazis."[4] The overt aim here was to appease the Arab countries in the Middle East and to rally the Soviet general and Jewish publics behind Moscow's Middle East foreign policy, a policy whose popular support was somewhat less than enthusiastic.

The second purpose was implicit: to deny the validity of a growing demand, made clear in extensive and large-scale petitions reaching the West, that Soviet Jews sought to emigrate and be reunited with their relatives in Israel. Speakers at the press conference formally declared that Jews were not subject to any discrimination or antisemitism and, presumably, were "equal in rights to all others in the 240-million Soviet family." And, for the first time, in a quarter of a century, they spoke of the services presumably rendered to Jewry by the Soviet motherland. A collective declaration incorporating these views was signed by fifty-two leading Jewish establishment figures.

The Soviet mass media, following the press conference, mounted a loud and vast campaign in which thousands of "citizens of Jewish nationality" took part through letters, or almost daily statements in *Pravda,* as well as in other Soviet newspapers. The peak was reached in late March and early April 1970, and then gradually dropped off, although it continued at a much lower level for nearly a year.

The campaign against Zionism afterwards dropped the Jewish component and took on a totally virulent and vulgar antisemitic character which helped spur the growing and massive exodus movement among Jews. Critics within the Soviet institutional establishment, particularly among academicians, found fault with the overt antisemitism and recommended returning to the technique of the March 4, 1970 press conference.[5] This approach was articulated at a conference in February 1976, held by var-

---

[4] *Pravda,* 5 March 1970; *Izvestiia,* 6 March 1970.
[5] Ibid.

ious institutes in the humanities of the Soviet Academy of Sciences in Moscow. The conference was oriented to improving methodology for combatting Zionism.

The main aim was to halt the exodus movement among Jews. The chairman of the conference, B. G. Gafurov, emphasized that a principal task of anti-Zionist propaganda was to counter the emigration of "youth and talent" from the USSR. Gafurov served as director of the Institute of Oriental Studies of the USSR Academy of Sciences and chairman of the permanent commission in the institute for research into the exposure and criticism of the history, ideology and practice of Zionism.

One strategy recommended was to use Jews for the "unmasking" of Zionism instead of the blatant and crude antisemitism masquerading as anti-Zionism. This view was advanced by the chief editor of the journal *Narody Azii i Afriki,* who stressed that the "unmasking of nationalism should be tactical."[6] In early 1983, the recommendation was to find expression.

Announcement of the Anti-Zionist Committee's formation was preceded, clearly deliberately, by preliminary public disclosures in a large-scale media effort designed to prepare the general community. TASS, on March 31, 1983 stated that eight prominent persons (all known to be Jews of the establishment) had appealed for the creation of a "Soviet Public Anti-Zionist Committee" in order to aid in exposing "the anti-people and anti-humanitarian nature of the diversionary propaganda and policy of Zionism." *Pravda* and *Literaturnaia gazeta* the next day carried the lengthy text of the appeal and the signatures.[7]

The appeal took on a sharply anti-Zionist tone, although with time this would pale before the harshness of the invectives which would later be used. The TASS appeal read:

> In its essence, Zionism is a concentration of extreme nationalism, chauvinism and racial intolerance, justification of territorial seizure and annexation, armed adventurism, a cult of political arbitrariness and impunity, demagogy and ideological sabotage, sordid maneuvers and perfidy.[8]

---

[6] A detailed report of the conference appeared in the samizdat journal, *Yevrei v SSSR,* 14 (1977). Also see E. L. Solmar, "Protocols of the Anti-Zionist Elders," *Soviet Jewish Affairs,* 2 (1978): 57–66.

[7] *Pravda,* 1 April 1983.

[8] Ibid.

The definition carried an international and anti-Soviet dimension. The appeal considered that imperialism uses international Zionism extensively as one of its shock detachments in the assault on socialism.

Details of how the anti-Zionist campaign would unfold were not specified, but the explicit belligerent intention of the authorities was made clear. A second intention was also indicated, although in quite indirect fashion, namely, that Jewish emigration would be taken off Moscow's agenda. The appeal observed, in a formulation not used previously, that "the Jews, citizens of the USSR, are part and parcel of the Soviet people." Implicit was the notion that they could not be induced to emigrate. Explicitly condemned was "Zionist propaganda," the alleged purpose of which was said "to interfere in their [Jews'] lives" by spreading "falsehood and slander against the socialist homeland." The appeal rejected any perception that there was such a thing as a "Jewish problem" in the USSR.

Yet a third intention could be read into the language and formulations used. By emphasizing the unity of Soviet Jews with the Soviet public, the Kremlin was signalling a determination to break all links and contacts with Jewry on the outside—"international Zionism." The media campaign against Zionism was already emphasizing that Soviet Jewish contacts with visitors could be construed as subversive.

The eight signatories were Col. General David Dragunsky, Lenin Prize laureate Martin Kabachnik, writer Genrikh Gofman, law professor Samuil Zivs, filmmaker Boris Sheinin, history professor Gregory Bondarevsky, philosophy professor and editor Genrikhas Zimanas, and writer Yuri Kolesnikov.

A striking feature of the appeal's authors and of the Committee leadership, once created, was that none of them had participated in specifically Jewish life or activity in the USSR. Missing, for example, was the name of Aron Vergelis, the editor of the Moscow Yiddish monthly, *Sovietish Heimland*. Nor was any of the journal's staff mentioned; nor was there mention of the editors and staff of the Yiddish newspaper in Birobidzhan, the *Birobidzhaner Shtern*. None of the half-dozen rabbis in the USSR was mentioned, including Moscow Chief Rabbi Yakov Fishman.

When criticism of the Committee began to mount in the Western world that it was merely a tool of the authorities, and not a very Jewish tool at that, Moscow must have entertained second thoughts and prevailed upon Rabbi Fishman to join. In a Hebrew-language broadcast, beamed to Israel on April 28 by Moscow Radio Peace and Progress, he was cited as declaring that "as a Soviet citizen...I do my duty by joining the Soviet Public Anti-Zionist Committee."[9] He went on to attack "Jewish capitalists" who "use others, boys and girls, whom they lure into their nets. So-called Zionists are rich persons who do not go to live in Israel but rather build factories to exploit the 'poor Jews.'" Rabbi Fishman was scheduled to appear at the Committee's first press conference on June 6, which was a Monday. But on the previous Saturday, TASS reported that he had died of a sudden heart attack at the age of seventy.[10] No prominent member of the active Jewish community replaced him on the Committee.

According to the *Pravda* announcement of the Committee's creation on April 21, what presumably sparked the decision was an "enthusiastic" public response to the appeal and a "meeting of representatives of a number of public organizations" held that day.[11] No names of representatives were listed but they came from special organizations including the All-Union Central Council of Trade Unions, Novosti Press Agency and the Soviet Committee for Solidarity with the Peoples of Asia and Africa. One can speculate on the basis of who were chosen as officers that Novosti, the important external Soviet instrument used for propaganda abroad, was especially interested. Named as a deputy chairman was Mark Krupkin, a deputy director of the Novosti Press Agency. Another deputy chairman was Igor Belayev, a non-Jew (apparently the only one on the Committee) who was the Middle East expert for *Literaturnaia gazeta*. The third vice-chairman was novelist Yuri Kolesnikov, about whom more will be said later. Samuil Zivs was chosen first deputy chairman. The distinguished scientist and human rights advocate, Andrei Sakharov, detailed in an American literary journal the extraordinarily unscrupulous and opportunistic traits of Zivs.[12]

That David Abramovich Dragunsky would be chosen chairman was scarcely surprising. Twice awarded the prized Hero of the Soviet Union medal during wartime, the 72-year old general had been frequently utilized by the Kremlin over the years as its "court Jew" to respond to charges of antisemitism. The number of Jews in high positions in the

---

[9] *Moscow Radio Peace and Progress* 28 April 1983 (Hebrew).
[10] TASS, 4 June 1983.
[11] *Pravda,* 21 April 1983.
[12] Andrei Sakharov, "Anatomy of a Lie," *New York Review of Books,* 21 July 1983.

armed forces had declined and disappeared during the late forties and they were no longer admitted into higher military schools.[13] Dragunsky was a rare Jewish survivor. Equally significant, he continued to render important military service to the state, administering the Vysstrel Military Academy which trained officers of Third World armies. Among graduates bearing Dragunsky's approving signature was at least one PLO military official.[14] A U.S. intelligence official observed: "He doesn't just propagandize against Zionists; he trains people to kill them."[15]

Shortly afterwards, the structure of the Committee took shape. It was comprised of thirty-seven members, some non-Jews, including the editor of *Yunost*, "a poultry farmer," and a political correspondent for *Izvestiia*. Among the Committee members was the writer Tsezar Solodar, whose articles reeked with propaganda ravings that must have been prompted by self-hatred. From the membership, a Praesidium of thirteen was chosen, including the officers. One Praesidium member was deputy to the Supreme Soviet identified as a "factory worker" whose name suggested that he was non-Jewish.

Initially, ambitious plans were projected. Dragunsky and Zivs in an interview with a Vilnius newspaper on May 6 said that branches were to be set up in each Union republic with additional branches in Moscow, Leningrad, Novosibirsk and Birobidzhan.[16] Scholarly, artistic and literary works, along with films, plays and paintings were to be produced for the Committee. Candidates for state prizes in the field of anti-Zionism would be put forward. Finally, it was hoped to create a working group of specialists on Zionism to assist in shaping opinion everywhere. But that was for the future. The present was to be taken up with a massive propaganda display.

It was in June 1983 that the Kremlin's purposes in setting up the Anti-Zionist Committee were made transparently clear. Propaganda on a major scale from a central platform and directed to a variety of audiences—this

---

[13] Korey, *The Soviet Cage*, 57.

[14] Raphael Israeli, ed., *PLO in Lebanon: Selected Documents* (New York: St. Martin's, 1983), 76, Document 10; William Korey, "The Soviet Public Anti-Zionist Committee," in Robert O. Freedman, ed., *Soviet Jewry in the 1980s: The Politics of Anti-Semitism and Emigration and the Dynamics of Resettlement* (Durham: Duke University, 1989), 30.

[15] *New York Daily News*, 7 July 1983.

[16] *Sovetskaia Litva*, 6 May 1983.

was the overriding aim. Neither public policy nor public activity was a primary concern. The Committee, according to *Izvestiia* in early June, had acquired an address—Fruzenskaya Naberezhnaya 46—but visitors to the site found few occupants and limited activity.[17] An announcement was made about preparation of a booklet on the "enthusiastic" public response to the establishment of the Committee.

On June 6, a major press conference was staged for the Committee in which star billing was provided for Dragunsky and, especially, for Zivs, with a minor, though significant and ominous part played by Kolesnikov.[18] The date chosen was deliberate. It was to mark the anniversary of Israel's offensive into Lebanon in June 1982. Israel, together with "international Zionism," were to be targets.

Yet, surprisingly, the major focus turned out to be the Soviet Jewish emigration issue. Clearly the outcry in the Western world had not been stilled and, indeed, was continuing to find expression at Madrid where the ongoing review conference of Helsinki Final Act signatories (which had begun in November 1980 and would conclude in September 1983) ineluctably called upon the Soviet Union to adhere to the provisions of the Final Act. Basket 3 of the accord had made "reunion of family" a cardinal concern. The provision of the Basket legitimized the right of emigration for Jews, Soviet Germans, and Armenians. Soviet Jews clung to the hope that they ultimately might obtain exit visas as they had during the seventies. The number being permitted to leave had drastically shrunk since 1979.

The USSR was determined to end both the internal and external clamor for emigration. Zivs, a specialist on international law, was assigned the responsibility for justifying the drastic reduction of emigration. He said that "the considerable decrease" in the number of people emigrating from the USSR was the result of the fact that the process of family reunion flowing from World War II had been "basically completed." It was as if an objective and unalterable fact had been revealed; Soviet policy or decision-making it was contended, had nothing to do with the drastic drop in emigration. The families that needed reuniting had found that this

---

[17] See *Insight: Soviet Jews* (London), 9, no. 5 (September 1983).
[18] The conference was held on the premises of the Soviet Union's Foreign Ministry. Its semi-official organ published an edited version of the proceedings; see *New Times* (Moscow) 25 (1983).

aim had already largely been consummated.

Novosti, reporting on the conference the next day, gave the presumably objective fact world-wide attention:

> Some Western correspondents insistently tried to find out why emigration of persons of Jewish nationality from the USSR has now fallen off so sharply. They were told that the people who had left were mainly those whose families had been split up during World War II. The process or reuniting families is, for the most part, now completed.[19]

It was a neatly contrived myth to justify previous Soviet emigration policy. The facts, of course, were quite different. The Kremlin had been prompted to allow Jewish emigration for a variety of reasons totally unrelated to families presumably split by World War II.

Equally fallacious was the argument that the reunion of families had been completed. Solid evidence existed that some 400,000 Soviet Jews still in the USSR had requested and received from relatives in Israel a *vizov* (affidavit), assuring the kinship affinity.[20] Acquisition of the *vizov* was the first step in the emigration process for a Soviet Jew. Moreover, some 10,000 Soviet Jews were known to have formally applied for an exit visa and had been refused, frequently more than once. There was solidly-based speculation that the actual number of so-called "refuseniks" was twice or three times this total.[21]

Zivs and the Committee, however, preferred to suppress the truth and to adhere to a myth that contained a solid humanitarian element. But after elaborating the seemingly objective fact of the completion of the reuniting process, Zivs felt compelled to add a subjective factor which only complicated and weakened his argument. As noted by him, the influence of Zionist propaganda upon Jews had diminished, thereby inhibiting a desire to emigrate. Novosti reported that many earlier emigrants had written letters to the Committee—which were then read out at the press conference—which disclosed how they had been deceived by Zionist propaganda to believe in "a life in paradise" in Israel. Instead their fate has been one of trauma and tragedy. In their letters, they

---

[19] Novosti, 7 June 1983.

[20] World Conference on Soviet Jewry, *The Position of Soviet Jewry: Human Rights and the Helsinki Accords* (London: Institute of Jewish Affairs, 1985), 5.

[21] Ibid. Estimates of the number of refuseniks were provided by the National Conference on Soviet Jewry.

condemned the Zionist "snarer of souls."[22]

If the process of reunion was completed, what was the point of arguing that Zionist propaganda was no longer enticing? It suggested the reality which was that the USSR was playing an active role in discouraging emigration. Still the Kremlin felt it essential to develop the line that Zionist propaganda must be vigorously combatted in order to bring an end to the aspirations for emigration. Indeed, this became a major program of the Committee, expressed both in policy statements and newly-published works. The thesis of a completion of a reunion process would soon be dropped. It was too feeble an argument, even if well-intentioned, to uphold.

Besides, there existed the critical anti-Zionist and anti-Israeli objective of the Committee spelled out in its very name and in the selection of the date for the holding of a press conference. The Committee, at the conference, framed the Zionist issue in the East-West context. The United States, under President Reagan, was waging "psychological war" against the USSR, and "international Zionism" played a vital part in that war. Jewish political power in the United States and Israel—as perceived by Moscow—was an integral and vital part of the presumed global assault upon the USSR and Communist Eastern Europe. Igor Belayev, the Soviet Middle East specialist, added—with some emphasis—that while the USSR recognized Israel's right to exist, it condemned the latter's "aggressive and adventuristic" policies.

If Israel and "international Zionism" were subjected to critical commentary, the criticism was nevertheless restrained. First, the primary emphasis was to justify the cutback in Jewish emigration. Secondly, the virulence of the typical anti-Zionist diatribes in the media, often accompanied by antisemitic stereotypes or blatant Judeophobia, was absent. While Zionism was criticized, Zivs tried to place it in the context of the emigration issue. The Committee's role, he said, was "to explain and help Soviet citizens understand the false and venomous nature of Zionist propaganda."[23]

Indeed, Zivs, whose comments largely dominated the proceedings, made a determined public effort to assume a negative and critical posture vis-à-vis overtly antisemitic Soviet books, especially with their canards

---

[22] Novosti, 7 June 1983.
[23] Ibid.

about alleged Nazi-Zionist collusion. One such book had acquired international notoriety in 1982—Lev Korneyev's *Class Essence of Zionism*. Angry commentary about the book in the Western world and particularly in left wing groups could be expected to impact upon various circles in the USSR who, in their contacts with the West, might feel a sense of embarrassment.

Zivs very much fits this category. Earlier, in an interview with Novosti, he had spoken of the need for high quality academic works of an "ideologically principled character."[24] The initial appeal of the Committee referred to "reasoned criticism" of Zionism as its aim.[25] At the press conference on June 6, not surprisingly, Zivs sought to disassociate himself and his Committee from Korneyev and similar Judeophobes. Referring to works which carried anti-Jewish stereotypes and innuendos, Zivs emphasized that the Committee would "struggle against improper expositions [about Zionism] in such books which unfortunately do appear."[26] Significantly, this telling public comment of Zivs was not recorded in the Soviet media, but were reported the next day by the *New York Times* correspondent, who was present at the press conference.

In sharp contrast were the comments of Kolesnikov. While Zivs hoped to avoid an all-out criticism of Zionism that could spill over into antisemitism, Kolesnikov opened up with a vituperative barrage directed against Zionism which, he alleged, had deliberately failed to protect Jews during the Hitler period. "On the contrary," Kolesnikov went on, the Zionists "had betrayed them by conspiring with the Gestapo and SS leaders." This was followed by an obscene allegation—that Eichmann was hastily executed by the Israeli authorities after his trial in order to prevent "the sacred secrets" of Nazi-Zionist collaboration from becoming public.

It was the Kolesnikov line (which had been only a minor theme in 1983) that would ultimately prevail. By 1984 a vicious antisemitism involving Kolesnikov's own writings would be in full bloom.

As early as the late summer and fall of 1983, it had become clear that the Kremlin would use the Committee as its propaganda instrument dir-

---

[24] *Sovetskaia Litva*, 6 May 1983.
[25] *Pravda*, 21 April 1983.
[26] *New York Times*, 7 June 1983.

ected both to the Jewish *and* the Arab world in dealing with Middle East issues. For Jews, both within and without the USSR, the Committee provided an automatic sanction for the Soviet Union's anti-Israel, pro-Arab policies. For the Arab countries, it offered a demonstration of how far Moscow was prepared to go in order to promote the Arab cause.

Thus, the Anti-Zionist Committee issued public statements appearing in the Soviet press condemning Israel's actions in Lebanon and the occupied territories. The Israel-Lebanese withdrawal agreement in May was denounced, and the attack on the El Khalil Islamic college in early August in which several persons were killed was sharply censured. Articles by top Committee members, such as Dragunsky and Mark Krupkin, appeared in leading Soviet press organs devoted to the condemnation of Israel and Zionism. In addition, the Committee took part in Soviet Hebrew-language broadcasts beamed to Israel.[27]

Particularly instructive was an interview with Dragunsky by Radio Damascus in late October.[28] The general sought to impress his Arab listeners with the impact of the Committee's pro-Arab activities. He related that it had already received 10,000 letters of which 1,250 came from outside the USSR, including Israel. He referred to "important" articles for which the Committee was responsible which had appeared in the Soviet press. He boasted that the Committee had become organizationally stronger. Finally, he acknowledged that the Committee had developed "close and extensive relations with the Arab world," especially Syria, one of the most militant "rejectionist" and anti-Zionist states in the Middle East. Its Friendship Treaty with the USSR was probably the only treaty in existence which specifically targeted Zionism as an "enemy" and called for its removal.

As initially conceived by the Soviet leadership, the Anti-Zionist Committee was to function on a defensive, propaganda level, justifying Kremlin policy primarily on the Jewish emigration cutback and secondarily on militant anti-Zionism. Besides the press conferences, newspaper articles and special broadcasts abroad, the Committee at the end of August and early September 1983 produced two brochures, both attractively packaged and published by Novosti. The first focussed upon

---

[27] *New Times* (Moscow) 21 (May 1983), and 28 (July 1983); *Izvestiia,* 6 August 1983; and *Pravda,* 28 July 1983.

[28] Radio Damascus 29 October 1983 (Arabic broadcast).

the June press conference and was entitled *The Anti-Zionist Committee of Soviet Public Opinion: Aims and Tasks*. The second constituted a collection of letters received by the Committee alleging nationwide support for it, particularly among Soviet Jews.[29]

Significantly, the Committee was deprived of any positive functions which might show a commitment to Jewish tradition and Jewish culture. The Kremlin had no intention—it was apparent—of creating another *Yevsektsiia* (Jewish Sections of the Party which had been active in the twenties), or another Jewish Anti-Fascist Committee (active from 1942 to 1948), both of which had promoted multifaceted, if politically circumscribed, Yiddish cultural and literary programs. Both institutions had been destroyed, in keeping with the party aim of facilitating the forcible assimilation of Jews.[30] It was hardly conceivable that the Kremlin would now wish to foster, in a systematic way, Jewish culture or identity. For that reason, the few Soviet Jews officially involved with Jewish culture and religion were not originally included in the Committee.

Precisely because the Kremlin's intention was to avoid Jewish identity, restraints were placed upon the expansion and extension of the Committee's structure, despite initial promises along this line. Little was reported in the Soviet press about the creation of new local branches. In November, rumors appeared in the West that branches had been set up in the Latvian cities of Riga and Daugavpils. Later, it was noted in the West that Zivs had sought to set up branches in Lithuania. However, corroboration of these rumors did not appear in the Soviet media.[31]

A second limitation on the Anti-Zionist Committee was more technical and related to its function in the international political sphere. It was appropriate for the Committee to be the tough, hardline anti-Zionist advocate, but supposing the Kremlin wished to send a message to American or Western Jews on detente? Dragunsky told an Arab foreign interviewer in October 1983 that the Committee was "now preparing an ap-

---

[29] See *Insight: Soviet Jews* (London), 11, no. 6 (1985), 1–2.

[30] For background, see Zvi Gitelman, *Jewish Nationality and Soviet Politics* (Princeton: Princeton University, 1972); and Gilboa, *The Black Years of Soviet Jewry, 1939–1953* (Boston: Little, Brown; 1971) 187–225.

[31] *Jews in the USSR* (London), 3 November 1983; *Agence Télégraphique Juive* (Paris), 3 January 1984.

peal to the Jews of the United States, exposing Israeli genocide actions against the Arabs."[32] This appeal never appeared.

Instead, the following month—November—the *New Times* of Moscow published an "Open Letter" to U.S. Jews from fifty-three "Soviet citizens of Jewish nationality."[33] It concentrated upon detente, an end to the arms race and a freeze on nuclear weapons. Such steps when realized would mark the "beginning of the road that should lead to disarmament." The Committee may have been instrumental in conceiving the idea and in advising as to who ought to be the signatories—at least one-half were associated with the Committee—but to sponsor the appeal would be inconsistent with the group's hardline purpose. At the same time, the Committee no doubt had a hand in a secondary point made in the Open Letter—that the raising of the issue of "concern for Soviet Jews" in the United States was allegedly harmful to detente. Finally, the Open Letter contained a call to American Jews to challenge the alleged aggressive policy of Israel and which posed "a threat to the very existence of that State." This, too, revealed a Committee purpose. Yet, the broad aim of the Open Letter made it essential to sever an direct linkage to the Committee.

From the beginning of 1984, the Committee's anti-Zionist propaganda function took on a much sharper form, indeed, becoming its dominant feature. The character of the new stress was established overtly elsewhere, and not intrinsically related to the Committee. On January 17, 1984, *Pravda* published an obviously pacesetting article on Zionism by one of its top commentators and specialist on anti-Zionist questions, Vladimir Bolshakov. The Bolshakov thesis, patently echoing the new Kremlin thrust, made Zionism the moral and political equivalent of Nazism.[34]

The equation was expressed and would continue to be expressed, on three levels. First, Zionism was said to have been the active supporter and partner of Nazism in the latter's rise to power and in its repressive policies, including the destruction of Jewry. The absurdity of the charge

---

[32] Radio Damascus, 29 October 1983 (Arabic broadcast).

[33] *New Times*, 46 (November 1983).

[34] *Pravda*, 17 January 1984. In February 1971, Bolshakov had called Zionism "an enemy of the Soviet people" Vladimir Bolshakov, "Anti-Sovetizh-professiia sionistov" (Anti-Sovietism: the profession of Zionists), *Pravda*, 18 February 1971.

was less consequential then its moral heinousness. Second, the purposes of Zionism and Nazism were said to be the same, establishing a particular ethnic group as the "chosen people," as superior to and dominant over all others. Hitler, it was argued, had actually borrowed his ideology from Theodor Herzl. Finally, Israel was declared to be following a bellicose foreign policy line, especially in Lebanon, that was similar to the Nazis and prompted by a motivation similar to that of the latter.

Two days later, on January 19, TASS reported that the Anti-Zionist Committee had held a press conference which condemned Israel (as well as the United States) for "barbarous aggression" in Lebanon.[35] It was the beginning of a year-long effort linking Zionism and Israel with Nazism and Nazi-like policies. The committee had become the intimate handmaiden of the Kremlin in its broader objectives.

The climactic expression of the new emphasis was an elaborate and remarkable press conference held by the Committee at the press center of the USSR Ministry of Foreign Affairs and heavily reported in the press (especially in *Literaturnaia gazeta* on May 23), and on radio broadcasts.[36] Moscow Radio, in its domestic service, underscored the Committee's preeminent objective: "The main thing in the work of the Committee is to expose the reactionary activity of contemporary international Zionism. At the press conference, the provocative role of international centers of Zionism was demonstrated convincingly."[37]

Dragunsky played the leading role in establishing the Zionist-Nazi equation. "We expose," he said, "the methods borrowed [by Israel] from the arsenal of Nazi war criminals such as concentration camps, keeping people in custody in unbearable conditions, summary beatings and murders, and Israel's institutionalization of terror as its state policy." Denounced, too, was the Israel-Lebanon peace agreement which, he said, had been imposed upon Lebanon and which violated its sovereignty.

But Zionism was not only portrayed as a Nazi-type aggressive power. It was also described as a Nazi-type subversive ideology striking at the Soviet Union itself through the "spurious slogan" of "defending Soviet Jewry." "International Zionist centers and their emissaries" were presented as responsible for the campaign for Soviet Jewry and for

---

[35] TASS, 19 January 1984.
[36] *Literaturnaia gazeta,* 23 May 1984.
[37] Radio Moscow, 15 May 1984 (Russian broadcast).

inveigling President Ronald Reagan to take part in it. The U.S. President joined the campaign of slander, Dragunsky claimed, in order to cover up U.S. violations of human rights, but also in order to win support among Jews "whose great-grandfathers fled the pogroms against Jews under the Tsarist regime to seek refuge overseas."[38]

A fascinating turn then took place in the Committee's press conference. Sharp criticism of the Kremlin's anti-Jewish practices in a variety of areas—education, culture, and emigration—was being articulated everywhere in the Western world. Some kind of response was thought to be essential. And the press conference was staged in such a manner as to present a flow of witnesses to deny allegations about Soviet antisemitism, and to link the allegations—the "slander"—to international Zionism.

Since discrimination against Jews in Soviet universities had become a major issue in Western academic circles, the Committee brought forth a young woman named Nataliya Grindberg who was studying at the mechanics-mathematics department of the University of Moscow. She asserted: "Western propaganda claims that young Jews are barred from higher education are lies." No statistics were offered and aside from her "personal" testimony, little of substance was advanced. The planned refutation, clearly, was quite weak.

On the cultural level, the Committee was able to summon the assistance of Aron Vergelis from *Sovietish Heimland* and Leonid Shkolnik, editor of the *Birobidzhaner Shtern*. The impact was greater than that offered by the Moscow student. Vergelis was accustomed to offering a version of Jewish cultural life that might appear impressive to the uninformed. Shkolnik described plans to commemorate the fiftieth anniversary of the establishment of the Jewish Autonomous Region. He failed to note the anomaly however, that only some 6 percent of the region's population was Jewish.[39]

The major emphasis was on the emigration issue where the argument was made that Zionist propaganda was the source of the problem and of personal tragedy. Several persons told harrowing tales. A Kishinev resident, Yefim Lecht, related how the Zionists induced his wife, who had a grave illness, to emigrate to Israel together with their young children.

---

[38] *Literaturnaya gazeta,* 23 May 1984.
[39] William Korey, "The Future of Soviet Jewry," *Foreign Affairs,* 58, no. 1 (Fall 1979), 80.

There she died shortly after attempting suicide. Lecht told the press: "The Zionist emissaries are mean and vindictive. I have found this out from my own experience. I know quite a few cases where, after failing to prod people into leaving for Israel, Zionists floated foul rumors to compromise the families of these people, sow suspicion and provoke conflicts."

A second witness, Ilya Tolmassky, related how his wife had emigrated to Israel and how she had failed to adjust to life in the Jewish state. Eventually she became ill and died. Tolmassky concluded that Soviet Jews must "fight against Zionism and lay bare the true essence of its propaganda."

A third witness, Gavriel Ilyaev, had just returned to the Soviet Union after living in Israel eleven years. From Tashkent, and now 75 years of age, Ilyaev related how he had to live in a damp basement in Jerusalem despite his asthma, how he never acquired sufficient money to buy more than the minimal basic foodstuffs, and how he had to start a new career—bookbinding—in his old age.

The point of these horror stories, clearly tendentious and a gross distortion of the mass emigration process which had involved over a quarter-million persons, was to demonstrate the evil of Zionist propaganda and how it no longer was effective. Zivs, in contrast to his previous posture which justified the emigration decline in objective terms, now stressed exclusively the failure of Zionist propaganda. But, inherent in the argument was the need for more horror stories and more "witness" demonstrations at press conferences so as to convince the uncertain and the doubtful. If the number of Jewish emigrants had drastically dropped, said Zivs, it was due to the fact that "the numbers of those who have understood their mistake and abandoned their intentions have been rising over the past year."[40]

Zivs could have added that the past year was one marked by massive publication of the supposed horrors of living in Israel. The Anti-Zionist Committee had been active in this endeavor. In any case, Zivs made it unmistakably clear that "the process of reuniting families has practically ended." Both Soviet Jews and Jewry abroad had to learn emigration was no longer a legitimate option. It was Zionism which was the enemy and which was responsible for the delegitimization of emigration. Indeed, 1984 marked the lowest point by far since 1970 in the Jewish emigration

---

[40] *Literaturnaya gazeta,* 23 May 1984.

pattern.

Illuminating the dominant ideological trend of the Committee oriented to an overall assault upon Zionism was the role assigned to Yuri Kolesnikov, an otherwise obscure novelist who, though Jewish, had written a particularly virulent antisemitic book, *The Curtain Rises,* published in 1979 by the strongly nationalist Military Publishing House in Moscow. It had received but one major review—in *Pravda*—and then seemed to disappear from public view.[41]

A review by General Dragunsky appeared on September 5, 1979; it was one of his rare published articles prior to 1983. Hailing the novel as "one of the first artistic works exposing that dangerous and current phenomenon—Zionism," Dragunsky indicated that it had established on a "documentary foundation" a linkage between "Nazi crimes" and the "Zionist top clique." That alleged linkage was scarcely "accidental," said Dragunsky, since both Nazis and Zionists "put the purity of the race higher than anything else."

For the next four years, nothing further was reported about the work. However, once the Anti-Zionist Committee was created with Kolesnikov as its vice-chairman, the Kremlin went to inordinate lengths to focus national and international attention upon both the author and his book. The reason was made patently clear. Soviet authorities, through massive promotion efforts, were underscoring the predetermined function of the Committee.

First, the Kolesnikov book was reissued in 1983 in serial form in two numbers of the literary weekly, *Roman-gazeta.*[42] Then, in 1984 it was translated into several foreign languages, including English and published by Progress Publishers. Finally, the book was lavishly praised by the Soviet press with *Ogonek* (the popular weekly published by *Pravda* in an edition of two million) devoting an unusual large-scale encomium to the book.[43] The review appeared on May 19, 1984 just four days after the Committee's press conference in which Kolesnikov himself appeared.

Valentina Malmi, the *Ogonek* reviewer, at the beginning established the

---

[41] For a detailed summary, see *Insight: Soviet Jews* (London), 10, no. 5 (September 1984). Initially published by the Soviet military in 1984, it was translated into several languages including English and printed by Progress Publishers.

[42] *Roman-gazeta,* 13–14 (1983).

[43] *Ogonek,* 19 May 1984.

principal theme of both the book and her review: "Italian Fascism, German Nazism, Romanian nationalism—and everywhere, everywhere, everywhere—the skillful and bloody strides of Zionism." She went on to emphasize that the author's main point, indeed, the "lesson of history" is that "the marching songs of the Fascist and Zionist youth were clearly similar." But if Fascism and Nazism were treated with scorn and sarcasm, Zionism was presented in more serious and deadly fashion. For Zionism, at its "essence," was seen as "misanthropic" which ineluctably "calls us to vigilance to be prepared to rebuff [it]." Clearly, Zionism was seen as a great threat to the Soviet Union itself.

Beyond the anti-Zionist obsession and undoubtedly undergirding it was Judeophobia itself. The typical Soviet anti-Jewish stereotype was given special emphasis by the reviewer. The Jewish characters were described as interested only in business: "commerce was life itself." And they exploited war for business, for "cash only."

The Kolesnikov book recalled the writings, fictional or otherwise, of the Hitler Reich. The novel's leading Jewish character, who was from Bessarabia, Haim Volditer, was introduced as a "halutz," whose task it was near the end of World War II to buy Czech machine guns from Romanian whores with American Jews' money in order to kill Arabs. He is brought into contact with the novel's central character, Rabbi Ben-Zion Hagera, the head of the local Jewish community in Limassol, Cyprus and an "extremely influential member of the Zionist Action Committee."

Rabbi Hagera was the very embodiment of evil even as he incorporated within himself every negative Jewish stereotype. Described in sinister terms as "the spitting image of Rasputin," he was rich and gross and simultaneously miserly and money-grubbing. A monumental hypocrite, this religious leader who also acted as the community banker, was the joint owner, with an unscrupulous police officer, of a local brothel. The identification of Judaism with prostitution resonated throughout the book.

Crude antisemitism of the Nazi and later Soviet variety was explicit in the discussions of the Zionist Action Committee. A key courier from the Zionist "Center" arrived to explain that "it is no secret that some of our coreligionist financial magnates hold the destinies of other people in their hands. In any case, their power to influence the policies of the rulers of these people is tremendous. That is why, by remaining in the countries of the Diaspora, they can and do render priceless aid to our cause." Here is made clear the "conspiracy" of the international Jewish financiers. Nazi Germany and the countries the latter dominated were, of course, an exception, noted the courier. But, he then observed that it "is our duty to save those well-off and influential people...until the time comes when they will again be able to say their weighty word in Germany." The last point was designed to clarify a secondary theme running through the book as to why, allegedly, the Zionist leadership frequently allowed poor Jews to be slaughtered while the rich were supposedly rescued.

Emerging in the discussions of the Committee and in the unfolding of the plot was the book's major theme: Zionist-Nazi collaboration. The novel's courier was asked how the Zionist "Center" regarded "the anti-Semitism of Herr Hitler." The answer took the form of an enthusiastic endorsement: "To put it bluntly, if this Adolf Hitler were not here today, then we Beitarim Zionists would have to invent him!" He went on to explain that "Yes, we Zionists are interested in encouraging anti-Semitism!" In this way, Jews are not allowed to forget "who they are" and are thereby motivated to become *halutzim* (pioneers) in Palestine.

The Nazi-Zionist linkage was drawn in precise, if somewhat absurd, terms. The German intelligence chief, Admiral Canaris, was portrayed as operating in the United States during World War I as a Jewish businessman with the name "Moishe Meyerbeer." The high-level Nazi official, Reinhard Heydrich, was shown to have descended from a Jewish grandmother. Especially stunning is the "revelation" that Adolf Eichmann was an agent of the Jewish Agency who had been deliberately infiltrated by the Jewish Agency into the Nazi movement as early as 1932.

Later, the novel had Eichmann secretly visiting Palestine in the guise of a correspondent for a Berlin newspaper. He then met with three agents of the Hagana special operations service. The following discussion was then offered to the reader:

> The Hagana men say that it is high time for the parties to get down to business. "Now, both of you and us can achieve a lot. But, for that, we need arms! And we want you to help us get them."
>
> Eichmann's spirits soared...the deal was fully in line with the purpose of his mission in Palestine.... It was then that a deal of tremendous international significance was struck between the SS Fuehrer and the Sherut Israel representative...the Nazis were establishing a "fifth column in Palestine to operate against the British; the Zionists were doing their utmost to bring closer the day when they would speak with the Arabs, and partly with British, in the

language of machine-gun fire."[44]

At approximately the time the Kolesnikov book was being given extraordinary attention in *Ogonek,* the author was offered a broadly national and international platform on which to express his views. On May 15, 1984 (four days prior to the *Ogonek* essay), at the Kremlin's stage-managed press conference for the Anti-Zionist Committee, Kolesnikov was given special attention. A correspondent from the weekly, *Nedelia*—put to him the following loaded question: "What can you say about the dirty methods used by the Zionists?" The novelist was succinct in his response: "the reactionary activity of international Zionism and the aggressive policy of the ruling circles of Israel toward the Arab peoples have been denounced by the world public as expansionist, terrorist, and racist." He went on to condemn "noisy gatherings" organized by the Zionists which use "falsehood and blackmail, bribes and promises, threats and even violence in order to continue enticing Jews out of the Soviet Union."[45]

Even as the vitriolic anti-Zionist campaign with its antisemitic overtones was being pursued, the Committee sought to cloak itself in some kind of Jewish garb, if only to provide it with a sense of legitimacy. With time, the Committee would seek to take on more specifically Jewish functions. Nonetheless, the additional roles performed in special dress did little to hide or minimize the seamier aspect of the Dragunsky group, so closely linked to the Kremlin's broader ideological and propaganda objectives regarding Zionism and Israel.

In late February 1984, the Praesidium of the Committee met and concerned itself largely with preparations for the 125th anniversary of the birth of Sholem Aleichem in the USSR.[46] The great Yiddish writer remained throughout Soviet history the solitary example and focus of public attempts to demonstrate the Kremlin's interest in things Jewish. While some cultural programs did emerge from the discussions, including a special evening on June 4 at Moscow's Central Actors' Building, it is significant that the Soviet press coverage given to the Praesidium meeting was limited. In addition, the meeting found it politic to couple its cultural

---

[44] Yuri Kolesnikov, *The Curtain Rises* (Moscow: Progress, 1984)(English).
[45] *Literaturnaia gazeta,* 23 May 1984.
[46] *Sovetskaia kultura,* 1 March 1984.

discussion with a condemnation of the Jewish Defense League for an alleged attack upon the Soviet Mission to the UN.

Similarly, the Committee at its May 15 press conference, directly involved both Vergelis and Shkolnik—two key figures in what remained of Yiddish culture in the USSR—for the first time. Both played prominent roles at the press conference and sought to document a certain vitality to Jewish culture in the USSR.

However, the next press conference of the Committee was given over almost entirely to a single issue—alleged Zionist-Nazi collaboration. The press conference was held on October 12 and largely focused on plans in the USSR to commemorate the fortieth anniversary of the victory over Nazism. The significance of the press event lay in the fact that it constituted a harbinger of developments for 1985 and, especially, of such developments as would affect the public perception of Jews in the context of a great patriotic ceremony.

Dragunsky opened the proceedings by contending that Zionists have made every effort to diminish the role of the Soviet Union in the historic destruction of Nazi Germany. Documentation for the unfounded charge was not produced. The Committee chairman added that it was "the victory of the Soviet Union that saved the Jews from total annihilation." If something of an exaggeration, the essential aspect of the assertion has been since World War II a staple of arguments advanced by Jews, including Zionists of every persuasion.

From the obviously political perspective of Dragunsky, it was convenient to distinguish between the actions of non-Zionist Jews and of Zionists during World War II. The former were presented as having fought against Nazism in the Red Army, the Allied armies, and in the partisan and resistance movements. In contrast, Zionists were described as having avoided fighting Nazism altogether and, instead, having collaborated with the Fascist enemy.

Stunningly, Dragunsky consciously neglected the massive documentation of the prominent and often key role of Zionists in the Warsaw Ghetto uprising, in the various resistance and partisan movements, and of course, in the Jewish Legion itself raised in Palestine. Instead, he and his colleagues on the Committee, including Zivs, Bondarevsky, and Rybalchenko pointed to various instances that, appropriately packaged and distorted, might bolster the argument of alleged Zionist-Nazi collaboration. Their contention was supported by two outside "experts"—Yulian Shulmeister, a senior lecturer at the University of

known for his virulent anti-Zionist writings, and a certain Yevgeniia Finkel, characterized as a resistance fighter during the Nazi occupation.

Among the examples offered of the supposed Zionist-Nazi collaboration were the "transfer agreement" of 1933, and the various contacts between representatives of the Gestapo and the Hagana. Leaders of the Jewish Councils (Judenräte) were described as Zionists who had betrayed the Jewish communities. Also at the press conference, Massimo Massara (described as an Italian historian) sought to demonstrate that Zionism and Italian Fascism had a close affinity.

A corollary of the thesis that Zionism had an ideological affinity with Nazism and had collaborated with it was the argument that Israel's actions, particularly in Lebanon, were Nazi-like. At the press conference, this theme was articulated by two Scandinavian members of the so-called International Commission of Inquiry into Israel's Crimes against the Lebanese and Palestinian People. The use of non-Russians, even when they may not be recognized as independent and distinguished experts, was designed to provide an aura of objectivity. Additional "evidence" of Israel's Nazi-like character was offered by Mark Krupkin, the Novosti executive, who cited the election of Rabbi Meir Kahane (the founder of the radical political party Kach) to the Knesset.[47]

The press conference of the Anti-Zionist Committee was to exert an impact on later, related media accounts emphasizing the heroic role of the Red Army in the war against Hitler. *Komsomolskaia pravda* on October 31 carried a response to a query about attempts made by "Zionist" propaganda to denigrate the Soviet contribution to the victory over Nazism.[48] The author, a certain A. Aleksandrov, reproduced passages from a previous, October press conference and went on to claim that "a criminal alliance of the Zionists and Nazis" had led to the massacre of six million Jews. He added that the Zionists were only concerned with Jewish victims of the Nazis and not with other nationalities, including Soviet citizens.

The last point was made again in *Izvestiia* on January 13, 1985 by the deputy chairman of the Novosti agency. His article, which referred to the Committee's press conference, claimed that Israeli school textbooks on recent history made virtually no reference to the Soviet contribution to

---

[47] *Novosti*, 12 October 1984.
[48] *Komsomolskaia pravda*, 31 October 1984.

the defeat of Hitler. Documentation of the allegation was not extended.[49]

That the provocatory Anti-Zionist Committee theme on Zionist-Nazi collaboration would become the dominant perception in the media was underscored on January 17, 1985 when TASS published the text of an interview with the Soviet Union's leading antisemitic propagandist—Lev Korneyev. Much of his earlier writings had been devoted to the collusion theme, and more recently, in 1982, Korneyev had questioned the number of Jewish victims of the Holocaust. He speculated that the published figures exceeded by as much as three times the actual size of the Nazi massacre of Jews.[50]

For over a year, little had been heard from Korneyev in the media, suggesting that the Kremlin leadership had been sufficiently embarrassed by his antisemitism as to warrant his being kept out of the major press organs. Criticism of Soviet antisemitism in the Western world had remained intense and Korneyev had been especially targeted, so only a few mild and inconsequential articles by him had been permitted to appear. Now, Korneyev returned with his usual vitriol. In the interview, he accused Zionist-Jewish bankers and industrialists of financing the Nazis. He also charged—as he had done earlier—that Zionists prevented Jews from joining the struggle against Fascism and that they shared responsibility for the Nazi extermination of Jews. That Korneyev would return to the public eye was hardly surprising given the kind of propaganda line intensively pursued by the "Jewish" Anti-Zionist Committee and especially by its vice-chairman, Yuri Kolesnikov. The Committee had, after all, set the pace for others to follow.

To divert attention from this rather malodorous function, the Anti-Zionist Committee sent a telegram to the United States Congress which charged the United States with being antisemitic. It read:

> It is a feeling of great concern that moves us to appeal to you, members of the US Congress. We have learned from an Associated Press report that 715 cases of anti-Semitic acts of vandalism, insults, threats, attacks on individual Jews and Jewish organizations were registered in your country in the past year.[51]

---

[49] *Izvestiia*, 13 January 1985.
[50] TASS, 17 January 1985.
[51] David Greenberg, "A Step Forward for the Anti-Zionist Committee," *Radio Liberty Research*, RL107/85, 9 April 1985.

The solicitousness was accompanied by a demand that American legislators "do everything possible to stop the growth of anti-Semitism in the USA [since] it is a disgrace to civilized society."

The diversion, drawn from Orwellian "doublethink," could only amuse. It was B'nai B'rith's Anti-Defamation League that had prepared the report on antisemitic incidents in the US upon which the Associated Press based its story.[52] That same report indicated that the antisemitic episodes were incidental, isolated, and far from the mainstream of American life. Quite the opposite was the situation in which discrimination against Jewish culture and against Jews, for example, in higher education or employment, was built into the very fabric of society.[53] Or, when provocatory antisemitic propaganda, masquerading as anti-Zionism, saturated the mass media, including the responsible central press organs.

In the late summer and fall of 1985—strikingly on the eve of the Reagan-Gorbachev summit—the Kremlin's anti-Zionist campaign sharply intensified. Inevitably, the Soviet Anti-Zionist Committee was called upon to play a central role in the campaign, now reaching unprecedented levels of public visibility. Especially important was the Committee-sponsored publication in August of a 300-page book of photos, illustrations and documents entitled *White Book*.[54] Designed to be an authoritative statement on the evils and horrors of Zionism, 200,000 copies were printed, and given extensive public attention in the media.

Some background on the publication of the *White Book* would be particularly pertinent as it throws light on the Kremlin's new-found determination to make the Anti-Zionist Committee the vanguard of its broad political campaign against Zionism. An earlier and smaller *White Book* on Zionism had appeared in 1979.[55] It was published by the principal legal group of the USSR, the Association of Soviet Lawyers (perceived as similar to the American Bar Association), in an edition of

---

[52] Anti-Defamation League, Audit of Anti-Semitic Incidents (New York: ADL, January 1985) The Associated Press carried the story on 17 January 1985.

[53] William Korey, "The Future of Soviet Jewry," *Foreign Affairs*, 58, no. 1 (Fall 1979): 70–2.

[54] It was published by "Juridical Literature," which gave it the sanction of the Soviet legal profession. Strong reviews appeared in *Pravda*, 10 August 1985; and *Sovetskaia kultura*, 31 August 1985.

[55] Association of Soviet Lawyers, ed., *The White Book: Evidence, Facts, Documents*, trans. by T. Gorshunova and Y. Grace (Moscow: Progress Publishers, 1981)(English).

150,000 copies. The book was trumpeted in the public media and vast numbers of copies were distributed to Communist Party cadres, bureaucrats, police and military officials.

The perspective of the two major contributors to the 1979 volume revealed something about the character of the *White Book*. One of the writers was Lydia Modzhorian, a specialist on international law who worked for the Institute of Oriental Studies of the Soviet Academy of Sciences and whose books and articles emitted a strong odor of bigotry. The other principal writer was E. D. Modrzhinskaia, who worked at the Institute of Philosophy of the Academy of Sciences. A prolific writer of anti-Zionist articles, she was the principal backer at the Academy of Sciences of the notorious propagandist Yevgenii Yevseev.[56]

On August 15, 1985, a TASS broadcast announced the publication of a new *White Book,* published jointly by the Association of Soviet Lawyers *and* the Anti-Zionist Committee. Unquestionably, the moving force in this effort was Samuil Zivs, a key figure in both organizations. For the Committee, it meant a significant upgrading of its status and prominence. The TASS broadcast provided an insight into the character of the book:

> Zionist leaders are responsible for the deaths of thousands of Jews annihilated by the Nazis. It is precisely the Zionists who assisted the Nazi butchers by helping them to make up the lists of the doomed inmates of ghettoes, escorted the latter to the places of extermination and convinced them to resign to the butchers.[57]

Another TASS broadcast later in August spelled out that the new book focussed on "the subversive activity of Zionist centers."[58]

The new *White Book* was given to anyone within or outside the USSR who raised questions about Jews. Thus, when Professor Nathan Glazer of Harvard University discussed the plight of Soviet Jews during the Helsinki-sponsored Cultural Forum held in Budapest in November 1985,

---

[56] Elena D. Modrzhinskaia and Vladimir F. Lapsky co-authored *Yad sionizma* (Moscow: Pedagogika, 1983), a viciously antisemitic work. Modrzhinskaia died in 1982, before the book's publication.

[57] TASS, 15 August 1985.

[58] Major reviews continued into September: *Trud,* 6 September 1985; and *Ogonek,* 36 (31 August–7 September 1985). Extensive excerpts were carried in *Argumenty i fakty,* 36 (3 September 1985) and 37 (10 September 1985).

the Soviet delegate who gave the official rejoinder offered Glazer the *White Book* as well as several other booklets so that he might learn the "truth."[59]

The new volume's introduction stated that the book was intended to reveal "the subversive activity of the Zionist centers," expose "the treacherous methods used by them," and show "the tragic fate of people who fell into the trap of Zionist propaganda." The work was perceived as "an awesome accusation" against Zionism which demonstrated the "irrefutable basis for a public verdict on the guilt of Zionism in tragic crimes."

A major segment of the book detailed how Soviet Jews have been "lured" by mischievous, deceitful and "blackmailing" Zionists into an "odyssey of torment and suffering." Another important segment allegedly documented the "collaboration" of Zionism with the Nazis. And a final segment picked up the latest theme of the Anti-Zionist Committee concerning the antisemitism supposedly raging in the United States and the West. Clearly, the official intent was to discourage and eventually halt the emigration drive within the USSR. Yet, the crude and distorted "documentation" bordered on open bigotry with the inevitable consequence of stirring racist animus.

To strengthen the increased status of the Anti-Zionist Committee, Soviet authorities arranged for the translation and promotion of General David Dragunsky's *A Soldier's Memoirs* with an introduction written, not surprisingly, by Samuil Zivs.[60] If the Zivs introduction was designed to portray Dragunsky as a characteristic "son" of the Jewish people, while the memoirs illustrated his patriotism and heroism, an afterword, written by Dragunsky, revealed his own mindset as well as the real aim of the memoirs.

In his afterword, Dragunsky discussed what he said was "the very first time I had come face to face with Zionism." Supposedly it occurred in 1956 at a ceremony in Paris to commemorate the victims of Nazism. At the very moment of the ceremony, Israel, together with Britain and France, "launched their aggression against Egypt." Dragunsky then related that he was approached by Israel Minister of Education Zalman Shazar. According to the Soviet general, Shazar "with off-hand

---

[59] Nathan Glazer, personal letter to William Korey, December 1985.

[60] David Dragunsky, *A Soldier's Memoirs* (Moscow: Progress Publishers, 1983).

impatience" said to him: "Mr. General, why does the Soviet Union oppose our lawful rights? We need land. We are crowded." Dragunsky added: "There before me stood one of the leaders of international Zionism. What could I have expected from him. All I could say was: 'Mr. Minister, what you have just said echoes the old Nazi claim of *Lebensraum*. Have you forgotten the price of Hitler's adventure?'"

The heightened status of the Anti-Zionist Committee found expression in foreign broadcasts over Radio Moscow, in frequent citations in the Soviet press and in the massive distribution of the Committee's booklets as well as the *White Book*. Foreign tourists visiting the Moscow synagogue received from a congregation official a free gift of four Committee booklets published by Novosti.[61] The material described, for example, "the foul role of Zionists as accomplices of the Nazis in exterminating millions of working Jews" or how "Zionism threatens to destroy the world's nations along with human culture and civilization." An indication of the Committee's new importance was the power extended to it to invite foreign experts as its guests. The first prominent Committee guest was remarkably revealing—Alfred Lilienthal, the well-known American anti-Zionist propagandist. In an interview in the journal, *Argumenty i fakty,* Lilienthal established his credentials by noting that "the Zionist lobby in Washington" had "influence over the President [Reagan] too."[62] Two months earlier, the journal had included parts of the *White Book*.

With the dialogue between the Soviet Union and the United States in 1987–1988 deepening and embracing a whole variety of areas—arms control, trade and cultural exchange—the operation of the Soviet Public Anti-Zionist Committee became increasingly anomalous. Its existence ran counter to the theme of detente and responsibility which Mikhail Gorbachev had sounded.

Moreover, its contacts with world Jewry were virtually non-existent. With its links to Soviet Jewish activism negligible and its connections with the Jewish communities abroad fatally compromised by an overt relationship with the propagation of antisemitism, the Anti-Zionist Committee functioned in a social vacuum.

Increasingly, Soviet diplomats abroad who had contacts with Jewish

---

[61] *Argumenty i fakty,* 47 (November 1985).
[62] Ibid. The article was entitled "I'm Becoming More and More Convinced that I Am Right."

leaders would drop hints of an early demise of the Committee. Indeed, as detente began to flourish, less and less was heard about the Anti-Zionist unit and many concluded that it had been put out of business. This was not the case. The Committee continued to exist and would be called from its dormant state from time to time to perform the functions which the Kremlin had initially assigned it, as the domestic purveyor of the demonology of Zionism.

Thus, in August 1989, after a score of Jewish activists founded a Zionist Union, the authorities arranged for the Anti-Zionist Committee to issue a statement through TASS ferociously attacking the Zionist Union as subversive and a violation of the international community's ban on Zionism through the UN's resolution defining Zionism "as a form of racism."[63] *Pravda* and *Krasnaia zvezda* gave full coverage to the Committee's text.[64] Clearly, as long as the demonology of Zionism held firm in important Soviet circles, the Anti-Zionist Committee would continue to play a vital role.

---

[63] TASS, 8 August 1989. It appeared in *Pravda* and other Soviet organs the next day.
[64] For the reaction of American Jewish leadership, see *JTA Daily Bulletin*, 18 August 1989. The following year, the Anti-Zionist Committee once again attacked the Zionist organization through TASS; see *Sovetskaia Rossiia*, 17 November 1990.

## Chapter 8

## Glasnost and the Demonology of Zionism

The consequences for Soviet Jewry of the Zionist demonology campaign were profound. Antisemitism had grown and had become a pervasive phenomenon in public life. Perceptions of Jews about encounters with anti-Jewish discrimination or acts of bigotry were a crucial indicator. While polls could not be conducted on Soviet soil, surveys of Jews who had emigrated during the seventies to Israel or the United States threw considerable light on attitudes.

One such survey conducted in 1980–1981 by Professor Zvi Gitelman of the University of Michigan is especially useful.[1] Four other surveys compiled results similar to Gitelman's. He had interviewed over 1100 former Soviet Jews who had emigrated during 1977–1980. In response to the question of whether they "had personally experienced antisemitism in the USSR," over 73 percent said "yes" with 33.2 percent of Jews from Russia proper saying they had "often" experienced antisemitism and 40.4 percent saying they had "sometimes" experienced it. The balance of 25 percent said they had "rarely" (21.2) or "never" (4.1) experienced it.

In the Ukraine, the overall figure ran somewhat lower—nearly 70 percent. Thirty-eight percent said "often" and 31.9 percent said "sometimes." A level lower were the percentages in the Baltics (26.8 and 36.9) and Moldavia (25.2 and 37.4). Lower still was Central Asia (13.1 and 34.3). Especially low were the perceptions of Georgian Jews (17.3 percent "often" and 20.5 percent "sometimes").

---

[1] Zvi Gitelman, "Perceptions of Ukrainians by Soviet Jewish Emigrants: Some Empirical Observations," *Soviet Jewish Affairs,* 17, no. 3 (Winter 1987): 11–21.

The most striking correlation in the survey was between the level of education and the perception of antisemitism. The higher one's education, the stronger was his or her perception of antisemitic encounters. It made no difference whether the respondent had been a member of the Communist Party. Reflected in this correlation were the difficulties experienced by Jews in admission to higher educational institutions and in obtaining high-level employment.

Reality corresponded with perception in a direct way. Enrollment in higher education was to reflect the new demonology. Jews may have been excluded from political life, from diplomatic or high-level military careers and from security branches of government, but, until 1968–1969, despite some quotas, they were able to enter university and pursue careers in science, technology and the arts (although not in fields that were sensitive to Party considerations, like history).[2] The academic year 1968–1969 showed that there were 111,900 Jews enrolled in higher education—a high point.[3]

A new policy was first signalled in a Polish ideological journal in June 1968.[4] Written by a top Party ideologue, Andrzej Werblan, the long article stated that Jews have "a particular susceptibility to revisionism" [reformism] and to "Jewish nationalism in general and *Zionism in particular*" [emphasis added]. He went on to add that the "concentration of people of Jewish origin" in Polish universities created a "bad political atmosphere." While Werblan focussed on Poland, the intention of his backers was broader in scope. A decade later, a former Polish "insider" revealed that the article was written on the "initiative" of the Soviet Party Central Committee in Moscow. Poland was to be "the first laboratory of official antisemitism in the Eastern bloc."[5]

That the Werblan thesis of the need to reduce the size of the Jewish student body in universities was probably perceived by Moscow authori-

---

[2] William Korey, "The Future of Soviet Jewry," *Foreign Affairs,* 58, no. 1 (Fall 1979): 71–2.
[3] Zev Katz, "After the Six-Day War," in Lionel Kochan, ed., *The Jews in Soviet Russia Since 1917* (London: Oxford University, 1970), 330–31.
[4] Korey, "Future of Soviet Jewry," 70.
[5] Ibid.; Hebrew University of Jerusalem: *Anti-Semitism in the Soviet Union: Its Roots and Consequences,* (Jerusalem: Centre for Research and Documentation of East-European Jewry, 1979), 1:30, fn. 1.

ties as applicable to Soviet education policy was suggested by data on university student admission practices.

From the academic year 1969–1970 onwards, the enrollment figures of Jews in higher education began to plummet. By the academic year 1976–1977—the last year in which the Brezhnev government chose to provide the sensitive data on enrollment—only 66,900 Soviet Jews were enrolled, It marked a drop of more than forty percent.[6] A similar percentage decline occurred at the post-graduate level. At Moscow State University and other flagship Soviet universities, the admission policies were especially tight. Between 1970 and 1975, the number of Jewish postgraduate students fell from 4,945 to 2,841. What the figures projected was a big drop, over the long run, of Jews in the sciences.[7]

A Soviet ideologist in education, Vladimir Mishin, wrote an important work in 1970, which justified limiting the number of students of each nationality in higher education to the percentage the nationality constitutes in the total population.[8] With the Jewish percentage in the population during the seventies and eighties declining, the discriminatory policy of Moscow was certain to produce especially low Jewish enrollment figures. A book of statistics covering Moscow only was published in 1982 showing that the number of Jews in higher education in the nation's capital between 1971 and 1981 was cut in half.[9]

Not until 1990 did new data become available on enrollment in higher education during the eighties. For the academic year 1984–1985, the total number of Jews had declined from 66,900 in 1976–1977 to 41,000.[10] Jews in higher education had dropped from 0.9 to 0.78 percent. Of significance, too, was data disclosing the enrollment figures of Jews in higher education for the academic year 1989–1990. As of fall 1990, the number of Jews in higher education was down to 35,400—this, despite

---

[6] Korey, "Future of Soviet Jewry," 71.

[7] Ibid., 71. For further details, see William Korey, "From Russia With Hate: A Bitter Centennial," *Moment,* 8, no. 3 (March 1983), 43–54.

[8] William Korey, *The Soviet Cage: Anti-Semitism in Russia* (New York: Viking, 1973), 318.

[9] Korey, "From Russia with Hate," 54. The book from which the data was drawn is *Moskva v tsifrakh* (Moscow: Vestnik Statistiki, 1982).

[10] *Narodnoe obrazovanie i kultura v SSSR* (Moscow: State Publishers, 1989). Data from this book was provided to the author by Professor Murray Feshbach, a demography specialist of the USSR.

glasnost and perestroika. Moreover, the drop occurred prior to the impact of significantly higher emigration levels.[11]

A very prominent American mathematician learned by 1990 from Soviet colleagues that several Jews in his field were turned down for doctoral degrees at Moscow State University "because of anti-Semitism." He was further advised that in the previous year the mathematics department at Moscow State University had changed "the entrance examination system" to "reduce the incidence of discrimination" with the result that "for the first time in many years, a good number of young Jewish students was admitted." However, the American scholar reported that he "just learned that the mathematics examiners recently voted to go back to the old system."[12]

The tightening of quotas in enrollment would, of course, affect future career opportunities for Jews. Prior to 1972, the number of Jews who entered the scientific technological intelligentsia was two to three thousand a year.[13] Since that time it dropped to about one thousand a year. The percentage of Jews in the workforce who had completed higher education declined from 12 percent in 1960 to 3.3 percent in 1987.[14]

Running parallel to the drop in the number of new Jewish scientists was the erection of new barriers in the specialized science fields. Andrei Sakharov noted in 1968 that the Soviet Academy of Sciences was applying antisemitism in its "appointments policy."[15] A secret 1970 Party directive—as reported by Roy Medvedev—recommended that Jews not be employed at "responsible levels" at various advanced scientific and security institutions.[16] The directive even applied to those who were listed as Russian in their internal passport or other documents, but whose father or mother had been Jewish. Werblan's formula on Zionist genes had come full circle.

---

[11] Ibid.

[12] Louis Nirenberg, "Human Rights of Mathematicians in the USSR," Letters to the Editor, *Notices: Bulletin of the American Mathematical Society,* 37, no. 6 (July–August 1990): 655.

[13] Korey, "Future of Soviet Jewry," 71–72.

[14] *IJA Briefing* (London), Special Issue, March 1990, 1, Table 2.

[15] Andrei D. Sakharov, *Progress, Coexistence and Intellectual Freedom* (New York: Norton, 1970), 11–12.

[16] Roy Medvedev, *Blizhnevostochnyi konflikt: yevreiskii vopros v SSSR* (Moscow, 1970). This samizdat essay is in the author's possession.

The selection of Mikhail Gorbachev as Party General Secretary in March 1985, did not bring a quick end to the official 18-year anti-Zionist media campaign. The enlightenment of his glasnost policy did result in positive and improved changes in many journals which heretofore had been in the forefront of hysterical anti-Zionism—*Ogonek, Sovetskaia kultura, Komsomolskaia pravda* are some examples—but the publication of hatemongering books had not yet halted.

In February 1986, a new star had arisen in the Soviet antisemitic firmament. He was Aleksandr Romanenko whose new book, *On the Class Essence of Zionism,* was officially published in Leningrad in an edition of 50,000 copies.[17] The work of 253 pages, claiming to be a historiographic essay on "scientific research" material concerning Zionism, is a rehash of traditional distortions and canards.

Once again Zionism was described in the Romanenko book as striving for world supremacy. Once again, Zionist ideology was portrayed as being rooted in reactionary Judaism and as advocating that "the Jews are superior to other peoples and their vocation is to rule over the whole of mankind." Once again, history was reinterpreted to discredit Jews. Even the expulsion of Jews from Spain in 1492 was presented as a "positive development, part of a national liberation movement." And, the Nazi era was supposedly perceived by the Zionists as a "unique historical opportunity" to achieve their aim of world mastery.

Later, in January 1987, an authoritative Party academic journal, *Questions of CPSU History,* severely castigated the Romanenko work as replete with "factual inaccuracies, distortions and errors," including the manipulation of quotations from the classics of Marxism-Leninism.[18] Especially disturbing to the academic researchers was the implication of the author that leading Party and state officials "have not noticed" the enormous influence of Zionism, and that fear of being accused of antisemitism had prevented academic critiques of Zionism. The reviewers found such hints as hostile ways for casting "doubt on the policies of the Party and state."

Nonetheless, the criticism of Romanenko did not extend beyond aca-

---

[17] Aleksandr Z. Romanenko, *O klassovoi sushchnosti sionizma* (On the Class Essence of Zionism: A Historiographical Survey of Literature)(Leningrad: Lenizdat, 1986).

[18] *Voprosy istorii KPSS,* no. 1, 1987. The analysis was conducted by three leading specialists on nationalism and Zionism—L. Dadiani, S. Mokshin, and E. Tadevosyan.

demia to the broad public arena. Indeed, the reverse was the case. A TASS Russian-language broadcast on Radio Moscow on May 22, 1987 extolled the book for revealing that "the Zionists have as their goal domination over countries and peoples."[19] Visitors found copies of the book displayed in bookstores in the major cities of Western Russia, especially Leningrad.[20] They reported that shelves were quickly replenished with copies after a number were sold.

But the Radio Moscow broadcast would be the last time that Romanenko or his work would be favorably reported upon in official organs. Hatemongering in these organs had become taboo as the liberal and humanitarian ideals of glasnost assumed a dominant role in the official media and in principal journals. With glasnost, a totally new outlook had taken hold. Indeed, a former major purveyor of the hate writings of Korneyev, *Ogonek* (now under the editorship of Vitaly Korotich, a strong supporter of glasnost), expressed regret over past articles: "unfortunately, in the recent past, the criticism of Zionism in the works of certain authors was not always conducted from a class position. Scientific analysis was replaced by ambiguous hints, and the concepts 'Jew' and 'Zionist' were often confused."[21]

More significantly, *Ogonek* emphasized that "anti-Semitism and its social roots were passed over in silence or received an incorrect evaluation." The harsh reality was that the existence of antisemitism had been simply denied, a view with which Gorbachev agreed in an interview given in February 1986. With glasnost, as one journal noted in 1988, all kinds of evils in the USSR which heretofore had been denied or suppressed, such as prostitution and drug addiction, were now acknowledged, along with antisemitism.[22] *Pravda* itself, in that year would criticize the antisemitism of Pamyat while *Izvestiia* would ridicule its notion of a supposed Zionist-Masonic conspiracy.[23]

---

[19] TASS, 22 May 1987; reported on Radio Moscow (Russian broadcast) on that day.

[20] Brought to the author's attention by visitors.

[21] Vladimir Nosenko and Sergei Rogov, "Ostorozhno: Pro vokatsiia," *Ogonek,* 23 (4–11 June 1988).

[22] Vladimir Ramm, "Antisemitizm," *Raduga,* no. 11, 1988, 80, cited in Zvi Gitelman, "Soviet Jewry in Transition," *Soviet Jewish Affairs,* 19, no. 2 (Summer–Autumn 1989), 5–6.

[23] *Izvestiia,* 18 June 1987.

Glasnost, or openness, of course, was designed to overcome the epoch of stagnation involving declining productivity rates, intellectual and ideological impoverishment, and a host of serious social and economic problems. Individual initiative in every field of endeavor would be spurred by the new openness. The impact was profound. The crimes of Stalin in gory detail were finally revealed, blank pages of history were filled, and hitherto unreported subjects became the grist of enlightened journalistic mills. Moreover, instead of command directives from above, individuals were encouraged to display private initiative in semi-capitalist cooperatives and in agriculture. Especially important was the impact upon political life where open election campaigns coincided with vigorous challenges from below to every kind of authority.

But glasnost also allowed the unprecedented sprouting of virulent antisemitic organizations, like Pamyat or Otechestvo, which were now given a public sanction. They were among the 60,000 grassroots or informal organizations either newly created or given some kind of official or unofficial recognition. Open antisemitic street rhetoric, activities and demonstrations became common. As noted by the poet Yevgeny Yevtushenko, glasnost "unfortunately...makes room for the development of very reactionary forces. We are seeing many of our dangerous microbes...like anti-Semitism."[24] If by mid-1986 the previously official state-sponsored antisemitism was diminished or ended, it was now replaced by the more palpable, uncontrolled populist bigotry which evoked a far greater degree of fear and anxiety among Jews than the controlled antisemitism of the state. Indeed, the era of glasnost was marked, at the end of the decade, with the sharpest intensity of fright among Soviet Jews since Stalin's Doctors' Plot. The resultant panic led to a vast exodus to Israel.

The circumstances in which glasnost was taking place contributed heavily to populist antisemitism. A deteriorating economic situation with increasingly fewer goods on the shelves of state stores, and worsening unemployment and underemployment, generated widespread anxiety. The anxiety was aggravated by the crumbling of the expectations that perestroika reforms would bring improvement. The result was a psychological atmosphere in which strong doubts that the economic situation would

---

[24] Stephen F. Cohen and Katrina vanden Heuvel, *Voices of Glasnost* (New York: Norton, 1989), 277. The figures on informal voluntary associations are in *Pravda,* 10 February 1989.

improve were expressed. Repeated public opinion polls recorded a growing degree of pessimism.

The situation easily lent itself to the search for scapegoats; the traditional social culture of Russia might easily find this in Jewry. A leading Soviet Jewish activist who served as editor of the *Jewish Information Bulletin,* Aleksandr Shmukler, appropriately commented: "The food stores are empty, people are hungary. People want to know why, so blame the Jews."[25] That which gave focus to the Jew as the source of distress was the emergence of an increasing number of capitalist enterprises, the so-called cooperatives. The phenomenon ineluctably deepened trends of economic and social inequality which ran counter to historic Russian cultural traditions of equality. Anger directed against the wealthier could be channeled against Jews even if Jews were not disproportionately represented among the cooperatives.[26]

A study of Soviet society under perestroika illuminated the attitude toward Jews as capitalist entrepreneurs:

> A Moscow worker who used to dream about having his own restaurant and becoming rich was cool toward perestroika. Why not open a cooperative cafe? We asked him. "Oh no, that's not for me," he said, adding a mindless Russian parrot-cry: "I'm not a Jew." Making money, in this deeply anti-Semitic nation, was something done by the Jews.[27]

A second circumstance, no doubt related to both glasnost and the deteriorating economic situation, was the emergence of strong centrifugal forces among the major non-Russian nationalities together with the heightening of ethnic tensions. Two aspects of the decentralizing nationalist process created deep uncertainties among Jews. As nationalism in the borderlands intensified, Jews with long memories could recall that their history with the predominant nationalities of the areas was hardly conducive to friendly relations.

Thus Ukrainian nationalism could not but evoke fearsome recollections of pogroms. *Rukh,* the dominant and liberal-nationalists popular move-

---

[25] Cited in *Jews in the USSR* (London), 17 January 1990.
[26] See Natan Sharansky, "The Greatest Exodus," *New York Times Magazine,* 2 February 1992, 46; Zvi Gitelman, *Anti-Semitism in the Age of Perestroika* (New York: HIAS, 1990, mimeograph).
[27] Dusko Doder and Louise Branson, *Gorbachev: Heretic in the Kremlin* (New York: Viking, 1990), 402–3.

ment in the Ukraine, even as it vigorously condemned antisemitism in its platform, nonetheless, recognized the hate phenomenon as a disturbing reality. It acknowledged in September 1989 that antisemitism had "maintained its position...among the denationalized masses whose thinking is based on stereotypes...."[28] Representing the "civically active citizens," *Rukh* concluded: "Down with anti-Semitism."

Similar recollections could apply to Byelorussia, to Moldavia, and even to Lithuania and Latvia. But, the popular movements in the latter two republics went out of their way to assure the small local Jewish communities of extensive defense, cultural, and religious support. Strong suspicions existed of popular Moldavian hostility. One unofficial slogan stated: "We'll drown the Jews in Russian blood."[29] As for the Moslem nationalities in Central Asia and the Caucasus, fears among Jews grew concerning a rising Islamic fundamentalism which would potentially carry a special edge of anti-Israel and, therefore, anti-Zionist fury. An unofficial slogan read: "Tatars to Kazan, Russians to Ryazan, we'll deal with the Jews ourselves."[30]

A corollary of the phenomenon of deepening centrifugal forces was the growing inability of the central government in Moscow to exercise effective control. Symptomatic was the inability of Moscow to protect Armenians from the rage of Azerbaijanis in Baku, and of Meskhetians from the anger of Uzbeks. The resulting massacres were seen by Jews as an index of Moscow's inability to protect them in the event rampaging mobs were to descend upon them. In one community in Uzbekistan—Andizhan—Jews suffered a mini-pogrom from Uzbeks in 1990.[31] But the fear was less among small communities in the various non-Russian national areas than in larger communities in Russia proper where a powerful nationalism had taken hold.

The circumstances of economic crisis and instability reminded thoughtful Jewish leaders of the immediate pre-Hitler era in Weimar Germany. The historical parallel was the source of great anxiety, and found

---

[28] *Literaturnaia Ukraina,* 5 October 1989. The *Rukh* statement was adopted on September 10, 1989.
[29] "Exodus: Revised Version," *The Economist* (London), 23 December 1989.
[30] Ibid.
[31] Vladimir Shlapentokh, *Moscow in the Aftermath of the Congress of People's Deputies* (Moscow, July 1989), mimeograph, 28.

expression in the major statement of the Congress of Jewish Organizations held in Moscow in December 1989, and in a major essay by Soviet Jewish scientist Vitalii Goldanskii.[32] Besides serving as director of Semenov Institute of Chemical Physics of the Soviet Academy of Sciences, he was a member of the Congress of Peoples' Deputies and of the Foreign Relations Committee of the Supreme Soviet. Goldanskii specifically compared "the Soviet Union in 1989–1990 to that in Germany in 1931–1933."

The most detailed analysis was prepared by Viktor Koretskii, an engineer and Jewish activist who found the historical parallels alarming. First, he called attention to "a very profound economic crisis" in Weimar Germany which had been accompanied by mass unemployment and terrible inflation that preceded the "ascent of the Nazis to power." In Russia, he noted that the economy stood "on the brink of crisis" with inflation growing and production levels decreasing.

More serious in the USSR was that perestroika placed in doubt the economic status of major groups. Reduction of the administrative bureaucracy, he said, threatened the stratum of eighteen million managers, which included highly placed representatives of the Party and state élite. Cost accounting methods will also affect executive personnel in industry, in the service field, in commerce. A similar phenomenon will affect the armed forces. As a result, one can expect, he thought, "the imminent appearance of a huge army of actually unemployed people," many of them lumpen proletariat. It was this category which had been most receptive to Nazi propaganda and who blamed their failure not on themselves but on Jews.

A growing mass of people, due to their aggravated economic situation and psychological features, he wrote, "will be ready to welcome and espouse Nazism." Koretskii doubted that the crisis could be quickly resolved. Rather, he expected a worsening of the situation in the mid-1990s related to fuel, energy, and raw materials. He concluded that this will "essentially lead to a further lowering of the living standards of all strata...." Under such conditions, "the slightest serious spark is sufficient to ignite the fires of national strife which can be quickly transformed into interethnic slaughter."

---

[32] Vitalii Goldanskii, "Anti-Semitism: The Return of a Russian Nightmare." *Washington Post*, 18 February 1990.

Another component which Koretskii would factor into his analysis of contemporary Russia was the presence of "an age old tradition of mass, popular anti-Semitism...." This made the Soviet situation "much more ominous." Secondly, the advent of intellectual antisemitism in the USSR during an earlier period and facilitated by the authorities aggravated the political and social scene. In his view, certain circles in the Party and state apparatus, seeing their power position threatened, were "ready to form an alliance with the dark forces and, when necessary, to rely on them."

A final factor, Koretskii held, was psychological stress. As with Germans in the thirties, the common man in Russia sought "strong and firm rule to restore order, welfare and stability." He was faced with "increasing political discord, alarming social changes, deepening economic crisis" and, very importantly, the necessity of deciding for himself. When added to the prevalent myth about the "good old times of Stalin," the thought process of the average person could lead to attributing all dangers to the intrigues of Judeo-Masons and to place hopes for salvation on strong authority. The myths of neo-Nazi and neo-fascist propaganda, he concluded, "can find a growing receptivity today."[33]

Goldanskii focussed more on social forces than on the objective situation. He compared the program of Pamyat with Hitler's *Mein Kampf* and he noted that a liberal Soviet newspaper, *Soviet Circus,* had printed a point-by-point comparison of Pamyat's manifesto with the program of the Nazi Party of the 1930s. In the opinion of Goldanskii, the Pamyat movement is the equivalent of Hitler's SA and SS (*Stürmabteilungen* and *Shützstaffel*).[34]

Pamyat (memory) was the focus of Jewish fears. An extremist expression of Russian nationalism, it was rooted in a social soil that had been nourished by rich nutrients of bigotry during 1967–1986. The vicious antisemitic chauvinism with the demonology of Zionism at its core, so pervasive in the propaganda of the Brezhnev era, took on a life of its own during glasnost. Pamyat was the most definitive expression of the

---

[33] Victor Koretskii, "The Situation of the Jews Resembles that in Germany in the 1930s," *Jews and Jewish Topics in the Soviet Union and Eastern Europe,* (Jerusalem), 3(10) (Winter 1989), 68–71.

[34] Goldanskii, "Anti-Semitism."

new extremism.

Significantly, the favorites of Pamyat from the beginning of glasnost were three of the leading specialists of the anti-Zionist media campaign— Yevseev, Begun, and Romanenko. A similar role was played by the lecturer Yemelyanov. Their views, of course, had not changed, even if they were no longer socially and intellectually acceptable to the dominant Gorbachev forces. They continued to preach variations of the doctrine of *The Protocols of the Elders of Zion* without, of course, referring specifically to this title.

Romanenko's connection with Pamyat and a general indication of his views were provided in a letter from a Moscow dissident.[35] According to the letter, Romanenko spoke in March 1989 before a large crowd assembled at the concert hall of the Moscow Physico-Technical Institute. He sought to show that the percentage of Jews in academic institutions was higher than that of Russians. More, in keeping with Pamyat's outlook, he complained that he was unable to find work as a historian because Jews were always selected ahead of him. Strikingly, the letter-writer observed that Romanenko was invited to give his lecture here by the first secretary of the Communist Party regional committee.

No longer would specific reference to the *Protocols* be avoided or excluded. A detailed report of a Pamyat meeting in December 1985 illuminated the openness with which extreme nationalists now carried and projected their outlook.[36] The audience at the Pamyat meeting in Moscow grew especially excited as Dmitri Vasiliev, its principal spokesman, after reading aloud a section of the *Protocols,* focussed on a map of the Moscow subway system. What he disclosed aroused the crowd's deepest fears and anxieties. Excerpted from the *Protocols* was a paragraph about how the Elders of Zion, at a climactic moment of their planned worldwide seizure of power, would use the underground passages "in every capital" for blowing-up national power structures "with all the organizations and documents of the country." The horrifying relevance was made clear when Vasiliev added that the map of the Moscow Metro revealed that "all the principal junctions are right beneath

---

[35] The letter was made available to the author by Helsinki Watch in New York.

[36] "A Lecture in Moscow," *Jews and Jewish Topics in Soviet and East-European Publications* (Jerusalem) 4 (Winter 1986–1987), 46–53; *Komsomolskaia pravda,* 22 May 1987; *Izvestiia,* 3 June 1987.

(Soviet) Party and government institutions."

Moscow's subway system had earlier aroused Pamyat's favorite, Valery Yemelyanov. In a special document prepared for the Communist Party Central Committee in early 1977, he reported that the grills of "the small white loudspeakers in all the stations and crossings of the Moscow Metro are...decorated with the same six-cornered Star of David which is so pleasing to the Zionist eye."[37]

Pamyat and its leaders saw things that others, less inclined to a conspiratorial turn of mind, did not. Vasiliev, in his speech, called attention to a moon motif on baby jackets. "The moon," he noted, "is a symbol of the Jews being protected." More threatening, however, were symbols hidden in the Soviet press—"coded menorahs" and "six-pointed stars"—all of which "betokens a presence." When one held a newspaper against the light, distinctive symbols became visible which disparaged Russia or proposed assaults upon it. Thus a news article might speak about the purity of the waters of the Dnieper River but, under the light, it displayed a skull; a newspaper headline might read "The Lessons of Chernobyl" but, against the light, a secret headline says: "This must become a tradition."

Hidden symbols were particularly noticeable in designs for a proposed monument in an area of Moscow especially treasured by the extreme nationalists—Poklonnaya Hill. Vigorously opposed to the building of any monuments there, Vasiliev commented that the competition entries on display at Moscow's Central Exhibition Hall all show "Masonic-Zionist and even fascist symbols."

Suspicion was cast on various sources. *Ogonek,* a major Party monthly in the forefront of the glasnost struggle and notably critical of Pamyat, had removed from its front cover the traditional Order of Lenin sign. The meaning to Pamyat was self-evident. Secret Masonic signs were everywhere: set squares and pairs of compasses, rectangles and plain squares; the two crossed roses on the cover of the liberal youth journal *Yunost.* Particular numbers, like 33, a token of "special Masonic initiation," or 21, assigned to someone the Masons had presumably condemned to death, were also suspicious. As noted by a writer in *Sovetskaia kultura,* an important ideological journal, "the hammer-and-sickle as well as the

---

[37] Valery Yemelyanov, *Memorandum to the Central Committee,* January 1977. The memorandum appeared in samizdat; a copy is in the author's possession.

Soviet five-pointed star are said to be Masonic symbols."[38]

Inevitably, Pamyat turned its attention to architecture.[39] It was in Moscow that the immediate danger appeared to exist. Whether the exposed system under government buildings or the bulldozed monuments and churches which had stood for patriotic Russian greatness—these were the core elements for unveiling the work of the secret enemy from within. The names of the "guilty" quickly surfaced: Lazar Moiseevich Kaganovich, a top Stalin aide, who was responsible for Moscow's reconstruction during the thirties; and Yemelian Yaroslavsky, alias Gubelman, Stalin's head of the Union of Militant Atheists.

Or there was Moisei Yakovlevich Ginzburg, the outstanding Moscow architect famous in the 1920s and 1930s for constructivism and functionalism. He and his colleagues were the "destroyers" of old and historic Moscow.[40] "But now," as one Pamyat leader intoned, "the time has come when we must save the homeland."[41] Kaganovich's partners-in-crime continued to destroy the holy places of "our" nation. A prominent geologist, Yevgeny Pashkin, speaking before a Pamyat meeting, saw "the main enemy of ancient Russian architecture as international Zionism, entrenched in the Main Department for Architecture and Planning in the municipality of Moscow...."[42] Yelena Degtyar, moderating at another Pamyat meeting, closed the discussion about who the conspirators of Moscow's cultural defacement were by reading out all the Jewish-sounding names in the directory of the Moscow architectural department.[43]

At another function Vasiliev, appearing before a standing room-only crowd in a big hall in Moscow, again targeted the enemy and its current plans. The harangue merits emphasis:

> Do you know that sinister forces are rebuilding our holy capital in such a way that the main streets will constitute a Star of David? Do you know that the Satanic forces want to make Russia a nation of alcoholics? But no one ever told you of the Judeo-Masonic plot to prepare our children for a life

---

[38] *Sovetskaia kultura*, 18 June 1987.
[39] "A Lecture in Moscow," 46; *Komsomolskaia pravda*, 22 May 1987; *Izvestiia*, 3 June 1987.
[40] *Komsomolskaia pravda*, 22 May 1987.
[41] Ibid. The comment was made by Pamyat council member V. Vinogradov.
[42] "A Lecture in Moscow," 46.
[43] Ibid., 53, footnote 8.

of debauchery. For the yogurt they are given every day contains not less than 1½ percent of alcohol.[44]

It was all spelled out in the *Protocols,* said Vasiliev. What this book revealed was a "Satanic conspiracy of Free-Masons and Zionists...to destroy our sacred country, its culture, all that is dear to us...."

The call to action by Vasiliev followed. "Unless we unite and smash these evil forces now—for there is very little time left—it will be the end of our people and our fatherland." His apocalyptic vision ineluctably required violence. In a hysterical address in Sverdlovsk, he called upon his listeners to "tear to bits" the secret enemy and to "throw them out." And, he warned, "We'll grind to dust anyone who stands in our way."[45]

Vasiliev summed up his perspective in an interview with an Italian journalist in 1988:

> We have reached the conclusion that it is no coincidence that we have been witnessing for years the destruction of our historic monuments, our traditions, and the customs of...the Russian people. There is clearly some evil force wanting to...destroy our culture...Zionism and Freemasonry.[46]

The journalist asked whether by "Zionist," he meant Jews, Vasiliev said:

> Yes, always these Jews, as though there were nobody else in this world. The Jews live everywhere, own the capital, live like parasites throughout the world, emigrate freely from country to country, and are always depicted as the most unfortunate nation.... It is enough to read the "Protocols of other Elders of Zion" [*sic*] to realize who created this situation. However, not all Zionists are Jews and not all Jews are Zionists. This is why we are not anti-Semitic[!][47]

Two events in the spring of 1987 brought Pamyat into the public limelight. In April, some 1500 of its supporters demonstrated outside the

---

[44] Ibid.

[45] *Sovetskaia kultura,* 18 June 1987; *Ogonek,* 21 (1987).

[46] Interview in *La Repubblica,* 26 February 1988, cited in Zvi Gitelman, *Anti-Semitism in the Age of Perestroika* (New York: HIAS, 1990, mimeograph), 26.

[47] Ibid. The separation of antisemitism from anti-Zionism was a standard device of Vasiliev. Thus, he would claim that he was not antisemitic and, therefore, was not in violation of Article 74 of the Russian Criminal Code. See an interview with him published in *Jews and Jewish Topics in Soviet and East European Publications,* (Jerusalem), 7 (Summer 1988), 36.

offices of *Moscow News* in central Moscow. They accused the editor-in-chief, Yegor Yakovlev, of harboring "Jews and Free Masons" on his staff.[48]

Far more significant was its demonstration in May, when some five hundred Pamyat members marched through the streets of Moscow, some carrying enormous banners denouncing the saboteurs of Mikhail Gorbachev's perestroika, condemning alcoholism, and calling for the preservation of the monuments of Russian culture.[49] Onlookers were given some sense of the organization's actual target when its various spokesmen blamed Zionists for the Chernobyl disaster, for the high level of drunkenness in Soviet society, and for the subversion of Soviet culture. Among the speakers along the line of march, besides Vasiliev, was the crackpot Jew-baiter, Valery Yemelyanov.

Initially, Pamyat was not antisemitic. Founded in 1980 by a number of employees of the USSR Ministry of Aviation Industry, its roots were profoundly nationalist with yearnings that went back to the Slavophilism of the nineteenth century. The original aim of the group was to preserve Moscow's historic and cultural monuments. Its name, Pamyat, carried a strong resonance evoking patriotic sentiments and, thereby, tapping a popular vein of support.[50]

But, in the following years, Pamyat was taken over by a leadership preoccupied more with the mythical enemies than with monuments and culture. Preservation of national and cultural landmarks was by no means dropped. Indeed, they were augmented by a special concern for combatting the evils of alcoholism, thus winning points with the new Mikhail Gorbachev thrust. But antisemitism—ever since 1985—had become the centerpiece of the Pamyat ideology, with the enemy portrayed as Judeo-Masonry or Masonic-Zionism.[51]

By April 1987, Pamyat had seized control of a major *official* cultural

---

[48] Dusko Doder and Louise Branson, *Gorbachev: Heretic in the Kremlin* (New York: Viking, 1990) 187.

[49] See *Moscow News,* 17 May 1987; *New York Times,* 24 May 1987.

[50] For background, see *Ogonek,* 21 (1987), 4–5; Walter Laqueur, *The Long Road To Freedom: Russia and Glasnost* (New York: Charles Scribner's Sons, 1989), 136.

[51] Ibid. For a characteristic early official Pamyat statement, see its "Appeal" of December 8, 1987 which was translated and published in *Soviet Jewish Affairs,* 18, no. 1 (1988): 60–70.

group—the Moscow section of the All-Russian Society for the Preservation of Historical and Cultural Monuments. On the eve of a conference to elect new officials, key leaders of the Moscow section who happened to be Pamyat members pulled a *coup* and succeeded in ridding the organization of anti-Pamyat leadership elements.[52]

How large a membership the organization now had was unknown and Vasiliev was reluctant to provide statistics to an interviewer from *The Guardian* of London, although he acknowledged it ran into "thousands."[53] In 1989, he told an American scholar that Pamyat had 20,000 members in Moscow alone, and many members in thirty other Russian cities.[54] Pamyat meetings filled large halls and tapes taken of these sessions were widely distributed through the mail. Meeting attendees appeared to cut across all age groups and social strata, including scientists and high level army officers.

The British interviewer found Vasiliev to be "a bulky, blue-eyed giant of a man with a bald crown fringed by long hair." A striking feature of his residence was the mix of tsarist and Bolshevist iconography— portraits of Tsar Nicholas II, Tsarina Alexandra, and Prime Minister Peter Stolypin along with volumes of Vladimir Ilyich Lenin. In his conversation, he embraced a devotion to Russian tradition, including the graves of saints and warrior monks, and disdain for "cosmopolitanism." Stolypin, who presided over the counterrevolution of 1906–1907, was one of his heroes just as he was for other Slavophil-oriented nationalists.

Jews were perceived by Vasiliev as the embodiment of cosmopolitanism. "No people," he told an interviewer, "have the right to proclaim

---

[52] *Ogonek,* 28 (1987), 31. Also see Laqueur, "Glasnost's Ghosts," *The New Republic,* 3 August 1987, 13–14.

[53] The precise wording of the Vasiliev description was provided by Martin Walker, Moscow correspondent of the *Guardian* (London). Also, Nicholas Bethell, "The Bell that is Rousing Ghosts of Hitler and Hate," *Mail* (London), 14 May 1989; Adam Karatnycky, "The Secret of Pamyat's Success," *Wall Street Journal,* 3 April 1989. For Walker's characterization of the "hate" mood in Moscow, see "Punk Perestroika," *New Republic,* 4 December 1989, 22, 26–27.

[54] John B. Dunlop, "A Conversation with Dimitrii Vasil'ev, the Leader of 'Pamyat,'" *Report on the USSR,* 15 December 1989, 12–16. Also see the perceptive interview with Vasiliev by Nicholas Bethell in the *Mail* (London), 14 May 1989.

themselves the 'chosen people'; it's an intolerable pretension."[55] He found them dominant in the professions and, even though they numbered less than one percent of the population, "they want to impose their views." Besides Jews, the enemy was to be found in freemasonry. Were there any in Soviet Russia? "Most certainly," responded Vasiliev and he pointed to Pamyat's critics in the media as evidence of the power of the Freemasons.

In his speeches, which one acute observer found fluent and self-confident, Vasiliev distinguished himself by citations from and praise for the *Protocols of the Elders of Zion*.[56] But he was careful on most occasions to make the "Zionists," not the "Jews," the enemy of mankind. In his formulations, he thought, he could not be considered as violating Soviet laws banning incitement to hatred of ethnic groups.

Diplomats in Moscow called attention to the tolerance displayed by Party authorities to Pamyat. One was quoted by the *New York Times* correspondent in Moscow as saying that "people of the Pamyat strain have some protection in the ruling circles of the Communist Party."[57] Another Western diplomat commented that Soviet leaders "don't want to come down too hard on Pamyat because some of the ideas they espouse are popular and respectable and supported by some of the leadership."[58] According to a longterm, keen observer of the Soviet scene, Pamyat, besides appearing to have "some sympathizers in the Party leadership," was reported to have support in the influential "political education" department of the army.[59]

Pamyat did not hesitate to publicly criticize prominent Soviet figures. A Pamyat board member in Novosibirsk, Aleksandr Kazantsev, for example, gave a number of lectures accusing several leading scientists of the Siberian department of the Soviet Academy of Sciences with being "clandestine supporters of Masonry and Zionism."[60] Kazantsev, himself

---

[55] For similar comments, see both the Dunlop and Bethell interviews, ibid.; Vassily Aksyonov, "Not Quite A Sentimental Journey," *New Republic*, 16 April 1990, 24.

[56] Dunlop, "Conversation," 15.

[57] Felicity Barringer, "Russian Nationalists Test Gorbachev," *New York Times*, 24 May 1987.

[58] Ibid.

[59] Walter Laqueur, "Glasnost's Ghosts," 14.

[60] *Sovetskaia kultura*, 18 June 1987; *Sovetskaia Rossiia*, 28 June 1987.

a scientist at the Novosibirsk Institute of the Physics of Semiconductors, charged that the USSR was becoming a "hostage of the Zionist-Masonry fifth column," and he apparently made public use of the *Protocols* in his lectures to demonstrate his thesis. Among his targets were Tatiana Zaslavskaia, the prominent sociologist and economist whose views had played an important part in Mikhail Gorbachev's perestroika. Possibly because of this, Kazantsev was expelled from the Party for slandering "top Party and state officials and leading scholars."[61]

Since the enemy, for Pamyat, was pervasive, it must be sought out everywhere.[62] All dissidents were perceived by Pamyat as Freemasons. Bureaucracy was a product of the international conspiracy of Zionism and Freemasonry. Academician Dmitri Likhachev, the world's leading specialist on ancient Russian literature, was called a "Zionist accomplice." So were Oleg Efremov, director of the Moscow Arts Theater, and Alla Pugacheva, a pop singer.

The great poet Andrei Voznesensky received a letter threatening his life which he said "looked as though it had come from Pamyat."[63] He had become a special target of antisemites when he helped organize a major exhibition of the paintings of Marc Chagall, many of which have Jewish themes. (Especially critical of the exhibition was the Pamyat favorite in Minsk, Vladimir Begun, who publicly denounced Chagall as a Zionist.[64]) At a public meeting of several thousand persons on perestroika, Voznesensky was sent a drawing of a defaced Star of David. But the poet would not be intimidated. He asked that the person responsible stand up. When no one rose, he shouted "Coward!" to the applause of the audience.[65]

According to an informed study of the Gorbachev era, Pamyat activists

---

[61] *Sovetskaia kultura,* 18 June 1987.

[62] Thus its early "Appeal" of December 8, 1987 spoke of *"enemies* who have entrenched themselves in every sector of the *Party....*" See *Soviet Jewish Affairs,* 18, no. 1 (1988), 61.

[63] *International Herald Tribune* (Paris), 17 December 1988.

[64] *Sovetskaia kultura,* 3 October 1987; John Russell, "Moscow's Remarkable Chagall Show," *New York Times,* 13 September 1987. Reznik, "The Rifle on the Wall," *The National Interest,* Fall 1989, 91; Kathleen Michalisko, "The Controversy in Belorussia over Marc Chagall," *Report on the USSR,* 19 May 1989, 20–3.

[65] An eyewitness provided the author with the information; see also *International Herald Tribune* (Paris) 17 December 1988.

"frequently resorted to fascist-style methods of intimidation, including threatening phone calls at midnight and pogrom-like actions. The apartments of several Jewish intellectuals were ransacked and their property was demolished by Pamyat gangs."[66]

In Sverdlovsk, members of a group similar to Pamyat—*Otechestvo* (Fatherland)—focused its attack upon a production of the local opera company. It was Aleksandr Pushkin's "Tale of Tsar Saltan," a fairy tale for children, which the group claimed had Zionist and Masonic symbols hidden in the scenery and costumes. When one of the snowflakes on a peasant woman's headdress was found to have six points (like the Star of David), the director and chief conductor of the company were accused of using "foreign," that is Zionist, symbols.[67]

Especially prominent among Pamyat's enemies was Aleksandr Yakovlev, one of Gorbachev's closest colleagues, formerly in the Secretariat and Politburo.[68] Fifteen years earlier he had won the undying hatred of chauvinist and extreme nationalist elements when he wrote a major ideological essay criticizing national prejudices including the tendency to glorify historical reactionary figures.[69] Vasiliev told a British Moscow correspondent that Yakovlev exemplifies the aims of the Freemasons.[70]

A letter to the editor of the journal *Sovetskaia kultura* illuminated the influence of Pamyat and the fear it engendered in various quarters. The writer, S. Filatov, described a meeting of Pamyat in Leningrad which he had attended. A speech by Vasiliev was found to be particularly shocking for it called upon his audience to war against Jews and Freemasons. Those in the audience who sought to challenge Vasiliev were thrown out of the hall by Pamyat strongmen. When Filatov complained to the police officer, he was stunned to hear from the officer that Pamyat enjoyed the

---

[66] Doder and Branson, *Gorbachev*, 187–88.

[67] Julia Wishnevsky, "Theater Attacked by 'Otechestvo' Received State Prize," *Radio Liberty Research*, RL477/87, 12 November 1987; *Sovetskaia kultura*, 18 June 1987.

[68] He was singled out in the initial Pamyat "Appeal" of December 8, 1987. *Soviet Jewish Affairs*, 18, no. 1 (1987), 63.

[69] Aleksandr Yakovlev, "Against Anti-Historicism," *Literaturnaia gazeta*, 15 November 1972.

[70] See Vadim Belotserkovsky, "The Nazi Movement in the Soviet Union," *Them*, September 1988, 6–7.

backing of fairly high-ranking Communist Party officials.[71]

Apparently, Pamyat's influence in strategically important Novosibirsk was even greater, at least for a period of time. There it was accorded recognition as a formal official society attached to the Academy of Sciences House of Culture.[72] But the political threat which Pamyat posed became more evident when one of its leaders began attacking researchers and advisers at Novosibirsk who were close to Gorbachev. Pamyat activities were seen as having "a scandalous nature" which aimed at usurping the prerogatives of local Soviets and other political bodies. Regional Party and Academy of Sciences officials met in mid-June 1989 and decreed the disbanding of the local Pamyat branch.[73]

But, of course, it was in Moscow that Pamyat, through its street demonstration of five hundred persons on May 6, 1987, acquired national and international attention. All the more was this the case when Pamyat officials like Vasiliev, along with Yemelyanov too, were granted an audience with Boris Yeltsin, the city's Party boss. At the time, Yeltsin, who had developed a reputation as a forceful populist and anti-bureaucratic figure, was seen as Gorbachev's principal ally in the capital. He had been brought by the Party General Secretary from Sverdlovsk to be the point man in the struggle for perestroika in the nation's largest concentration of bureaucratic forces. Besides serving as the secretary of the city's key Party Committee, Yeltsin was a candidate member of the Politburo. That his role and power were inestimably considerable was self-evident.

When Yeltsin allowed Pamyat a meeting lasting two hours, it was certainly seen as providing a major official national sanction for an organization whose very purpose is anti-Jewish bigotry.[74] If he later indicated that he was "appalled" by Pamyat's antisemitism, he nonetheless was willing to take seriously their comments on a variety of subjects including combatting alcoholism and bureaucracy.[75] Moreover, as reported in the

---

[71] *Sovetskaia kultura,* 23 July 1987.

[72] Anatoly Golovkov and Aleksei Pavlov, "O chem shumite vy" (What's all the noise about) *Ogonek,* 21 (May 1987).

[73] *Sovetskaia kultura,* 18 June 1987.

[74] *New York Times,* 24 May 1987; also see Walter Laqueur, *The Long Road to Freedom* (New York: Charles Scribner's Sons, 1989), 137.

[75] Barringer, "Russian Nationalists Test Gorbachev."

Moscow press, Yeltsin appeared willing to give serious consideration to a proposal "granting it legal status."[76]

A top advocate of glasnost, Vitaly Korotich, editor of *Ogonek*, which had assumed a leading role in exposing Pamyat, expressed his own personal dismay at the Yeltsin decision. Korotich related that "I've asked Boris Yeltsin why he allowed the May 6 demonstration and he told me there was nothing in the law against holding demonstrations in Moscow."[77] It was an evasive answer; most groups, particularly Soviet Jews, had been refused permission for demonstrations. Korotich reacted with puzzlement. "These are dangerous people," he said, and then went on to call them "our Le Pens," referring to the racist and proto-fascist group in France.[78]

If the meeting with Yeltsin testified, at the very minimum, to the acceptance of Pamyat, there were other indications which pointed to its respectability within the Communist Party. Various Pamyat meetings were held on Party premises and received formal approval from local or regional Party officials when held elsewhere. On at least one occasion, a Party First Secretary extended an invitation to a favorite Pamyat author to lecture at a Party-sponsored meeting.[79] Similarly, Pamyat-sponsored marches like that of May 6, were authorized by Party officials. Nor had it gone unnoticed that the formal head of the Pamyat governing body, Kim Andreyev, was a Communist Party member, a status which obligated him to fulfill Party discipline.[80]

Pamyat's "Proclamation" in 1988 holds the Jews responsible for a vast array of evils. It posed a series of questions:

- Who launched political terror in our country over the past 70 years?
- Who destroyed freedom of thought and violated the Constitution and

---

[76] William Korey, *Glasnost and Soviet Anti-Semitism* (New York: American Jewish Committee, 1991).

[77] Ibid., 36.

[78] Ibid. For an informed sketch of Korotich and of *Ogonek*, see Abraham Brumberg, "The Turning Point?" *New York Review of Books*, 28 June 1990, 56–7.

[79] Personal communication, Helsinki Watch research director Cathy Fitzpatrick to the author; see also *Komsomolskaia pravda*, 22 May 1987.

[80] Andreyev's Party role was emphasized in *Komsomolskaia pravda*, 22 May 1987 and especially in *Sovetskaia kultura*, 18 June 1987. He was removed from the Party by the end of the year.

democracy?
- Who profanes our history and culture?
- Who destroyed a great many landmarks that belong to the Russian people?
- Who ruined sacred historical landmarks, churches, Christian shrines and monasteries?
- Who destroyed our economy and our agriculture?
- Who caused the accident in Chernobyl?
- Who is responsible for the ecological disaster in our country?
- Who exhausted our resources of raw materials and sold them for next to nothing to the West?
- Who destroyed the Russian nation by means of ideology and alcohol?
- Who attacks us like a rabid dog with charges of nationalism whenever the word "Russian" is mentioned?
- Who tries to make the word "Russian" a synonym of enemy?[81]

The answer to all is Zionism, the "international center" which "controls the press" and has freemasonry as its ally. "We call to all Soviet people: Mobilize all your forces for a fight against the threat of Zionism in our country! Stop the machinations of those who would sell their country for thirty pieces of silver!" the proclamation urged.

A careful and large-scale poll sponsored by the West German journal, *Der Spiegel,* conducted in April 1989 by the Institute of Sociology of the USSR Academy of Sciences, showed that Pamyat's recognition factor was remarkably high. Nearly 80 percent of Muscovites had heard of it as compared with only 58 percent who had heard of the Berlin Wall.[82]

Judging from the results, one could conclude that one third or more of the Moscow population sympathized to some extent with Pamyat's anti-semitism. Seventeen percent of those polled reacted "very positively" or "positively" to Pamyat. Another 14 percent considered the organization "partly positively." While 47 percent judged Pamyat "negatively" or "very negatively," a sizeable 23 percent of the respondents said they "don't know."

The pro-Pamyat individuals, according to the poll data, appeared to come largely from the working class, especially those with a limited education. Komsomol members were more likely to be sympathetic to Pamyat than non-members. The most striking correlation related to atti-

---

[81] *Pamyat—Hatred Under Glasnost* (New York: Anti-Defamation League, 1989), 19–20.
[82] Robert J. Brym, "Perestroika, Public Opinion and 'Pamyat,' " *Soviet Jewish Affairs,* 19, no. 3 (Winter 1989), 23–31.

tudes about Gorbachev and perestroika. Pamyat sympathizers tended to be opposed to Gorbachev, were less critical of the prevailing Soviet system and more pessimistic about the future. A perceptive Western commentator on the data observed that it illuminated a major cluster of interrelated attitudes in Moscow: "authoritarianism, anti-Westernism, anti-Semitism and extremist Russian nationalism."[83]

Various schismatic groups broke away from the main body of Pamyat. One, headed by Igor Sychev, and sometimes called "Pamyat II," was denounced by Vasiliev as notoriously antisemitic and pro-Stalinist.[84] It was accused by him of shouting everywhere "Beat the Jews!" Vasiliev further charged that Pamyat II was created through the efforts of the Moscow Communist Party propaganda department in order to weaken Pamyat itself. Some indirect evidence tended to support a belief in the high Party connection. Various quarters in the Soviet press hailed the Sychev group as the "healthy wing" of Pamyat.[85] Sychev himself claimed to have good contacts with the KGB. On one hand, he spoke to visitors while in the presence of his sons dressed in tsarist uniforms and expressed reverence for the Tsar. On the other, he praised Stalin for his attempted "de-Zionization" which "unfortunately"—in Sychev's view—was left unfinished.[86]

Another splinter group, sometimes called "Rus," was headed by the notorious Valery Yemelyanov.[87] A third schismatic group, entitled "Patriot," was formed in Leningrad and officially recognized by the local authorities. It was headed by Aleksandr Romanenko, the well-known official antisemitic writer of the early eighties. Another schismatic group was also based in Leningrad; while retaining the Pamyat name, it was headed by Yuri Riverov who was said by Vasilev to be "a wild anti-Semite." The Riverov group was in fact expelled by the central council of Pamyat in Moscow. Adding to the sulphurous and explosive mix was a variety of other hate groups in a number of cities including youthful neo-Nazis, and Lubertsy, a type which resembled the punk and skinhead organiza-

---

[83] Ibid., 30.
[84] Dunlop, "Conversation with Dimitrii Vasil'ev," 13.
[85] *Novosti,* 12 November 1987; Julia Wishnevsky, "A Second 'Pamyat' Emerges," *Radio Liberty Research,* RL463/87, 16 November 1987.
[86] *The Economist* (London), 23 December 1989.
[87] Dunlop, "Conversation with Dimitrii Vasil'ev," 13.

tions in the United States. Particularly threatening were the so-called "Afghantsi" a small group comprising some veterans of the war in Afghanistan and which had come under the control of Pamyat.

On March 29, five new radical Pamyat groups which had emerged by 1990 formed a coalition under the umbrella of the "Popular Orthodox Movement of Russia Pamyat."[88] One, headed by Aleksandr Sveshnikov was called the Russian Orthodox National Patriotic Front Pamyat. It sought to join with Le Pen's National Front in France, LaRouche's European Party, the neo-Nazi Republic Party in West Germany and the Irish Republican Army to fight the "evil" of Zionism. Its foremost appeal was for "a German-Russian alliance which will finally put an end to Zionism," certainly, a strange call from alleged patriots of Russia who had been victims of Nazi Germany's destructive onslaught. These programs were outlined by the group's principal spokesman, Aleksandr Kulakov. For him, the October Revolution was nothing but a conspiracy: "Jews bear the collective responsibility for the 73-year old diabolical bacchanalia...." Conclusion: "Zionism must be destroyed."[89]

Especially militant and ferociously antisemitic was the Union of Proportional Representation-Pamyat, headed by Konstantin Smirnov-Ostashvili. A third group was the Russian Popular Party, led by K. Sidoruk, which was openly monarchist. Another one was the Russian Liberation Movement, led by Aleksandr Pobedinsky. It was strongly Orthodox, nationalist, pro-army and anti-perestroika. The final group was the Christian Patriotic Union, led by Yevgeny Pashnin. It held that Zionism was responsible for perestroika and for "the kike idea of democracy, so as to discredit the army and the Communists."

The coalition's platform embraced as its fundamental view the thesis that Jews were responsible for all the tribulations of the Russian people over the preceding seventy-three years. Therefore, the main task of the coalition was the renaissance of "Slavic Aryan" peoples so as to eliminate overt and covert Zionism in Russia and the world at large.[90]

What came through in the propaganda of Pamyat and its various splinter groups was the theme of the *Protocols:* Jews (or Zionists) seek dominance over society. Beyond that fundamental charge, Jews, or

---

[88] *Anti-Semitism in the USSR,* (New York: Anti-Defamation League, July 1990), 1–2.
[89] Ibid., 1.
[90] Ibid.

Zionists, were responsible for all the ills and difficulties that have plagued Soviet Russia. And, if no Jew was immediately apparent as the source of the problem, then it was some mystical and mysterious Freemason who could thus be labelled. Strikingly, Pamyat sought an idyllic and mystical past which would embody its values, and this turned out to be tsarism. Whatever happened after the overthrow of the tsars, whether democracy or Communism, was seen as antithetical to Russian interests.

In a special Hungarian Radio program broadcast on September 19, 1989, an insightful picture of Pamyat emerged. First, the broadcaster played a recording he had made at a mass meeting of Pamyat on June 8, 1989. Dmitri Vasiliev and Pamyat Chairman Kim Andreyev described the initial Pamyat emblem as a bell to signify a call for vigilance. This was replaced with a double-headed eagle, the symbol of the tsarist empire. The Pamyat uniform was then described: all black in order to emphasize, according to Vasiliev, the army-like character of Pamyat which was "fed up with undiscipline, immorality, corruption and soullessness under the aegis of democracy."[91]

Vasiliev frankly acknowledged his commitment to tsarism. The ruler, he said, "has always been the expression of the nation's wishes and the monarchy itself the embodiment of the power of the people." One thousand years of tsarism, he said, was always victorious as well as enormously rich. Food problems were simply unknown. Nor were there national problems.

The October Revolution had ruined this great historical achievement. Vasiliev said that he would like to ask Gorbachev "how was it possible to impoverish this enormous empire, to put it into the situation existing today in which it is bowing from the waist, begging for charitable donations." He would further ask "why had several millions died in Soviet concentration camps, why were these people shot in the heads, executed, tortured to death. In the name of what idea?" He poured out his personal sarcasm in responding: "So that on the 70th anniversary of Soviet power, sugar, washing powder and soap are restrained?" As for Gorbachev, he could not be elected tsar because he lacked "sufficient firmness" and has "no concrete program."

---

[91] "Soviet Opposition Groups Interviewed on Hungarian Radio," *BBC, Summary of World Broadcasts 5U/0568 B/5,* 22 September 1989.

Forms of democracy and democratic groups were sharply disparaged. Pamyat, he said, was "against all political doctrines, political parties." Instead, it sought "national consciousness" on "the basis of the cultural [and] historical development of the Russian nation." Vasiliev appeared to link democracy with Jews. Thus, he called a Soviet liberal group, the Democratic Alliance Party, "a purely Zionist organization." In his opinion, the group is a supporter of "cosmopolitanism which is alien, a crime against the nation."

Zionism was also linked by Vasiliev to the October Revolution. It was the Jews who practically carried out the revolution. Even the symbols of the revolution, he thought, were distinctly Jewish. Thus, the Red Star was a Jewish symbol, a Zionist sign. Allegations by Jews that they had been oppressed under the tsars were merely false. Pogroms, for example, were financed by rich Zionists. Their aspiration for domination had to be stopped. "Excuse me," he told the Hungarian interviewer, "we could not allow Russia to become Judaised throughout."

Public demonstrations, as in the unprecedented marches in Moscow of April and May 1987, were a crucial factor in bringing Pamyat to broad public attention. The Soviet Jewish leadership estimated in December 1989 that Pamyat had conducted some one thousand marches and demonstrations since 1986.[92] In Leningrad, the demonstrations in 1988 took the form of almost daily rallies in a popular park where Pamyat speakers harangued the crowds with virulent anti-Jewish appeals.[93] The incitatory character of these rallies was thought by Jewish activists to be responsible for some fifty incidents of Jewish cemetery desecrations.

What struck observers was the toleration of the police in response to these violence-charged public functions. On July 18, 1989, for example, a Sychev-Pamyat demonstration was held in Moscow at the site of the monument to Yakov Sverdlov, the first president of the Soviet state and Lenin's close comrade-in-arms.[94] Sverdlov was Jewish which probably explained why the monument was desecrated. Yet, none of the Party organs took note of the desecration or of the violation of a major Party

---

[92] Mikhail Chlenov, opening address to the Congress of Jewish Organizations in Moscow, 18 December 1989. A copy of the text is in the author's possession.

[93] Semyon Reznik, "The Rifle on the Wall," *The National Interest,* Fall 1989, 90.

[94] An eyewitness provided the author with the details; see also *Jews in the USSR* (London), July 1989.

image. Some speculated, probably correctly, about political influence being exerted on behalf of Pamyat.

Testifying to the political influence of Pamyat was the authorization given it to hold a demonstration on Red Square in Moscow during the first week of December in 1989. It was the first time an unofficial group had been permitted to hold a meeting in this highly visible and symbolically critical site. The significant development prompted Dmitri Zakharov, moderator to the popular, prime-time television program, "Vzglyad," to observe that Pamyat members have important sponsors.[95] This appeared to be a reference to Moscow's Party boss at the time, Yuri Prokofev, who was widely believed to be a Pamyat supporter.

A demonstration of Pamyat activity and the regime's initial response came on the opening of the historic Congress of Jewish Organizations on December 18, 1989. The seven hundred delegates and guests from foreign Jewish communities were confronted by some sixty Pamyat members shouting antisemitic epithets, waving placards and actually shoving the delegates. The placards and signs reflected Pamyat's purposes: "Zionists out of Russia" and "Who authorized a Zionist Congress in Moscow—Shame!" Strikingly, on the first day, the Moscow police stood by while "Pamyat continued to harass" the guests, according to a prominent American Jewish leader. He added that the police "behavior speaks for itself."[96]

Vigorous protests to the Foreign Ministry finally evoked a positive response. On December 20, Dr. Yuri Reshetov, head of the Foreign Office's Bureau of Humanitarian and Cultural Affairs, apologized to an American Jewish delegate and referred to the demonstration as "Pamyat terrorist acts."[97] Why no one was arrested went unexplained although Reshetov noted that the authorities were investigating a report that one of the demonstrators had held up a sign reading "Death to Jews." Presumably, if the term "Jews," instead of "Zionists," was used, and if there

---

[95] For details, see Isi Leibler, *Soviet Jewry 1990: Yet Another Turning Point?* (Melbourne: Executive Council of Australian Jewry, 1990), 5; Andrei Sinyavsky, "Russian Nationalists are Playing with Matches," *Guardian* (London), 22 February 1990.

[96] *New York Times*, 20 December 1989; William Korey, "A Fear of Pogroms Haunts Soviet Jews," *New York Times*, 29 January 1990, Op-Ed Page.

[97] This was reported by officials of the National Conference of Soviet Jewry who met with Reshetov.

was a death threat, then a case for incitement to ethnic enmity could be made. Nonetheless, the leniency of the police toward Pamyat demonstrators was evident from the first day.

By the second day—no doubt due to the protests and the embarrassment incurred from Western press coverage—security was beefed up. Sufficient police with firm instructions "assured...that any criminal act, or sign of inciting violence, would result in criminal prosecution."[98]

On the second day, the Pamyat demonstrators were joined by Keffiah-clad Palestinians determined to vent their anger. Their placards displayed photographs of Yasir Arafat, while the signs read: "We condemn Zionism," and "Zionism Will Not Succeed." The Palestine Liberation Organization supporters held two further demonstrations, the largest one occurring on the final day of the congress. According to a key source at the congress, the last demonstration became unruly prompting the police to finally use nightsticks to disperse the protesters.[99]

Two demonstrations in January 1990 were especially significant in documenting a more violent turn in Pamyat tactics. A television studio which carried a popular late-evening talk show that was shown across the country was planning to interview two liberal Supreme Soviet deputies. Pamyat conducted a threatening demonstration at the site of the studio. The deputies had to run a gauntlet of the mob, members of which jostled them and thrust incendiary leaflets into their hands. One leaflet called upon all who are interested in "bashing the Yids" to prepare for a nationwide pogrom on May 5. The deputies were overwrought by their experience. One read the text on television to a huge audience. The other commented: "The situation is no longer a joke; fascism is rampant in our country."[100]

On January 18, a meeting of Moscow liberal writers—*Aprel*—was broken up by Pamyat toughs yelling "Yids, clear off to Israel." The demonstrators promised to take over the country and conduct a pogrom:

---

[98] Ibid.

[99] Ibid.; Glenn Richter, "Jewish Congress, Jewish Concern." (New York, January 1990?), mimeograph. Richter is a leader of the Student Struggle for Soviet Jewry; another report is in Leibler, 6.

[100] An eyewitness account was made available to the author; some of it was reported in William Korey, "The Freedom to Hate," *Reform Judaism,* Summer 1990, 7; also see *Report on the USSR,* 9 February 1990, 37.

"Today we come with loudspeakers, tomorrow we will come with guns." When two Jewish women writers—a poet and a novelist—were openly threatened, a non-Jewish male novelist came to their assistance. He was severely beaten. One of the assailants read a statement declaring that Gorbachev's closest colleague, Aleksandr Yakovlev, has been a "hireling" of "world Zionism" since the time he served as Soviet ambassador to Canada.[101]

The threats had become palpable. If the new Pamyat platform constituted one long diatribe against "aggressive Zionism, Talmudic atheism and cosmopolitan usury"—all code words for Jewry—a leading Pamyat speaker at a rally in January screamed: "First we must deal with the Zionist problem, then we can tackle perestroika." How to deal with the "Zionist problem?" A Pamyat slogan provided an answer: "Get rid of all the Jews."[102]

At a rally of a Pamyat group—the People's Russian Orthodox Movement—in Moscow on June 6, 1990, the principal speaker told seven hundred participants that the Jews are "the main enemy of the Russian people." He threatened that the Orthodox Church will once again rise up "to slay its filthy enemies" with "sword in hand." In the meantime, he demanded an "immediate ban on all Jewish emigration until their fate has been decided upon by a supreme tribunal of the Russian people." Tumultuous applause followed.[103]

Adding to the general atmosphere of fear were reports that Pamyat was requiring that prospective members submit the names and addresses of five Jews.[104] Actually, it was sufficient for prospective members to submit only three names and addresses of Jews who were "trying to conceal their Jewishness." According to a Pamyat leader, "hidden Jews" who seek to attack Russian culture from inside the literary establishment were the nation's most dangerous enemies.[105]

---

[101] Vitaly Vitalyev, in *The Guardian* (London), 20 February 1990; Irina Ginzburg, "Russian Jews Fear for Our Lives," *New York Times*, 5 May 1990, Op-Ed Page.

[102] For the Pamyat platform, see "Manifesto of the National Patriotic Front, Pamyat," adopted on January 12, 1989.

[103] Eyewitness report of the event was made available to the author.

[104] See the disclosures of Soviet literature specialists, John and Carol Garrard, "Letter to the Editor," *New York Times*, 27 May 1990.

[105] Ibid; Goldanskii, "Anti-Semitism"; Irina Ginzburg, "We Fear for Our Lives," *New York Times*, 15 May 1990.

# Glasnost and the Demonology of Zionism 145

Not only was violence projected. A Pamyat program printed in the journal *Energetica* (published by the Moscow Energy Institute) insisted that it was essential "to prohibit Jews and their ilk from defending [university] dissertations, obtaining academic titles and degrees...."[106] Jews, the article said, must be numerically represented in the country's cultural and scientific hierarchy only in proportion to their "national representation." The purpose of the program, it was specified, was to de-Zionize the USSR.

Pamyat's reported platform made it evident that its target was quite broad: "Jews, including those who are trying to conceal that they are Jews, half-Jews, quarter-Jews, those married to Jews, etc." This would total—Pamyat said—9.69 percent of the Soviet population or 25 million people—hardly a tiny figure.[107]

A principal speaker at the Moscow Congress of Jewish Organizations, the Lithuanian-Jewish poet, Grigory Kanovich, wrote an article for the Vilnius edition of *Komsomolskaia pravda* which emphasized that "clouds of pogroms are gathering over our heads." He observed that "throughout our country...hatred of our people is secretly or openly gaining force." Particularly dismaying, Kanovich declared, was that "this incitement to murder takes place before the very eyes of all the Soviet people...who ignore the thugs and inciters." In the face of the explosive surge of hate, he offered one recommendation to Jews: "leave now."[108] In fact, emigration was escalating.

A poll of the several hundred participants at the congress underscored the anxieties of Soviet Jewish leadership. Taken by Aleksandr Benifand, executive director of the Jewish Research Center of the Soviet Sociological Association, it showed 35 percent of the respondents either "very often" or "often" experienced or were confronted with acts of antisemitism in the previous six months. Another 38 percent had such experiences "sometimes." Leaders from Russia, Byelorussia, and the Ukraine

---

[106] Vitaly Vitalyev, "Seeds of Racist Disaster," *Guardian* (London), 20 February 1990.

[107] Alexander Yanov "Letter to the Editor," *New York Times,* 10 June 1990. Vitaly Goldansky noted that Pamyat planned to search for Jewish progenitors to the previous tenth generation, while Hitler had determined that a person was Jewish if he were only one-quarter Jewish; see *Washington Post,* 18 February 1990.

[108] *Komsomolskaia pravda* (Vilnius), November 1989, cited in William Korey, "A Fear of Pogroms Haunts Soviet Jews," *New York Times,* 25 January 1990 25, Op-Ed Page.

experienced antisemitism far more frequently than those from other regions of the USSR; the range was 80–100 percent. The bulk of Soviet Jews—81 percent—resided in these areas. In the Baltic area where fewer than 3 percent of Soviet Jews lived, the incidence of antisemitic experiences was much less. But in Moldavia, the reported incidence was also high. Particularly striking was the fear of overt violence; 72 percent of Moscow's Jewish leaders and 94 percent of Leningrad's leaders believed that a pogrom was possible in the near future.[109]

A later poll in Moscow, conducted by the Institute of Sociology of the Academy of Sciences and supported by the American Jewish Committee, found that 17 percent of respondents thought that "most people are anti-Jewish" and 60 percent thought that "some are anti-Jewish." More critical was the 48 percent who believed that "anti-Jewish feeling is on the rise."[110]

---

[109] Union of Councils for Soviet Jews, *Anti-Semitism in the Soviet Union: A Status Report* (Washington DC, May 1990), mimeograph, 3, Appendix.

[110] *Moscow Survey of Political Tolerance and Anti-Semitism, February/March 1990* (New York: American Jewish Committee, 1990), mimeograph. The survey was analyzed by Professors James Gebson and Raymond Duch of the University of Houston.

## Chapter 9

## Political Uses of the Demonology of Zionism

A stunning feature of the escalating popular antisemitism was the support it received from intelligentsia circles that expressed strong nationalist views. As noted by Soviet historian Sergei Rogov in *Pravda* in July 1990, "this may be the first time in our history that Judeophobia has become popular in intelligentsia circles."[1] Such respectability of antisemitism was a powerful factor in providing Pamyat with moral and ideological sustenance. For the same reason, as the historian observed, it "evokes great alarm" among Jews and their supporters.

Contrast between the contemporary nationalist intelligentsia and their liberal forbears of the tsarist era is striking. Russia's most outstanding man of letters in the nineteenth century, Lev N. Tolstoy, had set the tone for the attitude of the creative intelligentsia of the pre- and post-revolutionary epochs. In a private letter which achieved wide circulation several years before his death in 1910, Tolstoy wrote:

> The Jew is that sacred being who has brought down from heaven the everlasting fire and has illumined with it the entire world. He is the religious source, spring and fountain out of which all the rest of the peoples have drawn their beliefs and their religions. The Jew is the pioneer of liberty.... The Jew is the pioneer of civilization.... The Jew is the emblem of civil and religious toleration.... The Jew is the emblem of eternity....[2]

Shortly after the pogroms of 1881–82, which had stirred the consciences

---

[1] Sergei Rogov, "Is There a Jewish Question Here?," *Pravda,* 22 July 1990.
[2] Cited in Salo W. Baron, *The Russian Jew Under Tsars and Soviets* (New York: Macmillan, 1964), 164.

of many liberal intellectuals, Tolstoy joined one hundred other distinguished members of the intelligentsia in a petition to Tsar Alexander III protesting the massacres of Jews.[3] The petition had been organized by one of Russia's leading thinkers, Vladimir S. Soloviev. Following the Kishinev pogrom in 1903, Tolstoy again made his anger felt: "The outrages of Kishinev," he declared, "are but the direct result of the propaganda of falsehood and violence which our government conducts with such energy."[4]

Maxim Gorky, the forerunner of "socialist realism," pursued the Tolstoy tradition. As a youngster, he had been outraged by the 1882 pogrom in Nizhny-Novgorod, and he later depicted it in his writings in forceful terms. The Kishinev pogrom spurred Gorky to denounce the upper classes as being "no less guilty of the disgraceful and horrible deeds committed at Kishinev than the actual murderers and ravishers." Their guilt lay "in the fact that not merely did they not protect the victims, but that they rejoiced over the murders."[5] Gorky wrote extensively against antisemitism, and it is a commentary on the thinking of Soviet officialdom that some two hundred to three hundred pages of Gorky's comments on Jews and the Jewish question were deleted from both a thirty-volume edition of his works published by the Soviet Academy of Sciences from 1948 to 1956 and from an eighteen-volume edition published from 1959 to 1963.[6]

What prompted Gorky's most vigorous intervention (along with that of scores of other Russian intellectuals) was the Beiliss blood libel case of 1911–1913.[7] In December 1911, they issued a manifesto the contemporary relevance of which was obvious:

> The eternal struggle of humanity for liberty, legal equality and fraternity and against slavery, hate and social discord has been with us from ancient times. And, in our times, as always, the same persons who uphold the rightless condition of their own people are the most persistent in exciting among them the spirit of religious and racial enmity.... The false story of the use

---

[3] Ibid., 61.
[4] Ibid., 70.
[5] Ibid.
[6] Boris Souvarine, "Gorky, Censorship and the Jews," *Dissent,* Winter 1965, 81–3.
[7] Maurice Samuel, *Blood Accusation: The Strange History of the Beiliss Case* (New York: Knopf, 1966), 242.

of Christian blood by Jews has been broadcast once more among the people. This is a familiar device of ancient fanaticism....[8]

It was signed by 150 leaders in the arts and sciences, including Count Ilya Tolstoy, the president of the Academy of Science, and Gorky.

A key figure in the drafting of the manifesto was the prominent novelist, Vladimir G. Korolenko. He had joined with Soloviev in 1882 in protesting against the pogrom of that time. Later, his novel *Yom Kippur* would sympathetically portray various Jewish characters. He gave special attention to the Beiliss trial, commenting pointedly, if somewhat optimistically, that "evidently Russian citizens finally understand that the Jewish question is not only a Jewish but also a general Russian question; that the untruth and corruption uncovered at the Beiliss trial is an all-Russian untruth and corruption...." Liberal lawyers from St. Petersburg gave expression to Korolenko's opinion by condemning "the slander of the Jewish people" and the attempt to propagate "racial and national animosity."[9]

In sharp contrast with the humanist views of Tolstoy, Gorky, and Korolenko was the outlook in the late 1980s of the major literary organs in Moscow (mainly controlled by the Russian Republic's Writers Union)—*Nash sovremennik* (Our Contemporary), *Molodaia gvardiia* (Young Guard), *Moskva* (Moscow) and *Literaturnaia Rossiia* (Literary Russia). Under glasnost, these periodicals had expanded greatly with circulation doubling to reach close to 2 million.[10] They set the tone and value system for important segments of the provincial press.

*Nash sovremennik* had been in the forefront of the anti-Zionist drive prior to 1986 and had even published the crackpot Yemelyanov (in a review of a book by hatemonger Vladimir Begun). The practice was continued despite glasnost or, perhaps, because of it. After November 1988, it became the only publication in the USSR which continued to print Begun.[11] A few months later, in February 1989, an exposé in *Sovetskaia kultura* demonstrated that Begun had plagiarized Adolf

---

[8] Ibid., 243.
[9] Ibid.
[10] Semyon Reznik, "The Rifle on the Wall," *The National Interest*, Fall 1989, 91; circulation estimates were from the research bureau of Radio Liberty.
[11] *Nash sovremennik*, 11, 1988.

Hitler's works.[12] Comparative textual analysis showed the remarkable similarities between Begun's works and those of the Nazi Führer.

Sergei Vikulov, the editor of *Nash sovremennik* in September 1989, had no hesitancy in defending Pamyat and sharply rebuked those journals that pointed up its antisemitic character.[13] The same could also be said for *Molodaia gvardiia* the organ of Komsomol. An article in November 1989 contended that Soviet Jewish organizations were "openly cultivating the feeling of superiority over other peoples" and "implanting Russophobia and chauvinism in the heads of Jewish youth." The provocatory essay cited a Purim play for Jewish children which was presumed to stir "misanthropic feelings." Its deputy chief editor, Vyacheslav Gorbachov, offered comments that would accord with utter obscurantism. He charged that Zionists and Freemasons have organized a conspiracy which was responsible for the failure of the Russian people to "compose or sing its own songs." The conspiracy, he further claimed, was the cause of "the destruction of the family and of corruption by sex, alcohol and drugs." In characterizing Freemasons, he described them as servants of the Devil, precisely the language of Pamyat.[14]

Similar views would find expression in other provincial Party youth journals as an outgrowth of a rather distinctive case involving the well-known actor, Nikolai Burliaev. He had written and directed a new film, *Lermontov,* about the prominent nineteenth century Russian poet. The film was severely criticized by a variety of Soviet newspapers and at a film-makers' congress. Burliaev contended that a conspiracy of Zionists and Freemasons was responsible for this. Burliaev then conducted a "holy struggle" campaign in favor of his film. In a series of interviews with provincial newspapers, especially Party youth organs, he accused the "new course" in Soviet cinema of serving the devil. One film writer, who had written a negative review in *Nedelia,* was sent a clipping from a provincial newspaper claiming that criticism of *Lermontov* was part of a conspiracy against Russian geniuses. A note accompanying the clipping read:

---

[12] *Sovetskaia kultura,* 25 February 1989.

[13] David Remnick, *Washington Post,* 31 July 1989; Julia Wishnevsky, "*Nash Sovremennik* Provides Focus for 'Opposition' Party," *Report on the USSR* (Jerusalem: Vidal Sassoon International Center for the Study of Antisemitism, January 1989, 4.

[14] "Ostorozhno: provokatsiia!," *Molodaia gvardiia* 10 (1989): 154–56.

"To a Yid and a Mason from the remainder of the Russian people!"[15]

During 1990, a high point in the journal's embrace of the *Protocols of the Elders of Zion* was reached. In June, an article in *Molodaia gvardiia* accused Gorbachev's close colleague, Aleksandr Yakovlev, of being the head of the Soviet Masonic Lodge, supposedly conspiring with world Zionism.[16]

Several months earlier, in March 1990, it had engaged in a highly questionable publishing venture. In Poland in early 1990 a forged excerpt of an alleged interview between Bronislaw Geremek, a leading figure in Solidarity, and journalist Hanna Krall had appeared. The fabrication had first surfaced in December 1981 after the Jaruszelski military coup. Geremek, who was born Jewish, was alleged to have told Krall, also a Jew, that "Jews are soon going to come back into commerce and industry in Poland," soon they would dominate the economy because they "will provide the money" as well as "the brains for this entrepreneurship." The forgery had been designed to serve the needs of reactionary and nationalist elements in Poland then striving to rid the country of "cosmopolitan" elements of Solidarity, which was said to be dominant in the Mazowiecki government. The forgery was circulated in the Polish Parliament.[17]

Significantly, *Molodaia gvardiia* published this Polish fabrication which recalled the earlier and more famous forgery, the *Protocols*.[18] That it chose to print the absurdity suggested that it had purposes similar to the purpose of the forgers of the Geremek-Krall interview, namely, to strike at both Gorbachev and Jewry by leaving the impression that the latter was once again secretly engaged in an effort to win domination of the economy.

The ideological orientation of the rightist journals was captured in a letter by Gennadi Kuznetsov to a prominent monthly literary journal in the fall 1988: "reactionary romanticism, advocating a patriarchal stance and isolation from the world at the end of the 20th century." He pointed out that "neo-Slavophil slogans" focusing on the struggle with foreigners and intellectuals "are close to the position of the neo-Stalinists." Positions espoused by *Nash sovremennik* and *Moldodaia gvardiia,* he concluded,

---

[15] Walter Laqueur, "Lermontov, or a Plot Exposed," *Encounter* 2 (1988): 66–8.
[16] *Molodaia gvardiia* 6 (1990): 184–94.
[17] *IJA Briefing* (London), 1, no. 2 (May 1990): 1–2.
[18] *Molodaia gvardiia,* 3 (1990).

were "a form of neo-Slavophilism, nationalist utopianism behind which arrant bureaucratism finds it easy to hide."[19]

*Molodaia gvardiia* and *Nash sovremennik,* with their articles subjecting Jews to ridicule or contempt and worse, provoked a stinging letter of protest sent to Gorbachev and signed by three hundred members of the Writers' Union. On September 29, 1989 the secretariat of the Writers' Union wrote to Gorbachev vigorously denying that the journals were antisemitic and, on the contrary, praising them as champions in the struggle against "the plague of Russophobia." A particularly vicious attack upon Jews followed. Noting that some Jews were guilty of Russophobia, the secretariat letter castigated the "arrogance of people who at any moment and without difficulty, can choose a better and more bountiful life abroad."[20]

Some of Russia's most popular novelists, who wrote for these publications had either joined the campaign in defense of Pamyat or gave overt expression to vulgar antisemitism. Viktor Astafiev, a well-known rural and nature novelist, vigorously polemicized against Jews as the enemies of a Russian national renaissance. He contended that Zionists, rather than Communists were responsible for the murder of Tsar Nicholas and his family.[21] Pamyat speakers picked up this accusation and publicly claimed that "the execution of the Tsar's family was committed as a Jewish ritual sacrifice."[22]

Of special importance was Valentin Rasputin, a national literary idol, who headed an environmental group which charged that the pollution of Lake Baikal in Siberia was connected with the Zionist-Masonic conspiracy.[23] From the very beginning of the attacks on Pamyat in the liberal press, Rasputin became an ardent defender of the group. He considered that the criticism of Pamyat was a leftist deviation and he denounced the liberal organs for having "lambasted the unfortunate Pamyat." The attribute "Black Hundred," he said, was totally incorrect in characterizing Pamyat antisemitism for they are "sincerely...if perhaps not in the right

---

[19] Josephine Woll, "'Glasnost' and Soviet Culture," *Problems of Communism,* November–December 1989, 47.

[20] *Jews in the USSR* (London) 17, no. 21 (November 1989).

[21] Reznik, "Rifle on the Wall," 90.

[22] *Sovetskaia kultura,* 25 February 1989.

[23] Reznik, "Rifle on the Wall," 90.

way concerned about the fate of the Motherland."[24]

Rasputin, in an interview with the *New York Times* made it plain where he stood on Jewish issues. In his view, Jews were responsible for the Bolshevik Revolution and, especially, for the terror that followed. With regard to both, "they played a large role and their guilt is great." Rasputin noted that "the crimes of communism are not so quickly forgiven." He added that, "in this country, those are Jewish sins because many Jewish leaders took part in the terror, in the repression of the kulak, of the peasants...."[25]

The rural novelist took pains to emphasize that Jews cannot be held responsible for the crucifixion of Christ, a traditional stereotype. The crucifixion, Rasputin held "is an ancient sin and no Jew today can be held responsible," yet in his general comments, Rasputin reflected not only a stunning ignorance of the Soviet Jewish plight, but revealed himself as a bigot as well, whose perception of the revolution and the terror of 1918–1920 was remarkably tendentious and one-sided. When he was named by Gorbachev in April 1990 to a newly-created and powerful Presidential Council, a kind of inner cabinet with important advisory functions, it testified less to his intelligence or experience than to his influence in nationalist circles. Gorbachev must have regarded the appointment as a method of coopting and thereby neutralizing a potential threat.

A third celebrated novelist, Vasily Belov, also focused upon rural life. His work, *Everything Lies Ahead,* had been characterized by a leading American authority on Soviet literature as "markedly anti-Semitic."[26] In Belov's essays and public speeches, he made clear his biases. When he addressed the First Congress of Peoples' Deputies in June 1989, he complained about the alleged concentration of real power in the hands "of those who control the media and who reflect the interests of certain groups" from the capital.[27] It was an allegation, noted the Soviet culture specialist, Josephine Woll, that was "often repeated at meetings of

---

[24] See Laqueur, *Long Road to Freedom,* 140–42; A Kuzmin, *Nash sovremennik* 3 (1988).
[25] Bill Keller, "Russian Nationalists: Yearning For An Iron Hand," *New York Times Magazine,* 28 January 1990, 18–21, 45–50. A correction in the initial translation was noted in the *New York Times,* 29 July 1990.
[26] Woll, "'Glasnost' and Soviet Culture," 47.
[27] *Pravda,* 3 June 1989.

extreme nationalists."[28]

Another illustration of the open involvement of popular novelists on behalf of antisemitism was the work of Valentin Pikul, one of the most popular historical fiction writers in the USSR.[29] His novels reflected a high degree of anti-Jewish bigotry. Typical was the novel *At The Outer Limit,* published in 1979 which portrayed the monk Rasputin as an instrument of a Jewish-Masonic conspiracy against Russia. In 1989, Pikul shed his fictional mask. Open bigotry was put on display in an interview with him published in *Nash sovremennik* in February 1989.

Pikul stated: "All of them together form a gang—Trotsky, Bukharin, Kamenev, Zinoviev, Kaganovich, Yemelian Yaroslavsky (Gubelman), Uritsky, Volodarsky, and Epstein—these are fanatics of mass murder," responsible for the "genocide of the Russians and other peoples." With the exception of Bukharin, all were Jews who, in Stalinist mythology, were the embodiment of Satanic evil. (How Bukharin's name was smuggled in is a mystery. Perhaps Pikul assumed that since he had been an opponent of Stalin, he must have been Jewish, or, since he was rehabilitated by the Gorbachev regime for which Pikul had little regard, perhaps it was taken for granted that he was Jewish.) Interestingly, Stalin was exonerated by Pikul for genocide. Stalin was presented as merely "a product of his times." What especially aroused Pikul's ire was the thought that these "fanatics of terror" were now being elevated into virtual sainthood.[30]

Nikolai Gulbinsky, writing in *Ogonek* in June 1989, appropriately observed that some literary people, like Pikul, "deal with historical themes, in order to substantiate their own ideas, ideas which have nothing whatsoever to do with history or, for that matter, with literature." The *Ogonek* article pointed out that V. Khatyushin had expressed similar views in another conservative-nationalist journal, *Moskva:*

> Trotsky dreamed of turning the country into a military-feudal state, so as to use it for the purposes of world revolution.... That is to say, he in fact dreamed of legalizing the idea of freemasonry power over the whole world.

---

[28] Woll, "'Glasnost' and Soviet Culture," 47.

[29] Ignacy Szenfeld, "Valentin Pikul'—the Soviet Vsevolod Krestovsky," *Radio Liberty Research,* RL278/79, 17 September 1979, 1–11. So extreme were Pikul's views that he was criticized in *Pravda,* 10 August 1979.

[30] *Nash sovremennik* 2 (1989).

A major obstacle to Trotsky was Stalin, who in all probability appreciated how adventuristic was this Masonic-Zionist conspiracy against mankind.[31]

Once again, the infamous Masonic-Zionist myth found expression in the demonology of which Trotsky was inevitably cast as an embodiment of evil. His Jewish origin, and his personality traits, often described in stereotypic terms, made the demonology transparent.

It was hardly an accident that Jews were perceived in the literature of the Russian nationalists as cosmopolitan, urban, atheist, Western, and not very Russian. Nor was it surprising that these presumed Jewish values were seen as epitomized in the Soviet "enemy"—Leon Trotsky—fanatic, terrorist, cosmopolitan, and internationalist, Satanic figure par excellence. Trotsky filled endless pages of Soviet literature and history. His presumed conspiratorial revolutionary nature was depicted as a "camouflaged cosmopolitan tendency."

One need not mention the many other writers who espoused antisemitism in their works; the syndrome is clear enough. One writer, however, does deserve special mention because of the prominence of his position and the distinctiveness of his outlook. Stanislav Kunyayev, editor-in-chief of *Nash sovremennik,* as early as 1980 revealed his bias when he wrote a poem about "Jews in the Pentagon" who were plotting to destroy the Russian people.

Especially mind-boggling was Kunyayev's thesis about the *Protocols of the Elders of Zion* which he advanced in the June 1989 issue of *Nash sovremennik.*[32] He called the *Protocols* a genuine document written with a "brilliant intelligence and an almost Satanic will." When questioned about the notorious forgery while visiting the Kennan Institute in Washington the following year, he indicated that whether the *Protocols* was a forgery or not was not consequential. What was decisive was the "truth" of the Elders of Zion.[33]

Kunyayev's bigotry was worn openly. The biggest criticism in his article was directed against "an immoral system by which publicists of Jewish origin use Russian surnames and write about the defects of the Soviet people." The fact that some Jews have taken on Russian surnames was his greatest concern even as it had become the object of a veritable

---

[31] *Ogonek* 23 (1989).
[32] Cited in *Washington Post,* 18 April 1990.
[33] *New York Times,* 18 April 1990; *Washington Post,* 18 April 1990.

crusade by Pamyat and other peddlers of hate. Overlooked was the reality that Stalin and his non-Jewish associates had also borne pseudonyms. It was the Jew with a Russian surname that burned deeply into the consciousness of the antisemite.

In sum, antisemitism embraced a broad segment of the intellectual community known as *pochvenniki* (nativists), who saw Soviet salvation in the Russian folk tradition.[34] Western culture was perceived as a corrupting influence to be rejected in favor of an ancient set of mores rooted in the Russian Orthodox and peasant tradition. While the *zapadniki* (Westernizers) sought to advance democratization and humanism, the *pochvenniki* aimed to exclude alien elements which they saw as emanating from a "powerful Zionist center." This was articulated in a major work by Igor Shafarevich, a mathematician and scholar, whose book, *Russophobia,* which originally appeared in *Nash sovremennik,* presented the Jews as always having been the enemy of the Russian people.[35]

The Shafarevich work exerted considerable influence in intellectual antisemitic circles. His reputation both as a leading mathematician and prominent dissenter during the seventies gave his views broad attention. In Shafarevich's opinion, "Great Russian" self-respect had been punctured by the "Little People" (i.e., Jews, in contrast to the "Great People"—Russians). This resulted from the effectiveness of the efforts by the Little People continually characterizing Russians as a nation of slaves who worship power and intolerance. In contrast, "the Jewish issue has acquired an incomprehensible power over people's minds...." He explained that "Jewish national emotions are the fever of the whole country and the whole world." This deleteriously affected disarmament talks, trade agreements and cross-border relations among scientists.

Shafarevich minimized the existence of genuine antisemitism. Instead, he saw Jews as maintaining a powerful lobby to prevent criticism by falsely charging antisemitism. The real victims of the Soviet state's policy, he argued, have been the Russians who were repeatedly slandered by the Little People.

The perceptive and analytical Professor Goldanskii, in examining the

---

[34] Tatiana Karasova, "Soviet Factors Clash Over Relations with Israel," *Jerusalem Post,* 12 October 1989.
[35] Igor Shafarevich, "Russofobia," *Nash sovremennik* 6 (1989). For an analysis by Andrei Sinyavsky, see the *Guardian* (London), 22 February 1990.

structure of antisemitic forces in the USSR, found that "the main organization serving as a coordinator of the monarcho-Nazi forces" was the Russian Republic's Writers' Union.[36] This central literary structure within the Soviet Union provided a powerful foundation for the journals which the Union controlled, and these, in turn, offered a headquarters for nonstop hate-peddling. The Union made possible peer-like sanction for anti-Jewish bigotry.

The Writers' Union had been under the control of conservative and nationalist forces since 1987. At its March 1988 plenum some of its prominent representatives, like Stanislav Kunyayev and Vladimir Krupin, defended Pamyat against the criticism of Yevgeny Yevtushenko, Yelena Lesota and Gavril Popov.[37] Another spokesman, Yuri Bondarev, denounced liberals for "mourning over" Russian history, and for sexual promiscuity among the young. Later that year, the righteous and vitriolic anger of the conservative-nationalist elements reached a crescendo. At a meeting of the board secretariat in Ryazan September 28–October 2, the floor was given almost exclusively to *Nash sovremennik* writers who denounced "cosmopolitan enemies of Russia" for allegedly corrupting Soviet youth and seeking to destroy the country's sovereignty, in language reminiscent of that of Andrei Zhdanov in the 1940s.[38]

Later, in December, at a plenum of the board held in Moscow, the targets were prominent perestroika supporters—Tatiana Zaslavskaia, Leonid Abalkin, Nikolai Shmelev and Otto Latsis, deputy editor of the leading Party journal, *Kommunist*.[39] This powerful journal was especially criticized because of an editorial in November that had castigated the writers' speeches at the Ryazan meeting as anti-democratic, anti-Western and, implicitly, antisemitic. Strikingly, the dominant elements in the Writers' Union articulated support for Pamyat or for its ideas. Yuri Bondarev, president of the Union, gave continuing expression to xenophobic views about threatening conspiracies against the USSR which reflected Pamyat ideology.

At a meeting in September of the board secretariat of the Russian

---

[36] Vitalii I. Goldanskii, "Anti-Semitism: The Return of a Russian Nightmare," *Washington Post*, 18 February 1990.
[37] Woll, "'Glasnost' and Soviet Culture," 46.
[38] Ibid.
[39] Ibid.

Republic's Writers' Union, sharp criticism was directed by a number of writers against journals which had been outspoken in their attacks upon Pamyat.[40] Sergei Vikulov, an editor of *Nash sovremennik,* particularly rebuked those journals that pointed up the antisemitic overtones of the organizations which defended Pamyat. And, soon afterwards, the prominent writer, Valentin Rasputin, expressed support for the organization while on a visit to Sweden.[41]

Professors John and Carol Garrard, who have prepared a study of the Writers' Union, conducted enlightening interviews as part of their research. They reported that they "were treated to the most breathtaking expressions of raw anti-Semitism" from privileged members of the Soviet Writers' Union. "Seemingly sophisticated and sensible persons," they observed, asserted that "Jews had been responsible for the terror-famine in the Ukraine...that [because] Lazar Kaganovich, a member of Stalin's Politburo, was a Jew [this] proved the Jews' guilt." The Garrards went on to emphasize that Writers' Union members have used the pages of journals under the Union's jurisdiction for the "worst sort of hatred of the Jews." Thus *Nash sovremennik* carried the allegation that the Jews themselves were responsible for the murder of Jews at Dachau and Auschwitz.

Indeed, the transcripts of meetings of the Writers' group, said the Garrards, "read like account of speeches at Nazi rallies in the 1930s." Such prominent Jewish figures in Russian literature as Isaac Babel, Boris Pasternak and Vasily Grossman were said to belong to "literature in the Russian language" not Russian literature proper. Anyone who opposed these views was condemned as a Jew, whether or not he or she was Jewish. In consequence, "the very word Jew has become a term of abuse."[42]

At a meeting of the Union in the late fall of 1989, one observer noted, accusations were hurled at Jews that reminded him of the perspective held by the tsarist Black Hundreds. Jews were charged with imposing the Bolshevik Revolution on Russia and of having murdered and

---

[40] Julia Wishnevsky, "*Nash Sovremennik* Provides Focus for 'Opposition' Party," *Report on the USSR,* 20 January 1989, 4.

[41] See Laqueur, *Long Road to Freedom,* 141. For Rasputin's specific radio comments on Vasilyev on June 26, 1988, see Boris Paramanov, "The Culture of Soviet Anti-Semitism," *Partisan Review* 2 (1990): 196.

[42] John and Carol Garrard, *Inside the Soviet Writers' Union* (New York: Free Press, 1990); their comments here are from their Letter to the Editor, *New York Times,* 27 May 1990.

"dismembered" Tsar Nicholas II and his family. One speaker predicted that the day of reckoning for the Jews was coming. Applause burst forth from sections of the audience. The same speaker emphasized the utter irresponsibility of Jews, who even after pursuing anti-Russian purposes, were preparing to emigrate to Israel with all their riches.[43]

Typical of the November 1989 plenum of the Writers' Union was the following, reported in *Nedelia:*

> Anatoly Buivolov: Let us speak about the Jews. The Jews are evidently the only national group interested in breeding strife among us.... I am not a member...[of Pamyat] but there are a lot of things in them which I like. Why are they everywhere where there is the smell of money...? And let us also speak about those who have changed their names and nationalities from Jewish ones and whose number is three times larger than the official figure.
>
> Tatiana Gluskova: The conflicts...in Moscow and Leningrad...are not...between the Russians and the Jews.... This is a conflict between Zionism, the worst form of world fascism.... How long will the Russian writers, the legitimate sons of the Russian land...the Russians with roots, languish under the heel of oppressors and usurpers?[44]

The Garrards saw in these developments "a parallel between Soviet society today and German society prior to the rise of Hitler." With a leadership lacking popular support and economic collapse imminent and with a sense of anger deepening over "the denigration of Russian culture" during much of the Soviet period, it was scarcely surprising, they found, that "the old belief in the Jew as the source of the Russians' troubles has reemerged."[45]

The vigorous backing of Pamyat in prominent literary circles could not but have consequences elsewhere, as became apparent during the summer of 1989. Heretofore, the major Party central daily press had been critical of Pamyat's bigotry. Now, for the first time, Pamyat was given a platform by a newspaper that had been among its most severe critics—*Komsomolskaia pravda,* the organ of the Young Communist League. Its

---

[43] Walter Laqueur, "From Russian with Hate," *New Republic,* 5 February 1990, 50; see also Josephine Woll, "Russians and 'Russophobes': Anti-Semitism on the Russian Literary Scene," *Soviet Jewish Affairs* 19, no. 3 (Winter 1989): 3–21.

[44] *Nedelia* 47 (1989).

[45] Garrard and Garrard, Letter to the Editor.

weekly supplement, *Sobesednik* carried a full-page article on June 23, 1989 by Aleksandr Shtilmark, a leader of Pamyat in a small town near Moscow—Kupavna. Shtilmark was a secondary-school teacher in the town.

According to *Sobesednik's* editors, the decision was based on the need to have a "constructive dialogue" with Pamyat. This was a line initially proposed by sections of the media after Pamyat had surfaced. On the second page of *Sobesednik,* a refutation of Pamyat's philosophy was published. The writer was a young sociologist, Pavel Kudyukin. In the view of the editors, a dialogue was appropriate because "maybe this is a case in which it is not the truth but a problem that lies between two polarized viewpoints."[46]

Yet, the Shtilmark article cannot but reinforce any ethnic specialist's view that constructive dialogue with Pamyat was an oxymoron. In an attempt to refute the charge of antisemitism, Shtilmark contended that it was Zionism, not Jewry, which was the enemy of the Russian people and its culture. What followed glaringly illuminated his thinking. He listed a group of names who constituted the Zionist criminals: "Lev Trotsky (Bronstein), Lazar Kaganovich, Yemelyan Yaroslavsky (Gubelman), Yakov Sverdlov, Lev Kamenev (Rozenfeld), Grigory Zinoviev (Apfelbaum)." It was the traditional listing found in the writings of antisemites. Shtilmark gratuitously added that the national composition of the Council of People's Commissars in the early years of the Bolshevik revolution looked more like the Israeli Knesset than a Soviet government. The posture of Shtilmark was little different from that of the anti-Bolshevik White armies in 1918–1920. Only the world "Jew" was missing, having been replaced by "Zionism."

Shtilmark went on to characterize the detrimental features of Zionism and its partner, Masonry, which constituted the enemy: "a putrid farrago of 'heavy metal,' pornographic films, video hits and all the other products of cosmopolitanism that poison the vestiges of our spirituality." It was the usual hodgepodge of bigoted stereotypes promoted by Pamyat and its conservative-nationalist supporters. Cosmopolitanism was the key term that echoed the Stalinist past of hatred and violence, which had fingered the Jew, not the Zionist, as the terrible enemy. The plea for a

---

[46] *Sobesednik,* 23 June 1989. For details, see *From Soviet Sources: Jewish Themes in the Soviet Media* (London), No. 0, 1989, 1–2.

dialogue with Pamyat supporters would seem to be misplaced.

If Pamyat's impact in the major cities was disturbing, all the more was this the case in provincial areas. Significantly, Shtilmark was a teacher from a small town. A more appropriate case study was provided by incidents in the fairly large town of Chelyabinsk in the Urals in the fall of 1989. Gregory Alpernas, a Jewish activist from Vilnius, visited the area and addressed the newly-formed Jewish Cultural Association of Chelyabinsk. He was reported by the local Chelyabinsk press as saying that the Jews "already run the world and they need only to take power into their own hands." The report was, of course, absurd. The press accused the Jewish Cultural Association of supporting "nationalist and Zionist" ideas. The warning was intended to dissuade the Association from hosting a similar speaker.[47]

The background to this event was particularly revealing. In October 1989, Chelyabinsk was flooded with a new leaflet entitled *Catechism of a Jew in the USSR,* a forgery which bore a striking resemblance to the *Protocols*. The scurrilous leaflet was known to have originated with Pamyat in Moscow. In patronizing remarks about various Soviet nationalities, most notably Russians, the *Catechism* addressed Jews urging them to "make things difficult for the Russians in as many petty and irritating ways as you can." Jews were further called upon in the forgery to "play on the Russians' softheartedness," and to avoid restoring Russian national monuments. Most important, Jews were urged "to take power into your hands." Finally, the forgery sought to demonstrate how the Jews were responsible for the Great Purge of 1936–1937 by listing the names (and wives' names) of the Jews in the government and the Party Central Committee during those years.[48]

When the local newspaper, the *Chelyabinsk Worker,* attacked Alpernas, it also carried a letter criticizing the Vilnius Jewish lecturer, citing extensively from the *Catechism*. The letter, with the heading "Under the Flag of Israel," was signed "S. Peysner"—an obvious Jewish-sounding name. The letter was accompanied by a so-called commentary written by N. Sheremet, the regional Party official responsible for ideology, as well as by an unsigned editorial comment. Sheremet's commentary stated that "if we look at things coolly, Peysner discloses the significance and

---

[47] *IJA Briefing* (London) 1, no. 2 (May 1990): 2–4.
[48] Ibid., 2.

content of the [Jewish] meeting." He chastised, as did the editorial, the Jewish Association for holding the meeting and the Soviet Cultural Fund for authorizing the lecture.[49]

A local Jewish activist later surmised that "Peysner" and Sheremet were one and the same.[50] Evidently the tradition of the *Protocols* and the use of forged Jewish names, made infamous by Lev Korneyev, continued to find a strong resonance in provincial areas. The episode was a startling one which revealed how a Party ideologist at the local level exploited glasnost for traditional antisemitic purposes.

On the national level, the leadership of the Russian Republic's Writers' Union exerted its climactic impact in a "Letter" by seventy-four of its most prominent members, published in *Literaturnaia Rossiia* on March 2, 1990. It was an extraordinary document which, in the words of the journal's editor, Ernst Safonov, constituted a desperate warning about the "dangers of Zionism as an ideology." The beginning was one long rather pathetic whine about the alleged put-down by liberal intellectuals of the Russian nation, of Russian patriotism and of those who expressed this patriotism in their writings. Included was a denunciation of the liberal intellectuals' concern with Pamyat and "Russian Fascism." In almost hysterical tones, the "Letter of the 74," denied that there was any basis for the notion of "Russian Fascism." It was a "phantom," a "counterfeit idea," a "lie," a "fiction," a "fantasy," "absurd," a "myth," and the "cheapest form of provocations."[51]

The "Letter of 74" then charged that "the fabrication of the myth of 'Russian Fascism' occurs against the background of the dynamic rehabilitation and...idealization of the Zionist ideology." The supposed "idealization" extended to both persons of "Jewish heritage" and political figures of Israel. What was apparent here, said the signers, was a racist phenomenon, an effort at cosmetizing the "criminal face of Zionism," and creating an image of a "supernation." Especially criticized was the attempt to repudiate the "Zionism equals racism" resolution of the United Nations.

Cited in the letter was a fascinating accusation made by academician Tatiana Zaslavskaia to the effect that Russia occupied first place in

---

[49] Ibid., 3.
[50] Ibid.
[51] *Literaturnaia Rossiia*, 2 March 1990.

"manifestations of anti-Semitism" as compared with other nationalities in the USSR.[52] The charge was violently denounced as one that required of Russians to be servile and submissive. Her reported perception was interpreted as accusing Russians of "inborn anti-Semitism." From the viewpoint of the signers, those who speak out against antisemitism display a "slavish attitude to Jews, past and present, Jews, foreign and domestic, including the imperialists and the Zionists."

Zionism as demonic ran like a red thread through the letter. It was the Zionists who were "primarily responsible for many pogroms, including the Jewish ones, and for the "pruning of the dry branches of the tree of its own nation" in the concentration camps and Jewish ghettoes during World War II. The malicious and obscene accusation of the anti-Zionist campaign of the seventies and early eighties was suddenly back in business articulated not by some obscure hatemonger but by presumably responsible writers.

At the same time, the "Letter of 74" rejected the reported rumors of explosive pogroms against Jews as nothing short of "forgeries." It denounced the very idea of a law that would specifically ban antisemitism as racist in character. Such a law, declared the signatories in hysterical terms, would really be "A LAW ABOUT THE GENOCIDE OF THE RUSSIAN PEOPLE." It was such a law, according to the "Letter of 74," which led to the "dangerous" effects of the 1920s and 1930s. What the signatories were intimating here—as spelled out in Pamyat literature and in the writings of its supporters—was that the Jews were somehow responsible for the collectivization and the terror against the Russian peasants.

The xenophobic nationalism of the Russian Writers' Union leaders and of the journals through which they channeled such strikingly benighted and anachronistic views has spread out in other social directions. Conservative forces, drawing upon Russian nationalist and religious tradition, began concentrating and focusing their forces in March 1989. Some established the Foundation for Slavic Writing and Slavic Culture in order to foster greater historical and cultural knowledge about cohesion

---

[52] Ibid. The "Letter" was referring here to Zaslavskaia's poll of Jewish delegates to the first Congress of Jewish Organizations in December 1989.

among Russians, Ukrainians and Byelorussians.[53] Extreme Russian nationalists participated heavily in its meetings. Earlier, in November 1988, many of the same groups organized an Association of Russian Artists in Moscow in order to "awaken, illuminate and strengthen the national self-awareness and spiritual powers of the Russian people."[54] Its goals were to encourage Russian folk songs and folklore, preserve Russian library and archival materials and restore Russian historical and cultural monuments. The group was also to promote "the education of the people in the spirit and respect for Russian history and the tradition of military duty." The Association sponsored a series of rallies early in 1989 under the rubric "The Voices and Colors of Russia" which at times "took on a decidedly anti-Semitic tinge."[55]

A more important group was the Union for the Spiritual Revival of the Fatherland, which was formally received by Yegor Ligachev.[56] Hostile to the aims of perestroika, it encompassed important officials of Russian Orthodoxy. One of the group's key officials, Vera Briusova, an open Pamyat sympathizer, believed that Jews, hiding behind Russian names, dominated Soviet society.[57] The "Jewish brain center" in the USSR was held responsible by her for the destruction of Russian village life and various ecological disasters.

Typical of the conservative-nationalist critique was the writing of Mikhail Antonov, a leader of the Union for the Revival of the Motherland who wrote frequently for *Nash sovremennik*. In an article in the August 1989 issue, entitled "There is a Solution! When and How *Perestroika* Will End," he sharply castigated the leading advocates of Gorbachev's economic and sociological reforms as "cosmopolitans." Clearly, Antonov had no concern that the term carried antisemitic overtones and was a throwback to the Stalinist era. In his view, the Gorbachev reformers were captives of a Western capitalist system that was oriented towards consumption and mass culture. The system, he said, had brought mankind to the brink of disaster. In contrast, he argued,

---

[53] See Woll, "'Glasnost' and Soviet Culture," 46; Douglas Smith, "Formation of New Russian Nationalist Group Announced," *Report on the USSR,* 7 July 1989, 5–8.

[54] Woll, "'Glasnost' and Soviet Culture," 46.

[55] *Moscow News* 6 (1989); *Ogonek* 7 (1989): 11.

[56] Douglas Smith, "Formation of New Russian Nationalist Group," 5–8.

[57] Ibid., 8.

Russia was the only country in the world with a "deeply thought-out" economic system rooted in moral principles, not the pragmatic urge for profits.[58]

Spewing forth antisemitic propaganda was not the only function of the militant nationalist forces. They also were determined to remove reformers in the literary field, and especially those who published writers on the Jewish Holocaust. Thus a bureaucratic assault was launched on the chief editor of *Oktiabr,* Anatoly Ananev.[59] The secretariat of the RSFSR Writers' Union had voted to dismiss Ananev on grounds of his editorial policy which included publishing, in the face of strong objections, major unpublished works of the late Vasily Grossman on the Holocaust. The subject was intolerable for the ultra-nationalists.

---

[58] Ibid., 7.
[59] Woll, "'Glasnost' and Soviet Culture," 45, fn. 24; *Moscow News,* 2 (14 January 1990) carries an interview with Ananev.

## Chapter 10

## Resisting the Demonology

Chauvinism, with roots deep in Russian history and tapping various nationalist, religious, nativist, and populist sentiments, was only one of two powerful pillars of support for Pamyat and antisemitism. The other pillar was rooted in the Communist Party and, therefore, in more recent Soviet history. Neo-Stalinist and conservative forces, especially to be found in the bloated Soviet bureaucracy, saw in perestroika a powerful challenge and threat to their perception of Communism. Gorbachev was increasingly perceived as undermining the socialist basis of a great revolutionary tradition. For many in the Party, a deepening ideological instability seemed to place their world, their history, and their status in jeopardy.

With each major political step by Gorbachev towards a more open society, resistance mounted, ineluctably involving the political uses of antisemitism by neo-Stalinist forces. A central turning point in the struggle was a historic letter in *Sovetskaia Rossiia* by Nina Andreyeva, a Leningrad chemistry teacher in a technical institute. It appeared in this conservative organ of the Russian Republic Party Central Committee on March 13, 1988.[1] The moment was opportune, for Gorbachev was about to leave on an official visit to Yugoslavia; his closest colleague and principal ideologist, Aleksandr Yakovlev, was on an official visit to Outer Mongolia; and Defense Minister Dmitri Yazov was in Geneva, meeting

---

[1] *Sovetskaia Rossiia,* 13 March 1988. According to the Italian Communist Party newspaper *L'Unità,* the initial draft of the Andreyeva letter was more openly antisemitic; See Kevin Devlin, *"L'Unità* on 'Soviet History' of Andreeva Letter," *Radio Liberty Research* (Munich) RL215/88, 26 May 1988.

with the U.S. Secretary of Defense.[2]

The Andreyeva letter, in one long paean to Stalin, extolled him as a trail-blazer in a variety of fields and chastised the anti-Stalinist doubters, critics and advocates of glasnost. If the Stalinist period had been "extremely harsh," the Party nonetheless prepared young people for labor defense "without demoralizing their spiritual world." She then took a crack at Jews and Jewish aspirations. It was a period, she said, when "imaginary relatives were in no hurry to invite their fellow tribesmen to the 'promised land' turning them into 'refuseniks' of socialism." Andreyeva targeted cosmopolitanism (the code word for Jewry) as responsible for the undermining of Soviet patriotism.

Andreyeva's bigotry was etched more sharply in an interview in July 1989. She said that while there were less than one percent Jews in society, "then why is the Academy of Sciences...and all prestigious professions and posts in music, culture, law, why are they all Jews?" At her institute in Leningrad, *only* Jews, she said, defended their thesis "illegally." She was convinced that "certain Zionist organizations are carrying out their work here.... They are clever conspirators. I know that our Leningrad professors...go once a month to the synagogue and give them money.... This goes on, this constant mutual aid. In this way, Jews keep getting into the Institute."[3] Domination, conspiracy, clannishness—central elements of the *Protocols*—were again writ large.

According to a recent study of the Gorbachev era, the letter bore the imprint of Yegor Ligachev, the most powerful figure in conservative ranks of the Communist Party, who, in Gorbachev's absence, was serving as acting general secretary of the Party.[4] The study further contended that the letter was heavily edited by journalists with close links to this top Party conservative. On March 14, the day after the article appeared, Ligachev called a meeting of Soviet editors to discuss Party policy. He praised the *Sovetskaia Rossiia* article and criticized glasnost. On the same day, TASS drew the attention of editors across the country to the Andreyeva letter which, in effect, was a call for them to reprint it. At least

---

[2] Dusko Doder and Louise Branson, *Gorbachev: Heretic in the Kremlin* (New York: Viking, 1990), 304.

[3] Interview conducted by David Remnick, *Washington Post,* 28 July 1989; also appeared in *International Herald Tribune* (Paris), 2 August 1989.

[4] Doder and Branson, *Gorbachev,* 304–10.

forty-three newspapers, including the hardline East German *Neues Deutschland,* did precisely that. Viktor Afanasyev, *Pravda's* top editor and, at the time, a supporter of Ligachev, called a staff meeting and chastised his staff for ignoring a piece that important.

The "anti-perestroika manifesto"—as Gorbachev supporters later dubbed the Andreyeva letter—now took on a critical twist prompted by the Ligachev meeting with key editors. Party lecturers hinted that the Andreyeva message represented a new line. One lecturer at a Party group meeting of Leningrad TV criticized Gorbachev by name as responsible for unrest in Armenia and Azerbaijan. Some in the military, *Moscow News* later noted, also gave their support to the Andreyeva line. The conservatives seemed to be moving towards a showdown.[5]

By the second day of Gorbachev's visit to Yugoslavia, he was alerted to the Ligachev gambit. Gorbachev returned to Moscow on the 18th and Yakovlev on the 19th, with the mood in the capital uncertain and some intellectuals saying that Gorbachev's policies were in great jeopardy if the Andreyeva line was not overturned.

On March 31, Yakovlev prepared a response which was sent to *Pravda*. The issue was then brought to the Politburo. Gorbachev, after outlining the role of Ligachev in the Andreyeva affair, said he could not continue without an unequivocal endorsement of his policy by the Politburo. The Yakovlev draft was given to each member and Gorbachev dramatically left the meeting for his dacha. He placed his career in balance.

The Politburo backed him. Ligachev was given a mild formal reprimand while Gorbachev's policy of glasnost and perestroika was given full support. On April 5, the Yakovlev draft was published in full in *Pravda*. The blistering unsigned editorial called the Andreyeva letter "backward-looking" and the work of "blind, die-hard, dogmatists."[6]

By no means did the final *Pravda* editorial end Andreyeva's career. On the contrary, she had become the darling of the neo-Stalinist and conservative forces in the Party. When the Union of Russian Workers was established by Party stalwarts in Leningrad in 1989, she was quickly embraced as the group's favorite.[7] The Union rapidly spread throughout

---

[5] Ibid.

[6] *Pravda,* 5 April 1988.

[7] See *Sovetskaia molodezh,* 22 June 1989; *Leningradskaia pravda,* 8 June and 14 June 1989.

the country. Its influence as a potential opponent of Gorbachev's perestroika was not to be discounted.

The willingness of the anti-perestroika forces to link criticism of Gorbachev with antisemitic aims was illustrated by a December 1989 interview with Nina Andreyeva in the Hungarian daily, *Magyar Hirlap.* While charging that Gorbachev had deviated from Leninist norms and then commenting that "nobody is irreplaceable," she went on to accuse unnamed Zionists for pushing to attain power in the USSR. Reformers were also said to be attempting to restore capitalism in the USSR.[8]

In August 1989, Andreyeva had also given an interview to a Spanish newspaper, *El País,* in which she compared Gorbachev with Alexander Dubcek, the former Czech leader, (at that time Speaker of the Prague Parliament), whom she called a "counterrevolutionary." She had no hesitancy in asserting that the workers are demanding that Gorbachev's mask be removed from his face to reveal his bourgeois nature.[9] It was a line consistent with that of Ligachev in the latter part of 1989, when he was championing workers' interests that he claimed were being undermined by perestroika reforms. In his view, the Congress of People's Deputies represented not worker interests but the intelligentsia. He urged the convocation of a genuine workers' congress.[10]

The popularity of Stalin as symbol of socialism, according to a prominent Soviet historian, Yuri Afanasyev, was a "widespread phenomenon. You might call it folk Stalinism." It resulted from the absence of a democratic tradition in Russia, he said, with the consequence that "people admire a strong-arm leader, a strong boss and they associate Stalin with that kind of leadership." Afanasyev went on to say that many people who had lived under Stalin had had a "positive experience." They believed "that the socialism they were building would bring a radiant future." Stalin was their focus. "If you take away Stalin, you take away everything—their happy memories, their beliefs, their hopes." He concluded that over the years, "their consciousness was profoundly mutilated and

---

[8] *Magyar Hirlap,* 8 December 1989; cited in *Report on the USSR,* 15 December 1989, 40.
[9] *El País,* 20 August 1989; cited in *Report on the USSR,* 8 December 1989.
[10] See Roy Medvedev and Giulietto Chiesa, *Time of Change* (New York: Pantheon, 1989), 303.

deformed."[11]

An initial test of the strength of nationalist, neo-Stalinist, and conservative elements came in 1989 with the elections to the Congress of People's Deputies. The defeat suffered in the elections by these elements along with local Party officials led to a new strategy. Consolidation of the opposition forces was projected. During the summer and fall of 1989, two new organizations emerged, each representing the growing resistance to perestroika—the United Front of Workers of Russia and the Joint Council of Russia. United in their respective ranks were Party apparatchiks and conservative Russian nationalists, joined by elements of the working class with a strong conservative bent.[12]

In assaulting Gorbachev's reforms, they used a mixture of Russian nationalism and Stalinism, as well as traditional Marxist formulas. Targets were the cooperatives, leasing in agriculture, and self-financing of enterprises. All were perceived as violations of Marxism and a major turn toward capitalism. Economic innovations of Gorbachev's followers were seen as a mere Slavonic imitation of the decadent West which had the effect of undermining the social justice character of Soviet society.

The ideological core of the criticism was also an antisemitism drawn from the *Protocols* but which used the language of Stalinism. That language emphasized phrases like "enemies of the people" and terms like "conspiracies." The newly-aligned forces stressed the existence of a Judeo-Masonic conspiracy to which all the reformers were linked. The conspiracy was portrayed as a thrust against Marxism-Leninism, and described in vivid terms such as Russophobic and unpatriotic. Disclosures flowing from the investigation and correction of "blank spots" in past historical works and in conventional wisdom were especially challenged as Russophobic and unpatriotic.

Despite Pamyat's aggressiveness, and its wide support in nationalist, neo-Stalinist, and conservative circles, its growing influence had yet to be translated into electoral victories for seats in the Congress of People's Deputies or for local soviets in Moscow, Leningrad, or elsewhere. In the national campaigns, Pamyat and its rightist supporters won between 7 and

---

[11] Stephen F. Cohen and Katrina van den Heuvel, *Voices of Glasnost: Interviews with Gorbachev's Reformers* (New York: W. W. Norton, 1989), 110.

[12] Elizabeth Teague, "Worker Unrest in 1989," *Report on the USSR,* 26 January 1990, 12–13.

*Resisting the Demonology*                                                                                         171

11 percent of the votes, depending upon the particular region.[13] Although in absolute numbers Pamyat-supported candidates received several million votes, only a few seats were won in local and regional bodies and none in the national body.

In the 1989 election for the Congress of People's Deputies, Pamyat-backed candidates won no victories.[14] In the campaign, Pamyat activism focused on intimidating political supporters of liberals such as Vitaly Korotich, editor of *Ogonek*. Wherever he campaigned, Pamyat supporters appeared with placards depicting a crossed-out six-pointed star and the words: "Korotich is the Goldstuecker of *Perestroika*." (Eduard Goldstuecker, who was Jewish, was one of the principal advisers to Alexander Dubcek during the Prague Spring. The fact that he was Jewish enabled the Kremlin to train their heavy anti-Zionist guns upon him and Dubcek as well.) Korotich had already come under attack from Pamyat as "the mouthpiece of the Jews" when his journal criticized *Molodaia gvardiia* for its antisemitic policies.[15]

During the local Moscow elections in December 1989, Pamyat members campaigned hard against liberal candidates. They distributed handbills featuring Mother Russia caught in a Star of David held aloft by a hairy man with a giant nose.[16] Their efforts were not very successful; only ten deputies of Moscow's 468-member City Council were sympathetic to their perspective.[17] But it was also clear that they were playing for influence beyond their members by pursuing disgruntled soldiers and the United Front of Workers. Thus, Vladimir Yakushev, a founder of the Front and Pamyat fellow traveler said he opposed Gorbachev's economic reform on the grounds that "all of the drafters [of Gorbachev's economic program] were, how shall I put it, of a certain nationality."[18]

---

[13] See Julia Wishnevsky, "Patriots Urge Annulment of RSFSR Elections," *Report on the USSR*, 6 April 1990, 18–21.

[14] Ibid.

[15] *Jews in the USSR* (London) 18, no. 21 (November 1989); see Nicholas Bethell's column in the *Mail*, 14 May 1989.

[16] "The Long Shadow: New Fears of Anti-Semitism in Eastern Europe and the Soviet Union," *Newsweek*, 7 May 1990, 36.

[17] John B. Dunlop, "Moscow Voters Reject Conservative Coalition," *Report on the USSR*, 20 April 1990, 15–17; "The Maggots in Communism's Decay" (Editorial), *New York Times*, 6 May 1990.

[18] *Newsweek*, 7 May 1990, 36.

In the election to the Russian Republic's Congress of People's Deputies held in March 1990, they did poorly. Of the seventy sympathizers of the Patriotic Bloc (comprising all the ultra-nationalist groups) who ran for sixty-five seats in the RSFSR Congress of People's Deputies, only two were elected.[19] Such stalwart rightists as Ernst Safonov, editor of *Literaturnaia Rossiia,* and Nikolai Doroshenko, editor of the antisemitic in-house organ of the Writers' Union were defeated. Others defeated included Salina Litvinova, the author of a number of articles supporting Pamyat and attacking Jews; Dmitri Barabashev, a Central Committee bureaucrat who made public attacks upon the Zionist menace and upon Aleksandr Yakovlev; Viktor Novikov, the director of the Sovetskaia Rossiia Publishing House; and Stanislav Kunyayev, editor of *Nash sovremennik.*

The rout of the reactionary nationalists in the local Moscow and RSFSR elections constituted a repeat of the 1989 election results to the Congress of People's Duties. The rightist forces must have anticipated the March results because, on January 24–26 1990, several chauvinist groups met to devise a common tactic for "a quiet seizure of power" over the course of the next four years.[20] Included were Pamyat, the Interfronts from the Baltic States, and Yedinstvo, headed by Nina Andreyeva. The closed meeting was organized by the All-Union Council of Trade Unions and the ideological department of the Moscow City Komsomol Committee.

Election results were not the entire story. What the future would bring remained uncertain, especially under circumstances of economic crisis and interethnic tensions. That antisemitism was being overtly used for political purposes carried a dangerously explosive potentiality. It was certainly clear that among the Soviet intelligentsia a fierce and unpredictable struggle was under way between those with an obscurantist and viciously antisemitic drive and those who regarded antisemitism first and foremost as a symptom of society's illness.

One of the most perceptive refuseniks, Inna Joffe Uspensky of Moscow, was able to sum up prevailing attitudes among Soviet Jews in early November 1989 when vast numbers were seeking invitations and affidavits from Israel: it is "the fear of what might happen rather than any

---

[19] *Moscow News,* 12 (1990), 4.

[20] Julia Wishnevsky, "Patriots Urge Annulment," 21.

actual incident that worries all my friends. Suddenly, everybody around me is either leaving or talking about leaving."[21] And Jews were not the only ones being threatened. Non-Jews who criticized antisemitism were warned. Yuri Afanasyev reported that he was told: "I'm either a Jew or a Mason or that I've been bought by the Jews."[22]

Besides, Pamyat propaganda and activity carries more than an immediate incendiary possibility. Aleksandr Yakovlev told an American scholar that its "ideas are a strange mixture of crude, pre-revolutionary pogromism and illiteracy" to which "well-known techniques of demagogy" are added.[23] Examples of Jewish fears abound.

Even as Soviet television was broadcasting the admirable pro-Jewish film, *Komissar,* members of the Patriotic Front, a Pamyat splinter group in Leningrad, were handing out leaflets on November 7, 1989 with the slogan "Today should be a day of national mourning; this is what the Yids have brought us to."[24] Implied was the notion that the Bolshevik seizure of power in November 1917 was a plot of the Jews. Leningrad had become a hotbed of anti-Jewish sentiment. A leading Jewish activist from that city, Semyon Frumkin, observed: "Manifestations by neo-Nazi thugs are now part of the Leningrad scene; all our protests are to no avail."[25]

A group of sixteen activist Jews representing almost every Jewish study and cultural organization wrote to the Supreme Soviet complaining of the propagation of racist ideas in publications which were daily and openly distributed in Pushkin Square and Arbat Street in Moscow and at the Kazansky Cathedral in Leningrad.[26]

Endless warnings of violence and pogroms inevitably had taken an enormous psychological toll. Jewish activists desperately appealed to the authorities to halt the threatening Judeophobic marches, demonstrations, and leaflets inciting to murder. The response of Soviet authorities to the Pamyat and antisemitic challenge until 1990 was extraordinarily timid

---

[21] The citation was provided the author by the National Conference on Soviet Jewry. It was initially published in *Jews in the USSR* (London), 18, no. 21 (November 1989).

[22] Cohen and van den Heuvel, *Voices of Glasnost,* 99.

[23] Ibid., 66.

[24] *Jews in the USSR* (London), 18, no. 21 (November 1989).

[25] Ibid.

[26] Ibid.

despite their linkage to anti-perestroika forces of powerful neo-Stalinist bureaucratic circles in the Party and potent chauvinist forces both in and out of the Party. In one case, Vasiliev was summoned by the KGB on May 28, 1988 and was given an official warning against stirring up national hatred.[27] In addition, according to an interview with *Moscow News,* the Leningrad city public prosecutor, Dmitri Verevkin, observed that Pamyat's meetings in the public park were finally halted because they were seen as a violation of the USSR Constitution.[28] Later, the same newspaper reported that in September 1988, the Leningrad prosecutor's office held a discussion with the Leningrad leaders of Pamyat who were informed that Soviet law "forbids the propaganda of national discord."[29]

Some observers were struck by the contrast between the silence of the Congress and the Kremlin's top rulers with the posture of Vladimir Ilyich Lenin, the founder of the Soviet state. Faced by a burgeoning antisemitism linked to right wing monarchist forces in 1918–1920, he had categorically denounced antisemitism. In a historic address broadcast to the Russian people in March 1919, Lenin had cried: "Shame on those who foment hatred toward the Jews...."[30] He had personally drafted the language in a decree of July 1918, requiring that "pogromists and persons inciting to pogroms be outlawed."[31]

From the seat of state power, the Kremlin, no strong criticism was forthcoming. Instead, silence prevailed at the first Congress of People's Deputies. In spring 1989, three Jewish members—Kanovich, the writer from Lithuania; and Vitaly Ginzburg and Oleg Gazenko, both from the Academy of Sciences—drafted an appeal asking the Congress to adopt a resolution condemning antisemitism and creating a special committee to follow up on the issue.[32] While more than two hundred deputies

---

[27] *Argumenty i fakty,* 23 (1988); cited in *Jews and Jewish Topics in Soviet and East European Publications* (Jerusalem), Summer 1988, 35.

[28] *Moskovskie novosti,* 52 (1988); cited in Dunlop, 13, fn. 5.

[29] Ibid.

[30] William Korey, *The Soviet Cage: Anti-Semitism in Russia* (New York: Viking, 1973), 21.

[31] Ibid., 65

[32] The episode is described in Vladimir Shlapentokh, *Moscow in the Aftermath of the Congress of People's Deputies* (Moscow, July 1989), Mimeograph, 29.

joined in signing the petition, it met with a totally negative response from the presidium of the Congress. The appeal was never brought before the Congress; indeed, it was stricken from the list of petitions submitted to the presidium.

Passivity of Soviet officials did not inhibit Jewish leaders. Especially impressive was the urgent appeal by an "establishment" Jewish journal which was created in August 1989. *Vestnik yevreiskoi sovetskoi kultury* (Bulletin of Soviet Jewish Culture) printed its appeal on October 11, 1989 and addressed the Supreme Soviet. It was signed by thirty-two prominent Jewish and non-Jewish writers, playwrights, poets, editors, scholars, film directors, composers, and artists. Included were such internationally famous names as Yevgeny Yevtushenko, Leonid Kogan, and Tatiana Zaslavskaia.

In introducing the "Appeal by Soviet Citizens to the USSR Supreme Soviet," the *Vestnik* editorial board said: "we find it necessary to declare loudly and clearly that the threat of very grave anti-Semitic excesses, including pogroms, exists in the Soviet Union." The Appeal gave the strongest emphasis to the fact that "the problems of Soviet Jews and anti-Semitism are still being treated with an embarrassed silence." This was followed by a broad summary of the antisemitism during the Stalin and later Brezhnev eras with respect to higher education, job opportunities and cultural rights.[33]

It was the strong opinion of the Appeal signers that "in order to face the future with a clear conscience, the Supreme Soviet must openly condemn today this shameful period in our history, a period connected with the covert approval of anti-Semitism, a phenomenon that led to the gradual destruction of Jewish culture in the USSR and of the Jewish national ethos."

But silence has prevailed not only concerning the past of antisemitism. The current situation of Soviet Jews, the signers stated, "has not yet been settled." Strikingly, the "vital problems" of many Soviet nationalities may have been addressed by the Soviet government and Party officials, the Appeal noted, "in sharp contrast...the subject of Jews and antisemitism is the sole exception." Reference was made specifically to a letter of two hundred People's Deputies submitted to the Congress of Deputies which "was...ignored."

---

[33] A copy of the *Vestnik* appeal is in the author's possession.

Two months later the Congress of Jewish Organizations meeting in Moscow adopted a strong resolution on antisemitism which specifically denounced anti-Zionism (and anti-Zionist propaganda campaigns) as merely an "approved form of anti-Semitism, the slogan of all anti-democratic movements, the tool for stirring up the hatred between nations." The Congress demanded that the Supreme Soviet and the Communist Party Central Committee adopt and publish a condemnation of antisemitism in the USSR. Such a statement should also contain an evaluation of the prevailing forms of Soviet antisemitism and offer "concrete measures [to] guarantee the security of the Jewish population in the USSR."[34]

The Congress also resolved to denounce "the veil of silence" drawn by the Soviet authorities over the massacre of one and one-half million Soviet Jews by the Nazis. It called on Moscow to erect monuments to the victims of the Holocaust at various sites, using voluntarily collected donations.

Mikhail Gorbachev, in his public career, rarely felt compelled to comment on antisemitism in the Soviet Union. His first, made nearly a year after he was appointed general secretary of the Party, was hardly a profound observation. Responding to a question posed by the French Communist newspaper, *L'Humanité*, in February 1986, Gorbachev declared that antisemitism is "impossible in the USSR" because it is "prohibited by law and constitutes a crime."[35]

Not that Gorbachev was totally in error. Article 36 of the Soviet Constitution prohibited the advocacy of racial or national hostility and contempt, and Article 74 of the Russian Criminal Code—replicated in the criminal code of each Soviet republic—made the "inciting [of] national discord" a crime carrying penalties of incarceration for several years.[36] But since the twenties, no one had been charged with antisemitic incitement, let alone convicted and sentenced. After the Bolshevik revolution and through War Communism and the New Economic Policy (NEP) convictions and sentences for the stirring up of antisemitism were not

---

[34] A copy of the resolution is in the author's possession.
[35] *L'Humanité*, 25 February 1986.
[36] Korey, *The Soviet Cage*, 51, 82.

unusual.[37]

The only other references Gorbachev made to the subject were brief and seriously flawed. At a plenum of the Party Central Committee in January 1987, and in his book, *Perestroika,* published that year, he bracketed antisemitism and Zionism as examples of unacceptable forms of national chauvinism.[38] This came very close to linking Zionism with racism and providing the UN resolution with appropriate legitimization. Thus, even when the Soviet leader appeared to condemn antisemitism, he offered a protective cloak for those who engage in anti-Jewish bigotry. All that they had to do was frame their assertions and actions in anti-Zionist terms. The demonology of Zionism was more than sufficient to cover a multitude of vicious stereotypes.

Gorbachev's earlier perceptions of the problem and the hold of the demonology itself no doubt restrained him from responding to the requests of Kanovich and the petitions which came from a variety of directions including his strong supporters among the intelligentsia. An indifference appeared to prevail at the apex of society. As described by the prominent writer Yuri Nagibin in May 1989 in *Nedelia* (the weekly supplement of *Izvestiia*), what existed with respect to Pamyat was "a protective non-intervention on the part of the leadership."[39]

Certainly, toward the end of 1989, Gorbachev must have become aware of the growing threat to perestroika and to the image of the Soviet Union from abroad. In an article in *Pravda* on November 26, 1989, Gorbachev stated that the Party must resist "populist demagoguery, nationalistic or chauvinistic currents or unruly group interests."[40] Three days later, *Pravda* carried an editorial endorsing his views.[41]

The absence of specifics emptied the warning of any effectiveness. A top level scientist, Vitaly Goldanskii, warned in late January 1990 that

---

[37] See Solomon Schwarz, *The Jews in the Soviet Union* (Syracuse: Syracuse University Press, 1951), 274–89.

[38] Mikhail Gorbachev, *Perestroika, New Thinking for Our Country and the World* (New York: Harper and Row, 1987), 121–22.

[39] Cited in Semyon Reznik, "The Rifle on the Wall," *National Interest,* Fall 1989, 91. The Gorbachev response to the petition of Kanovich and others is described in William Korey, "A Fear of Pogroms Haunts Soviet Jews," *New York Times,* 25 January 1990, Op. Ed.

[40] *Pravda,* 26 November 1989.

[41] *Pravda,* 29 November 1989.

"the monarcho-Nazis seem to be meeting no serious opposition—indeed, more often sympathy and connivance from important Party and government leaders of the USSR." What disturbed him was the failure of the Party in its new platform on ethnic problems adopted in August 1989, to make any reference at all about previous Soviet antisemitic campaigns—anti-cosmopolitanism (1949), the massacre of the Jewish writers and artists (1952), and the Doctors' Plot (1953). In contrast, he observed that the new platform took scrupulous note of the crimes against other Soviet nationalities. In the face of the growing danger of the "monarcho-Nazis," Goldanskii warned of the possibility of "a wave of pogroms" and an "orgy of chauvinism and racism."[42]

A turning point came in February. Several steps were taken which, while modest, pointed to a more vigorous response to antisemitism. The chief of the KGB in Leningrad, where Pamyat was especially threatening, declared on local television (and carried by TASS) that "pogroms or any kind of outrages" will not be tolerated. Indeed, he warned, "drastic measures" will be taken against the preachers of antisemitism, should they move toward violence.[43] Soviet Foreign Minister Eduard Shevardnadze promised a Western Jewish visitor that Moscow "will not tolerate pogroms" and "we will do everything in our power to protect the Jewish community."[44] Again, in February, *Izvestiia* chastised anti-Gorbachev conservative forces which "disseminate appeals for pogroms." The government newspaper assured readers that "the pogroms will not take place and Gorbachev will not resign."[45] (The reference to the thought of a Gorbachev resignation grew out of extremist demands that called for pogroms at the very same time as they appealed for the general secretary to resign.)

In mid-February, Moscow prosecutors finally initiated a criminal investigation of Pamyat on grounds of "inciting national and racial hatred

---

[42] *Washington Post*, 18 February 1990.

[43] Radio Liberty, *Report on the USSR*, 9 February 1990, 37. The indicated date of the appearance of the Leningrad KGB chief on local television was January 27. The Jewish Telegraphic Agency reported the event in the *Daily News Bulletin*, 31 January 1990. KGB nationally warned against pogroms in *Izvestiia*, 9 February 1990.

[44] Jewish Telegraphic Agency, *Daily News Bulletin*, 1 March 1990.

[45] *Izvestiia*, 9 February 1990.

*Resisting the Demonology* 179

and strife," according to *Literaturnaia gazeta*.[46] What would emerge was as yet uncertain. The basis for the investigation was a Pamyat publication which called for a cutback in advanced degrees and in appointments in culture and political life for Jews.

Two months later, Gorbachev took two separate initiatives which pointed in opposite directions. On the one hand, he chose for his newly-created inner cabinet (the 16-member Presidential Council) two major defenders of Pamyat: Valentin Rasputin and Veniamin Yarim, the head of the right wing Union of Workers. While this appeared to offer a strong signal of encouragement to nationalist and Stalinist forces, Gorbachev may have had in mind a strategy of coopting and neutralizing anti-perestroika forces.

On the other hand, the Soviet president finally gave some expression of concern regarding antisemitism. Asked in April about "abnormal conditions of life" for Jews in the USSR (following an address to a Komsomol congress) he stated that extremist manifestations of chauvinism, antisemitism and other undefined "isms" should not be allowed "to occur."[47] While very much welcome, it was scarcely the strong repudiation which Jews and his active supporters of perestroika sought.

But even the modest statement provided a long-awaited signal. Article 74 would finally be brought into play. According to *Moscow News* in April, proceedings had been initiated for the very first time under that article.[48] It was directed against a woman in Leningrad who sent notes to her Jewish neighbors reading "Death to Kikes!"

In June 1990, the reaction of the authorities to antisemitic activities became significantly more pronounced. One key official in the Ministry of Internal Affairs, Col. Anatoly Sereda, told TASS on June 13 that "deplorably there are separate manifestations of anti-Semitism in our country. We do not deny this." He went on to add that "law enforcement bodies" are taking the necessary measures to curb manifestations of chauvinism, nationalism and antisemitism.[49] Interestingly, the word

---

[46] *Literaturnaia gazeta*, 21 February 1990.
[47] *Komsomolskaia pravda*, 12 April 1990. For the reaction of the American Jewish leadership, see Jewish Telegraphic Agency, *Daily News Bulletin*, 16 April 1990.
[48] *Moscow News*, April 1990; cited in *Anti-Semitism in the Soviet Union: A Status Report* (Washington DC: Union of Councils, May 1990), 24.
[49] *TASS*, 14 June 1990. Sereda was interviewed on June 13.

"Zionism" as an evil was missing.

As an example, Sereda stated that "criminal proceedings have recently been started in Novosibirsk in connection with the circulation of antisemitic leaflets in the city which were put into the postboxes of local Jews." He added that the procurator's office in Moscow was investigating criminal cases in connection with the acts of some members of Pamyat.

Significantly, during the same month of June, Boris Yeltsin decided to intervene. In his first press conference after being selected president of the Russian Republic, he decried the growing fascism and antisemitism, saying that "the situation has deteriorated because of lack of legislation."[50] A law was needed to "block those organizations which are developing into Fascist-type groups," and if the All-Union Supreme Soviet does not adopt such legislation, he warned, then the Russian Republic's Supreme Soviet will.

It was clear that Yeltsin may have been attempting to rectify his blunder of May 1987, when he had chosen to meet with Pamyat. Perhaps he was also responding to the pressure of the liberal intelligentsia who had thrown their full weight behind his candidacy. In any case, as Gorbachev's major critic on the left, he had placed the latter on the defensive morally, if not politically. Gorbachev's hesitancy in seizing the moment for moving more urgently was becoming increasingly untenable especially since the rightist forces were exploiting antisemitism as a means for placing perestroika itself in jeopardy.

The 28th Party Congress in early July gave Gorbachev and his supporters an opportunity to respond to the challenge of Yeltsin if not to the seriousness, even dangers, of the moment. The resolution on "Nationalities Policy" read:

> It is the duty of Communists to oppose the ideology and political practices of national extremism. The Congress resolutely condemns any kind of chauvinism, Russophobia, antisemitism, the propaganda and practice of national intolerance and discrimination, and demands that the state should respect and protect the national dignity of its citizens.[51]

The reference to antisemitism was unprecedented. The word had never been mentioned in any policy resolution of the previous congresses of the

---

[50] *Jewish Chronicle* (London), 8 June 1990.
[51] The resolution, entitled "Democratic Nationalities Policy: Peace and Concord Among the Peoples," was adopted on January 17, 1990.

Communist Party. The fact, too, that it was not paired with Zionism, as had been the case in statements of Party leaders since Brezhnev, was encouraging. Disturbing, however, was the addition of the term Russophobia; this was the language of Shafarevich and the strongly nationalist members of the Writers' Union. To a significant degree, that term was directed against Jews as supposedly hostile critics of Russian culture.

The Party had taken a forward step, yet it was circumscribed by additional, provocative language. The decision reflected developments at the Party Congress. The principal theoretician of glasnost and perestroika, Aleksandr Yakovlev, the bane of Pamyat and rightist forces, was compelled to face a massive verbal onslaught. Anticipating the militant opposition, he chose to resign from the Party Central Committee in order to devote full time to the new Presidential Council. Gorbachev paid a high price for the partial victories he won at the Congress.[52]

What may very well have strengthened the initiative to obtain a specific repudiation of antisemitism was an unprecedented development outside the USSR. International agreements specifically denouncing antisemitism had never been previously adopted, but during June, a Helsinki-sponsored "Conference on the Human Dimension," was held in Copenhagen, and chose to deal with the issue. The thirty-five member states (including all of Europe except Albania, and North America) agreed to "clearly and unequivocally condemn" antisemitism. They declared their firm intention to intensify their efforts to combat this phenomenon in all its forms and, therefore, would "take effective measures, including the adoption...of such laws as may be necessary, to provide protection against any acts that constitute incitement to violence against persons or groups based on...[racial] hatred, including anti-Semitism...."[53]

Significantly, after the initial proposal on the subject of antisemitism was drafted by Canada and circulated among the Helsinki signatories, the Soviet Union joined in co-sponsoring the draft. It was an unexpected de-

---

[52] Yakovlev's influence continued to decline; the Presidential Council never got off the ground. He publicly warned against a rightist dictatorship; see Francis X. Clines, "Ally Who Soured on Gorbachev Warns of a Stalinist-Style Coup," *New York Times,* 16 August 1991. Concerning his deeper political vulnerability, see Julia Wishnevsky, " Aleksandr Yakovlev Quits the Central Committee," *Report on the USSR* (Munich), 27 July 1990, 5–8.

[53] Stephen J. Roth, "CSCE Outlaws Anti-Semitism," *IJA Research Report* (London), 6 (1990), 5–8.

velopment. Heretofore, the USSR had resisted such proposals in international bodies.

The high point in the Kremlin's response to criticism of its failure to deal with the rising trend of antisemitism came on July 22, 1990, with a long article in *Pravda* by Sergei Rogov, who had previously written a major exposé of Judeophobia in *Sovetskaia kultura*. It was a searching analysis of a problem that was now recognized as threatening to perestroika itself. That the article appeared in *Pravda* testified to the seriousness with which the Gorbachev regime now took the threat. Decisions of the Party Congress and of the Helsinki Conference prompted the new thrust.

The *Pravda* article began with a remarkable degree of frankness. Heretofore, said Rogov, even asking whether there is a Jewish problem in the USSR "would be met with extreme hostility." The answer would always be: "There's no such problem here...the issue has been resolved in the Soviet Union once and for all...." Reality had finally thrust itself into Soviet consciousness. With Jewish emigration rising to unprecedented levels reaching two or three times the 1989 rate, and with rumors of pogroms spreading from city to city, it would have been "stupid" to deny the existence of a Jewish problem.[54]

For the first time, *Pravda* acknowledged that "hidden forms of discrimination" against Jews had begun in the forties and reached a climax with the "disgraceful fight" against cosmopolitanism. These "crude violations" of Lenin's nationality policy were now surrounded by a "conspiracy of silence." Even as Jewish cultural needs were no longer satisfied, "daily anti-Semitism was practically never censured."

But this was only the tip of the iceberg. *Pravda* now for the first time presented a penetrating analytic summary of the anti-Zionist propaganda campaign of 1967–1986 (though without specifying these dates.)

> Considerable damage was done by a group of authors who, while pretending to fight Zionism, began to resurrect many notions of anti-Semitic propaganda of the Black Hundreds and of Fascist origin. Hiding under

---

[54] Sergei Rogov, "Sushchestvie-li nash yevreiskii vopros?" (Is there a Jewish problem here?), *Pravda,* 22 July 1990. Two years earlier, Rogov had joined in warning against the resurgence of the "Black Hundred" and of the *Protocols of the Elders of Zion.* See Vladimir Nosenko and Sergei Rogov, "Ostorozhno; provokatsiia!" (Beware: provocation!), *Ogonek,* 23 (4–11 June 1988).

Marxist phraseology, they came out with coarse attacks on Jewish culture, on Judaism, on Jews in general.[55]

For the first time, the Kremlin appeared to acknowledge that the anti-Zionist campaign which it had organized and which featured Ivanov, Yevseev, Begun, Korneyev, Bolshakov, Yemelyanov, Romanenko and others had resurrected themes used by the Black Hundreds, and the *Protocols*.

Rogov then turned to the current scene. "An entire array of extremist groups has arisen," he noted, and they shamelessly use antisemitic propaganda including "such classical canards" as the *Protocols*. Pamyat, he noted, is in the forefront of this effort and has not hesitated to dig up "the myth about a 'Jewish-Masonic-Bolshevik plot' against Russia." The *Pravda* article catalogued the allegations made by Pamyat. Jews were blamed for the murder of the tsar's family; for Stalin's oppression; for the violence of collectivization; for wasting Russia's heritage; for the ruin of the ecological system.

Of even greater significance was the willingness of *Pravda* to take on the backers of Pamyat among the literary publications. "Unfortunately," observed Rogov, the current "political anti-Semitism arms not only the new 'Black Hundreds.'" He pointed out that "an entire array of literary publications...have openly associated themselves with anti-Semitic publications." Rogov went on to add that "they publish the most odious fabrications." He expressed the view that this is the first time in Bolshevik history that Judeophobia has "become popular in intelligentsia circles." It was the unprecedented "respectability" of antisemitism, commented Rogov, which "evokes great alarm."[56]

*Pravda's* emphasis on the alarm posed by the burgeoning antisemitism was matched by its focus on the target of the bigotry. Jews were not the enemy; rather, the target was Gorbachev's reform program. Pamyat, said the article, "resurrected anti-Semitism as a weapon against perestroika." Similarly, the race-baiting by the literary publications was described as "an attempt to halt the process of consolidation of our society on the platform of perestroika, to poison one part of our society against another." At the same time, the author expressed grave concern about the massive proportions of Jewish emigration which, he believed, was

---

[55] Ibid.
[56] Ibid.

sparked by the hate phenomenon. Anticipating a level of emigration significantly larger than the prevailing trend, he sought means that would permit the "Jewish question" to be solved, not through emigration but "by democratic means within the Soviet Union itself."

The *Pravda* article was extraordinarily significant; not since 1965 had either of the flagship Soviet newspapers—*Pravda* and *Izvestiia*—delivered a full-scale blast at antisemitism. And the critique was broad and detailed. Nothing was hidden from public view. The danger was made crystal clear.

The publication of the *Pravda* article was a clear signal of a more determined leadership to move against the violence-prone modern Black Hundreds. Not surprisingly, on July 24—two days after the article had appeared Moscow opened the case against Konstantin Smirnov-Ostashvili, whose black-shirted Pamyat-splinter gang, had broken into a meeting of liberal writers—the Aprel group—on January 18, physically abusing several and threatening violence against Jewish and other writers.

It was the first court case involving Article 74 and was seen by all sides as a test of the government's determination to prosecute fascists, of the law's effectiveness, and of the resistance of Pamyat. Poet Mark Kabanov, who had been present on January 18, now observed that "regardless of the outcome of the trial, its significance is important. At least this is the first open battle at the judicial level." Another observer, a woman who had videotaped the January 18 fracas, called the trial "very important" because "it would be the start of a very strong anti-Fascist movement." Writer Oleg Feinstein commented: "It will set a precedent."[57]

Supporters of Pamyat similarly saw the trial as significant. A woman backer at the court said:

> I support him because he fights for Russia. He's fighting against Zionism and this is important.
>
> The media is in their [Zionist] hands. The television, the radio and the press. Culture and art, too. You won't find one worker among them....

Pamyat leader Aleksandr Kulakov stated "they are trying to do away with

---

[57] *Philadelphia Inquirer*, 25 July 1990; "The Rekindled Evil of Anti-Semitism," *Los Angeles Times*, 26 July 1990, editorial; *Los Angeles Times*, 27 July 1989.

somebody who openly expressed his views."[58]

The principal prosecution attorney, Andrei Makarov made evident that the trial had transcended the matter of simple guilt. "My main goal," he said, was "to reveal the character" of the organization behind Smirnov-Ostashvili and disclose "what danger it may pose to the country." It was also intended to indicate that "fascism is growing in the Soviet Union." Makarov was assisted by two public participants permitted by Soviet law, Yuri Afanasyev and Yuri Chernichenko, prominent liberal intelligentsia members.[59]

From the beginning, Pamyat packed the courtroom and organized demonstrations outside of it. The intent was clear: to use the trial to give broader and greater emphasis to their ferocious antisemitism. At every opportune moment, Pamyat supporters in the courtroom shouted and demonstrated for Smirnov-Ostashvili, virtually turning the courtroom into a circus. The presiding judge, A. Muratov, who was young and had never before presided over a case in a city-wide court, had considerable difficulty in keeping order and maintaining decorum.[60]

Overt antisemitism was a tool of the defendants. At the opening session, Smirnov-Ostashvili demanded the removal of his court-appointed lawyer and his replacement by a foreign lawyer on grounds that the Moscow legal collegium was dominated by Zionists. He wondered aloud to the press as to "what his [the prosecutor's] nationality is" and proceeded to add that while Russians died fighting in World War II, "the Jews sat in Alma Ata and Samarkand, safely behind the lines." Outside the courtroom in the hallways, Pamyat supporters distributed hate literature. One of the pamphlets charged that the "Zionists killed 100 million Russians and now they are pressing the case against Smirnov-Ostashvili." If they win, the pamphlet added, "they will begin a new repression of Russian national movements."[61]

Symptomatic of the bigotry were the following comments by the defendant's supporters. An army colonel in full military dress, visibly drunk, shouted that Jews were responsible for the Bolshevik revolution

---

[58] Interview with Leonid Kelbert, *Hadassah Magazine,* 19 (February 1991), 17–21.

[59] William Korey, "Message from Moscow: Success and Pessimism," *Hadassah Magazine,* 19 (February 1991), 22–23. Interview with Andrei Makarov, August 1990, New York.

[60] Walter Ruby, *Forward,* 16 August 1990; see also *Jerusalem Post,* 18 August 1990.

[61] Ruby, *Forward.*

and for the killing of Tsar Nicholas. And he praised Stalin for taking strong action against the Jews. A Russian Orthodox monk declared that "the biggest pogrom of all was in 1917 and that was carried out by Jews against Russians." Another Pamyat partisan shouted: "Russian villages are dark and hungry while the Jews get rich. Who is making our gas and benzine disappear? The answer is as obvious as the sun in the sky."

Of special interest was the bombshell which Smirnov-Ostashvili dropped at the very opening of the trial; it illuminated the strategy that would be followed and the core of the ideology that sustained Pamyat. He revealed to the judge that he had sent a letter to the Austrian embassy in Moscow asking Austrian President Kurt Waldheim to appear as a witness on his behalf. He explained that Waldheim had been secretary-general of the United Nations when it had adopted the "Zionism is racism" resolution. Thus, Waldheim was in a position to "tell us what Zionism really is."

With the trial expected to last into 1991, Pamyat intended to have a field day focussing public attention upon the resolution associated with Moscow's leadership at the UN in 1975. Indeed that resolution remained a central element in the continuing demonology of Zionism in the USSR. Pamyat and its supporters, by embracing anti-Zionism, sought to shield themselves from the law. Ideological rationalization was provided by the UN resolution capriciously defining Zionism as a "form of racism."[62] In the face of this sanction and because the Kremlin, too, was caught up in the coils of the prevailing Soviet demonology, it was difficult to initiate the prosecution of violent antisemitism.

A test of Gorbachev's commitment to the new Helsinki injunction on antisemitism and to the new Party policy would well have to be his willingness to discard an obscurantist demonology. Soviet agreement to support Western initiatives for repeal of the UN "Zionism equals racism" resolution, too, would demonstrate the kind of commitment that would enable Soviet Russia to become part of the "European common house," a consummation desperately sought by the Soviet president.

Beyond the need to exorcise the demon and demystify Zionism, there was the accompanying need to provide an educational program that would cope with widespread ignorance about Jews and Jewish history in

---

[62] A typical Pamyat poster distributed in Moscow in November 1989 cited the UN resolution as the basis for its public campaign against Zionism.

the USSR, especially about the Holocaust and the role of Jews during World War II. It was precisely this yawning vacuum that permitted bigotry to fester and demonology to flourish. At the CSCE Copenhagen human dimension meeting, the Helsinki signatories urgently called for educational programs to combat "racial prejudice and hatred."[63]

History textbooks in the USSR for elementary and high school students made no reference to Jews, ancient Israel, or Jewish history. As for the greatest trauma of the contemporary epoch—the Holocaust—"blank spots" exist in the pages of Soviet historiography. In November 1987, while General Secretary Mikhail Gorbachev was ushering in a major change in Soviet historiography by rehabilitating some victims of Stalin's purges, a young Leningrad Jewish activist deeply familiar with historical subjects, Semyon Dyskin, formally asked the Central Committee of the Soviet Communist Party finally to permit publication of the famous *Black Book* which documented the fate of Soviet Jewry under the Nazis. Compiled by the writer-journalists Ilya Ehrenburg and Vasily Grossman during and immediately after World War II, the book had been suppressed for over forty years. Copies of the letter were sent to the Supreme Soviet and the State Publishing House.

Dyskin stunningly noted that as of 1987, the Russian language had no equivalent for the English word "Holocaust" or the Hebrew word "Shoah." Since not a single official book devoted to antisemitism had appeared in the USSR in over half a century, the young writer asked, "what has been done in the Soviet Union in order that the tragic lessons of the past are not forgotten?"[64]

It was not only the Holocaust which was unexamined in historical works. So, too, were Jewish heroism and Jewish martyrdom. "Where can the Soviet reader obtain information about the historical struggle of the Jews against Fascism?" he asked. Or, "about the revolt of the Warsaw Ghetto and about the unprecedented uprising in the Treblinka concentration camp where a small group of Jews managed to destroy the camp and escape to bring the incredible and horrible truth to the world?"[65]

At the historic Congress of Jewish Organizations in December 1989, the participants drafted a resolution which bitterly complained that "there

---

[63] Roth, "CSCE Outlaws Anti-Semitism."
[64] See Korey, *Soviet Cage,* 90. A copy of Dyskin's letter is in the author's possession.
[65] Ibid.

are no historical studies and publications in the USSR devoted to the genocide of Soviet Jews; in the school books the tragedy of the Jewish people is not mentioned."[66] Such basic information as the number of Soviet Jewish deaths—one and one-half million—was unknown. Also absent was the heroic role played by Jews in Moscow's great victory over the Nazis. Jews won more medals of valor than any other nationality, except the Russians. This, despite the fact their percentage in the population was quite small.

The Congress's appeal for an educational campaign that would focus attention on the consequences of racial hatred and antisemitism found an echo in a decision of the Copenhagen meeting obligating Helsinki member states to create educational programs aimed at combatting "racial prejudice and hatred." The burgeoning problem of Pamyat demonstrated, if nothing else, how urgent a priority this requirement was. But whether Moscow would respond was quite another matter.

---

[66] Resolution of the Congress of Jewish Organizations, December 1989, Moscow.

## Chapter 11

## The Malady Lingers On...and On.

It is a measure of how deeply-rooted the demonology of Zionism has reached into Soviet society that, several months after coming to power, Mikhail Gorbachev had no hesitancy, in his most intimate political circle, to refer to the historic Jewish national movement in a shockingly bigoted manner. The setting was a meeting of the top Communist policy-making body, the Politburo on August 29, 1985. Gorbachev had already served in that body for some time and knew its members intimately. On March 11, he had been chosen by the group as the general secretary of the Party's Central Committee, the very apex of the power structure.

A critical focus of the Politburo session of August 29 was whether Yelena Bonner, Andrei Sakharov's ailing wife, should be permitted to go abroad for medical treatment. While agreement was reached approving the medical request, at the same time the KGB chief, Vladimir Chebrikov, made it clear that Sakharov himself must never be permitted to leave because he "knows in detail all the steps in the development of our atomic weapons." What made Sakharov especially dangerous, noted Chebrikov, was the presumed fact that his "behavior is formed under the influence of Bonner."[1]

What the KGB head had left unsaid was that Yelena Bonner was half-Jewish (her father Armenian; her mother Jewish.) When the Soviet media, in the fall of 1973, had conducted a massive vituperative campaign against Sakharov—undoubtedly prompted by the KGB—special

---

[1] For recently disclosed Soviet archival excerpts from Politburo meetings, see *New York Times*, 8 February 1993.

reference was made to Bonner as a Zionist.[2] Of course, the allegation was absurd since she had no connection with any Zionist movement or ideology. But the incitatory term had been intended to signal her Jewishness. The media drive, at the same time, had also striven to emphasize that Sakharov was manipulated by his wife, the demon Zionist.

The most striking feature of the Politburo discussion in August 1985 was Gorbachev's comment, which came immediately after Chebrikov's observation that Sakharov was "under the influence" of Bonner. The general secretary forcefully and pointedly noted: "That's what Zionism is." It was axiomatic in Gorbachev's thinking that Zionism operated in dangerously conspiratorial ways. It will be recalled that Gorbachev, in his book, *Perestroika,* and in his major policy speech to the Party early in 1987, stressed an equation between antisemitism and Zionism as paired expressions of chauvinist excrescence.[3]

The demonology of Zionism permeated the highest political level of Soviet society, including some of its most enlightened members (in 1986 Gorbachev became the principal advocate of glasnost); it permeated the general citizenry much wider and deeper. An extensive survey of the population conducted by the Soviet Center for Public Opinion and Market Research during September 21–November 12, 1990 demonstrated the extraordinary impact of the demonology. Over 4200 respondents—an unusually large sample from ten republics—were interviewed.[4]

Especially striking were responses to questions about Zionism. Fully 50 percent—a clear majority of the sample—thought that the Soviet Union "should be more resolute in fighting Zionism and Zionists in the USSR and all over the world." Only 7 percent disagreed with this view while a whopping 37 percent had no opinion on it.

What made the perception of Zionism particularly intriguing was the fact that the respondents elsewhere in the questionnaire reacted rather warmly to Israel. A significant 64 percent expressed the opinion that the

---

[2] Andrei Sakharov, *Memoirs* (New York: Alfred A. Knopf, 1990), 385–92.

[3] Mikhail Gorbachev, *Perestroika* (New York: Harper and Row, 1987), 121–22.

[4] Lev Gudkov and Alex Levinson, *Attitudes Toward Jews in the Soviet Union: Public Opinion in Ten Republics* (New York: American Jewish Committee, 1992). The study was commissioned and published by the American Jewish Committee; analysis of the data (27 pp.) was followed by 80 detailed charts.

USSR should "renew diplomatic relations with Israel." And 44 percent—a plurality—said that they would like to "visit Israel as a guest, on invitation, or as a tourist." Clearly, a fundamental dichotomy had characterized what would ordinarily be perceived as linked, if not unitary, objects—Zionism and Israel. The logical linkage was severed by a demonology that made rational thinking and perception of Zionism impossible.

Indeed, when a question was posed about a definition of Zionism, the largest single group expressing an opinion (22 percent) declared it to be "the policy of establishing the world supremacy of Jews." That, of course, was precisely the definition in the *Protocols of the Elders of Zion* and of much of the Kremlin's anti-Zionist propaganda during 1967–86. An additional eight percent defined Zionism as "the ideology used to justify Israeli aggression in the Middle East." Only nine percent thought Zionism to be a "movement for the return of Jews to their historical homeland." Fifty percent had no opinion on a definition.

Another question sharpened the focus by explicitly asking whether the respondent had ever heard "about a 'world Zionist conspiracy' to establish Jewish domination over other peoples"; 27 percent said "yes." When further pressed as to whether the respondent believed that "such a conspiracy really exists," only seven percent answered in the affirmative, but a huge number (68 percent) said they didn't know.

While the hostile image of Zionism was especially striking in the survey, the poll also indicated that a considerable percentage of the inhabitants of the USSR—about 40 percent—manifested some degree of negative feeling towards Jews, usually in the form of holding and expressing negative stereotypes. Still, a significant minority (10 percent) was described by the poll analysts as "strongly anti-Semitic." The respondents in this category thought that "Jews are mainly responsible for the present problems of our country," or that they "are mainly responsible for the disasters of the Revolution and mass repressions," or that they "are mainly responsible for making Russians as well as other peoples in this country drunkards." A disturbing six percent of those polled would go so far as to advocate Jews being eliminated from society.

That basic human rights education or, rather, the lack of it contributed significantly to the negative image of the Jew in Soviet society is suggested in responses to a couple of survey questions. Sixty-one percent of the respondents could not name a single Jew who has "contributed greatly to world culture and science." This staggering percentage reflected the deliberate attempt by Soviet authorities to diminish or exclude the role of the Jew in history, except as a negative force. A second question about the Holocaust revealed an extraordinarily high percentage who answered "don't know" to a question about "how many Jews...were exterminated by the Nazis." The figure was 73 percent, which illustrated, and illuminated, how effectively Soviet society had suppressed teaching about the Holocaust.

Lack of education was reinforced by limited experience; 43 percent of the respondents, in answer to a question as to whether they have "any Jewish relatives or friends" said "none at all."

A particularly disturbing revelation in the survey has to do with attitudes of educated people. Generally, surveys of antisemitism elsewhere tend to indicate a correlation between the degree of negative stereotyping about Jews and the level of the respondent's education. The more hostile views were usually held by those with limited education, and the converse. In the USSR this was not the case; a segment of highly educated respondents living in urban areas expressed strongly antisemitic views.

Thus, respondents with academic degrees were one and one-half to two times more likely than respondents with a completed secondary education and two to three times more likely than respondents with an incomplete secondary education to hold Jews mainly responsible for "disasters" of the Revolution and for the USSR's current problems. This data reflected the previously-indicated outlook of broad segments of the *pochvenniki* and nationalists that were dominant in the Russian Writers' Union and who controlled major nationalist organs of opinion.

To some extent, popular antisemitic views reflected the anti-modernization syndrome of the urbanized strata with a medium level of hostility. The highest degree of antisemitism, the survey revealed, was to be found in precisely those republics with such characteristics—Byelorussia, Moldavia and the Ukraine. This order of listing reflected the degree of attitudinal hostility in each. Nearly 30 percent of the respondents from those republics exhibited hostile antisemitic views.

The perception of Jews in the survey merit some limited attention even if the size of the Jewish sample was too small to provide precise reliable analysis. Of the Jews interviewed, 59 percent believed that "more than half" the people in the USSR are "against Jews;" 58 percent contended that they "witnessed hostile or unjust attitudes" towards Jews in the street, in queues, or in public transport; 62 percent reported the same experience at work or in state offices. Concerning the future, Jews reflected a fearful and pessimistic outlook: 71 percent believed that "antisemitic sentiment has increased in the Soviet Union in the last 2–3 years." The same high percentage was convinced that "pogroms against Jews" were "likely to occur" in 1991.

It was, however, the Zionist-demonological feature of public opinion that was particularly striking, and that the press continued to reinforce. Just prior to the survey, in August 1990, *Pravda* carried a TASS dispatch citing a newly-released statement of the infamous Anti-Zionist Committee denouncing a small, recently-established Zionist group in Russia and warning against the spread of this evil.[5]

Shortly after the survey was completed, the Anti-Zionist Committee was once again sending out notices to the Soviet public in provocatory language. It advised the populace that Jewish groups, under the cloak of fighting antisemitism, had set up a nationwide spy network. The new deputy head of the Committee, German Smolyanin, spelled out the extent of the network: "we estimate these groups are active in fifty cities of the Soviet Union."

The potentially incendiary implications of such assertions would become apparent when the media elaborated upon them in odd ways. On November 30, 1990 *Pravda*, taking note of the Committee's observations, commented that since there were 1,500,000 Jews in the USSR, no one could be sure how many of them were Zionists.[6] Could not this statement be understood as a warning that a large number of Jews were Zionists and, therefore, "enemies of the people"? On December 7, *Sovetskaia Rossiia* gave expression to the danger of the Zionist conspiracy taking on a palpable reality. "Zionists were infiltrating into the highest echelons of the state," cried the conservative newspaper in almost hysterical terms.[7]

So concerned had Soviet Jews become about the incendiary use of the word "Zionist" and "Zionism" in the media that the representative of their central body, the Vaad, raised the subject with the chairman of the Congress of Peoples' Deputies, Anatoly Lukyanov at a meeting he held

---

[5] *Pravda*, 9 August 1990.
[6] *Pravda*, 30 November 1990; see also *Jews in the U.S.S.R.*, 19, no. 23 (12 December 1990).
[7] *Sovetskaia Rossiia*, 7 December 1990.

in November 1990 with representatives of ethnic minorities.[8] It was also attended by Gorbachev himself. The Jewish spokesman urged that the media be asked to define Zionism by its accepted meaning—the national aspiration of the Jewish people—and thereby, end the negative connotations associated with its perception in Russia.

It was, of course, Pamyat that cultivated and exploited Zionist demonology. The hate group may have constituted a serious threat to the political system, and its promotion of the *Protocols* a clear challenge to the Russian legal code on racial incitement, but at the heart of the security structure of the USSR, it had warm friends and protectors. A Soviet television show on July 6, 1990 illuminated this strange relationship. The program was a talk show in which studio guests were asked questions by the viewing audience. On that day, Vladimir Kryuchkov was a studio guest and he was asked how the KGB regards and deals with Pamyat.[9]

The reaction of the KGB chairman was anything but hostile and angry. Even a modest concern was absent. Instead, he began with two generalizations: first, that Pamyat embraces several different things; and second, that there are several different Pamyat organizations. At this point, Kryuchkov chose to focus on the particular but unnamed "useful" and "patriotic" Pamyat group. He said nothing about other Pamyat groups which may have been perceived as "not useful" or "unpatriotic." What the viewing audience would have undoubtedly comprehended, given the nature of the response to the question, was that Pamyat hardly merited concern or criticism; and, indeed, the unnamed Pamyat group was to be embraced. Kryuchkov went out of his way to say that the unnamed group's activities were to be hailed.

The *Izvestiia* article which recorded the extraordinary, if dismaying, television episode pointedly posed the intriguing question as to which Pamyat group the KGB chief referred. The journalist Pavel Gutionov, a

---

[8] *Jews in the U.S.S.R.* (London), 19, no. 23 (12 December 1990), 6. In Byelorussia, the vicious use of the term "Zionists" was possibly even greater than in Russia. It was especially used by Romanenko in a key Party organ in Minsk. See Institute of Jewish Affairs, *Intelligence Report*, no. 3 (June 1991).

[9] Pavel Gutionov, "What is Wrong with My 'Memory?'" *Izvestiia*, 12 July 1990; see Yelena Bonner, "On Gorbachev," *New York Review of Books*, 17 May 1990, 17. In this article, Yelena Bonner emphasized the thesis that Pamyat groups "are intertwined to some degree with the [Soviet] state Party apparatus."

well-known commentator, noted that he had followed Pamyat pretty closely, and had met with the leaders of its different groups. He sharply added: "I cannot possibly understand who did Mr. Kryuchkov have in mind?" The query was followed by the names of leaders of four separate Pamyat groups, each of whom was wilder and crazier than the next— Vasiliev, Sychev, Yemelyanov, Smirnov-Ostashvili. Gutionov flatly added: "I am not aware of any others." The implication was clear: extremist antisemites were not perceived as dangerous by the state's authority on security; on the contrary, at least one of them is to be lauded.

The Kryuchkov interview may have been the most blatant *public* example of KGB bigotry. An internal organ, *Pogranichnik,* published by the KGB Border Guards, pointed in a similar direction.[10] On December 12, 1990, it attacked the liberal democratic press in Russia, notably *Ogonek* and *Moscow News,* suggesting that they were controlled by the Zionists. The major thrust of the article was an endorsement of President Saddam Hussein of Iraq, and a strong condemnation of the Moscow democratic media for its criticism of him. How anti-Zionism was a principal guideline of KGB thinking and policy-making was disclosed in public testimony in Moscow by a former high KGB official, Valentin Korolev.[11]

Especially troubling was the relationship between the military leadership and extremist nationalist groups and publications with distinctive antisemitic overtones. Thus the Ministry of Defense under Marshal Dmitri Yazov (also a Politburo member) arranged for the placing in military post libraries and reading rooms such chauvinist journals as *Nash sovremennik* and *Molodaia gvardiia.*[12] Even more disturbing was the outlook of the official historical journal of the Defense Ministry with its quarter-million readers. Under the editorship of Major-General Viktor Filatov whose views were decidedly racist, the *Military-Historical Journal* had published in 1990 parts of Adolf Hitler's *Mein Kampf,* apparently authorized by Yazov himself. Early in 1991, Filatov planned to publish the notorious

---

[10] *Pogranichnik,* 12 December 1990, cited in Adrian Karatnycky, "Soviet Diplomacy's Smiles Turn to Snarls," *Wall Street Journal,* 21 February 1991.
[11] *Stolitsa,* 40 (1990); *RFE/RL Daily Report,* 22 October 1990.
[12] *Ogonek,* 1 (1991), as reported in Institute of Jewish Affairs, *Intelligence Report* 1 (February 1991).

*Protocols of the Elders of Zion;* he told an interviewer from the *New York Times* that he considered the *Protocols* to be both authentic and true.[13]

It was Yazov and Kryuchkov who were to join with the leading Party bureaucrats in an initiative to seize power, end Gorbachev's glasnost and perestroika and return the USSR to authoritarian rule. What their chauvinism and anti-democratic perspective would have meant for Jews is almost self-evident.

In December 1990, Foreign Minister Eduard Shevardnadze, sensing the unfolding of a rightist conspiracy, warned that a "dictatorship is coming."[14] The occasion was a speech at the Supreme Soviet where he announced his resignation as foreign minister. Shortly afterwards, on December 22, the organ of the anti-perestroika forces, *Sovetskaia Rossiia,* called for a special state of emergency to stem the tide of "disintegration" engulfing the USSR. A couple of weeks later, the same journal advocated military intervention to ensure "national salvation."[15]

By the summer of 1991, the rightist publications became ever more shrill in their demand for a military dictatorship. *Den,* an especially militant journal under the editorship of Aleksandr Prokhanov, in May carried a round table discussion of the editor with four top military officials.[16] The hint of arbitrary military rule was scarcely hidden. On June 17, Prime Minister Valentin Pavlov openly demanded emergency power and he was vigorously supported by Yazov and Kryuchkov.

The most striking evidence of the Soviet military's support for the flagrant type of antisemitism espoused by Pamyat was a small book which it published in June 1991, two months prior to the attempted coup. Entitled *The Black Hundred and the Red Hundred* by Viktor Ostretsov, the work constituted a glowing panegyric about the Black Hundreds and the Union of the Russian People, which is described as "the most popular and democratic organization in Russia."[17]

History was turned upside down by Ostretsov. Pogroms either had not taken place in tsarist Russia or they were the fault of the Jews. The Black

---

[13] *New York Times,* 7 January 1991.
[14] *TASS,* 20 December 1990.
[15] *Sovetskaia Rossiia,* 22 December 1990.
[16] *Den,* May 1991; see also *Moscow News,* 40 (1991).
[17] Viktor Ostretsov, *Chornyi sot i krasnyi sot* (Moscow: Military Publishing House, 1991).

Hundreds had the objective of promoting the self-defense of peasants and workers, not to provoke pogroms; it was the Jews who had initiated attacks on the populace. As an example, the author pointed to what had appeared as a symbol of an anti-Jewish pogrom in Bialystok in June 1906. According to Ostretsov:

> Jewish militants from the Bund organizations, armed with guns and bombs, attacked the unarmed Russian population. At high noon, those militants started shooting at a religious procession, in which many local peasants participated, and then a bomb was thrown.

The Bialystok example, said the author, was duplicated in Gomel where only 2 Jews were killed as compared with 4 Russians, and in Kiev where, during the supposed anti-Jewish riots of October 18–21, 1905, the Jews constituted a mere twenty-five percent of those killed and thirty-five percent of the wounded. The author concludes:

> It is high time to say loudly so that all Russia and all the world could hear that there were no pogroms in our country; what happened was a forced self-defense against the animal-like, carnivorous and insatiable Jew.

Readers could quickly learn from the book what the future of Russian Jewry would be were the program of the Union of the Russia People to be realized. Jews would be "immediately pronounced foreigners, without rights and privileges." Identified in the work as a signer of the Union's "Statute" was V. Purishkevich. Additional research by readers would reveal this leading reactionary landlord to be the first who cried in the Duma: "Kill the Kikes, Save Russia." It would become the slogan of Black Hundreds as they engaged in pogroms.

Particularly impressive was the size of the edition—one million copies. Clearly, a mass readership in the military forces was anticipated. The work had only forty-eight pages and was written in the simplest language, and thus could be easily assimilated.

Lenin and his Bolshevik colleagues would certainly have been stunned beyond belief that the Soviet military had become an apologist for their principal enemies—the Union of the Russian People. But it is a measure of how far xenophobic nationalism and antisemitism had made inroads into one of the basic pillars of the regime that this work could be published without any apparent serious opposition. Pamyat could derive enormous satisfaction from the fact that what it had claimed as its spiritual forerunner was now endorsed at the highest military level. The connection between the Soviet military and Pamyat was probably even closer. According to a knowledgeable Moscow source, the author of the work was an active member of Pamyat.

One month after the remarkable apologia for the Black Hundreds was published, the highest military authority took an additional step linking the armed forces with chauvinism and antisemitism. On July 7, 1991, Minister of Defense Marshal Yazov issued a highly unusual directive (No. D-12) ordering all units of the Soviet Army and Navy to take out subscriptions for *Nash sovremennik*.[18] The Yazov order went significantly further than the 1990 Ministry of Defense decision requiring a fixed number of copies of this monthly journal—100,000—be subscribed to by the military.

The armed forces' embrace of rightist and antisemitic publications was extended to other areas as well. Two military printing plants were given as a gift to the Russian Writers' Union, whose reputation as a hate propagator has earlier been described.[19] Printing plants were invaluable in the new, perestroika economy which rested upon the thesis that all publications must be self-supporting. And, since the number of subscribers was crucial for the sustenance of publications, the military's guarantee of a sizable subscription rate was also extremely helpful. And, if the Writers' Union had a problem of finding adequate space for its convention, the Ministry of Defense could easily provide the required premises. It was scarcely surprising that principal speakers of the Writers' Union, at its congress in December 1990 lauded the support given the Union by Yazov and the Ministry of Defense.

A closer look at aspects of the Writers' Congress in December 1990 was as revealing of the military's symbiotic relationship with antisemitic writers as it was disturbing.[20] The meeting place itself, the hall of the Red Army Theatre, evoked considerable intriguing commentary from the speakers. Since the building, erected in the thirties, had the shape of a pentagon, several leaders of the Writers' Union complained that it was built by "Kike-Masons." The reception room to the main hall contained a large number of copies of Hitler's *Mein Kampf*, the *Protocols* and various other antisemitic works, which were openly on sale to the attendees.

---

[18] The directive was published in *Moskovskaia pravda*, 4 October 1991.
[19] *Literaturnaia Rossiia*, 51 (1990).
[20] *Maariv*, (Tel Aviv) 4 January 1991.

At the sessions, antisemitic writers like Feliks Chuyev spoke openly of how "only the army and the Communists of Russia will save us." Participants chose the occasion to depose the Union's chairman, Sergei Mikhalkov, who had served in that post for twenty-seven years, and to replace him with a virulent nationalist, Yuri Bondarev. Among democratic intellectuals, he was perceived as having distinctive fascist tendencies. A significant *military* resolution adopted by the body demanded that Soviet aid not be given to the forces opposing Saddam Hussein of Iraq.

The military and security forces were not alone in utilizing and exploiting antisemitism. Just as significant was the role of the Communist Party bureaucratic apparatus which had organized and supervised the vast propaganda campaign against Zionism together with the anti-Jewish discrimination pattern in university admission and employment practices. Egregious Party behavior was given sharper documentation when the failure of the coup on August 21 prompted Communist Party officials in Moscow and Leningrad to seek to destroy papers which, according to a well-informed report in the *Daily Telegraph* of London, showed close links between the apparatus and extremist Russian nationalist and antisemitic groups.[21]

A particularly disturbing "dirty tricks" device was utilized during the 1990 elections for the Congress of People's Deputies. Agents of the city prosecutor in Leningrad found in that city's Party headquarters (known as Smolny) precisely numbered packets of antisemitic leaflets. These were specifically used against non-Communist candidates who had non-Jewish names. The intent was clear: to focus a spotlight on a Jewish candidate while suggesting that he was shielding his real name from the public, and, thereby, engaged in traditional conspiratorial activities.

The climactic signal of rightist intentions came on July 23 with the publication of an extraordinary appeal, "A Word to the People," in *Sovetskaia Rossiia*, the flagship organ of the Party hardliners.[22] According to the appeal, Holy Russia is "sinking into nonexistence" with "our home" "already burning into the ground, the bones of the people... being ground up and the backbone of Russia... broken in two." Demagoguery of an extreme chauvinist kind could not be more blatant. What was urgently needed was a "nationalist movement" that would "halt

---

[21] *Daily Telegraph* (London), 31 August 1991.

[22] *Sovetskaia Rossiia*, 23 July 1991.

the catastrophic collapse of the state." Signers included the commander-in-chief of the army ground forces and the deputy minister of internal affairs. The well-known political extremist whose bigotry was easily recognized, Vladimir Zhirinovsky, publicly announced his personal support and spoke of "a military coup" as "the last step to save the state."[23] Acknowledged as a special favorite of the KGB, Zhirinovsky was the head of the Liberal Democratic Party. In 1990, his candidacy for the Russian presidency had won some six million votes, a not inconsequential figure.

Had the coup of August 19–21 succeeded, it would have placed in power those forces determined to crush an emerging democracy. Antisemitism would have been greatly strengthened. Not surprisingly, Soviet Jews displayed a very deep sense of anxiety, and their younger members played activist roles in the resistance movement. Public demonstrations on behalf of Yeltsin included numerous Jews.

The collapse of the coup in Moscow and Yeltsin's heroic victory ended the immediate danger confronting Soviet Jewry even as it greatly weakened the threat to democracy. Still, the defeat of the rightist conspirators was hardly a consequence of massive fervor and partisanship for the democratic forces. Outside of Moscow and Leningrad, public apathy was all too apparent. The supporters of the coup, of which there were many, did not suddenly vanish. Indeed, the newly-chosen head of the KGB, Vadim Bakatin, told a group of Yeltsin backers that it would simply not be possible to incarcerate all the fascists in Russia because that would require the building of more concentration camps than even Stalin had erected.[24]

Bakatin's comments were disclosed by Dr. James Billington, the Librarian of Congress and distinguished historian of Russia, who had been present in Moscow during the coup and its aftermath. That the new KGB chief, appointed by the returned Soviet president, Mikhail Gorbachev, represented a major departure for the Kremlin was made quite evident. He spoke publicly about cutting back its huge manpower, opening its files to responsible inspection officials and researchers, and generally

---

[23] *TASS*, 30 July 1991. For a characterization of Zhirinovsky, see Paul Quinn-Judge, "Russia's David Duke," *New Republic*, 11 November 1991.

[24] James Billington, "The True Heroes of the Soviet Union," *New York Times*, 30 August 1991, Op-Ed.

conducting a refreshing shakeup of what had been the principal pillar of totalitarianism.

Regrettably, Bakatin did not long remain in office. With the removal of Gorbachev by Yeltsin in December and the disintegration of the USSR, the KGB reformer lost his job. His planned radical overhaul of the agency was rapidly aborted. Yeltsin's choice of a replacement to head the newly-dubbed Ministry of Security was a traditional, conservative police official. Soon, the Ministry, with the old KGB officials occupying most of their previous positions, began in various respects to resemble its predecessor.[25] Bakatin, interviewed in *Izvestiia,* shortly after his removal, caustically observed that it would be an error to think that "our special services have become safe for our citizens."[26]

Certainly, nothing was undertaken to respond to the challenge of a growing antisemitism and the organizations like Pamyat which gave voice to it. But a few weeks after Bakatin related how numerous the fascists in Russia were, a leading Soviet Jewish public figure, Colonel Yuri Sokol, told a seminar in Moscow on September 25 that, with reference to antisemitism, "the situation in this country is very dangerous...it reminds me of what was happening in Fascist Germany."[27] Especially needed was a strong and vigorous condemnation of bigotry and extremist nationalism. Such condemnation, in keeping with CSCE recommendations in Copenhagen and implied at the Paris summit, should be undertaken at the highest political level of the state, but both Gorbachev and Yeltsin were reluctant to address the issue with determination.

Indicative of that reluctance was the way they each handled a sharply-posed question on the subject at a satellite telebridge, sponsored by ABC-TV on September 5.[28] A rabbi in Houston, Texas asked whether antisemitism in the USSR would become weaker or stronger, and went on to inquire about Pamyat, "a very, very strongly anti-Semitic organization." Yeltsin avoided altogether an answer to the first question. Given the fact that the query was plainly and clearly formulated, the failure to respond

---

[25] Alexander Rahr, "The KGB Survives under Yeltsin's Wing," *RFE/RL ResearchReport,* 1, no. 13 (27 March 1992), 1–4.

[26] Paul Quinn-Judge, "Spooked," *New Republic,* 16 March 1992, 19.

[27] Jewish Telegraphic Agency, *Daily News Bulletin,* 27 September 1991.

[28] Transcript of the telebridge, *New York Times,* 7 September 1991.

to it was patently deliberate. What was the Russian president seeking to avoid and why?

Equally mystifying, but far more disturbing, was his response to the more general question about Pamyat. Yeltsin chose to answer it with two interlinked assertions. First, he stated that he had "had dealings with Pamyat for quite a long time...." Second, he observed, Pamyat was becoming "different" from what it had been. Specifically, it was ceasing to be as "extreme" as it had been, a view which, in fact, conflicted with all available information about Pamyat.

The gratuitous comments about Pamyat were startling. Dismaying, too, was the revelation that the president of Russia was maintaining ongoing contacts with an uninhibited hate organization. Why, and with what consequences? Since the telebridge, Yeltsin has never disclosed why he answered as he did. Was he seeking, at this early stage, to build bridges to rightists and especially strong nationalists with whom Pamyat enjoyed a frequently symbiotic relationship? This seems altogether likely and probably explains his continuing failure later to speak out against bigotry.

Gorbachev's response was not much better. He restricted himself to addressing the question about antisemitism, which he thought was "lessening," hardly a very perceptive comment. Concerning Pamyat, Gorbachev said nothing. All that he would say was that he was "opposed to chauvinism and nationalism." Like Yeltsin, Gorbachev was no champion of the struggle against racism as required by the Helsinki process. Jewish activist Col. Sokol put it rather succinctly: "Gorbachev and Yeltsin have great difficulty in pronouncing the word 'anti-Semitism.'"[29]

Even after the collapse of the coup, Pamyat and extremist nationalist elements had no hesitancy about spreading its message of hate and they obviously could count on friendly or perhaps indifferent government officials for that purpose. Most striking, indeed mind-boggling, was an action taken by Pamyat at the historic meeting in Moscow of the Commission on Security and Cooperation in Europe (CSCE) Conference on the Human Dimension (September 10–October 4, 1991).[30] It was the very first Helsinki assemblage in the Soviet capital and the CSCE

---

[29] Jewish Telegraphic Agency, *Daily News Bulletin*, 27 September 1991.

[30] Commission on Security and Cooperation in Europe, *Moscow Meeting of the Conference on the Human Dimension of the Commission on Security and Cooperation in Europe, 10 September—4 October, 1991* (Washington, DC: CSCE, 1991).

delegates who had gathered along with numerous non-governmental organization representatives were especially enthusiastic about the defeat of the totalitarian forces which had attempted the coup of August 19–21.

A solitary note of hostility to Yeltsin's democratic victory could be heard, and it emanated from what was called a "parallel conference" conducted by non-governmental organization representatives on September 26–27. Parallel conferences were characteristic features of CSCE meetings. They allowed NGOs to dramatize and document violations of human rights in the various CSCE states. For the very first time in CSCE history, and in sharp contradiction to what the Helsinki process represented, an open appeal to bigotry was sounded in one area of the parallel conferences.

That area had been taken over by an obvious Pamyat front group with the odd name of "Alliance of Victims of Political Reprisals of 1985–90's, Slavic Assembly." The advertised topic of this meeting "Genocide of Russian and Other Slavic Peoples of the USSR," but the focus was solely upon Jews, or rather "Zionists," who were declared to be the practitioners of genocide against the Slavs.[31]

Aleksandr Romanenko, a Pamyat favorite who had written a notorious hate book on Jews, was the group's principal speaker. Others who addressed the session denounced Yeltsin whose first name was said to be "Baruch," not "Boris." The intent was clear: to depict him as a Jew and, therefore, not to be trusted. The audience was told that Russians should "unite with Communists against Jews" and "with Christians against Jews—but not with Christians who are converted Jews." Underscored were Pamyat's themes of nationalism and Orthodoxy.

Materials distributed to the session's participants were equally overt. One Pamyat leaflet showed a two-headed Jewish monster representing Gorbachev and Yeltsin. Other documents sought to expose and ridicule "Soviet Zionism" and the Jewish religious ritual of male circumcision. *Der Stürmer*-type cartoons were displayed depicting the Persian Gulf War as a Zionist plot to enhance "Greater Israel." A second cartoon characterized Soviet Communism itself as the creation of "Zionists under the mark." Incitement to violence was not eschewed. In one cartoon using

---

[31] A detailed report on the meeting was drafted by Jewish activists who attended the proceedings anonymously. A copy was presented to the author by the activists during his stay in Moscow, 10 September–4 October 1991.

medieval stereotypes, Slav and Muslim warriors join to strike a serpent defined as the traditional Jew; in another, a mighty Slav soldier kills the "Jewish devil."

How this type of parallel conference, unheard of in CSCE history, could have been approved in the face of decisions taken by CSCE itself in June 1990 at Copenhagen, is more than a bit puzzling. The Moscow meeting was the responsibility of a secretariat composed entirely of Soviet officials. It is difficult to believe that these officials were ignorant of Pamyat or Pamyat maneuvers.

A second example in Moscow of the official tolerance of bigotry was the permission granted a well-known hate advocate to enter the premises where the CSCE sessions were held in the face of tight security arrangements which limited access solely to those conducting CSCE business. The notorious political proto-fascist, Vladimir Zhirinovsky, was able, shortly after the opening of the Moscow meeting, to enter the lounge used by the numerous reporters and correspondents, and to harangue them with his basically xenophobic and authoritarian message.[32] His demagoguery was frequently compared to that of Adolf Hitler during the early thirties.

These incidents, together with various other episodes of antisemitism in the USSR, prompted a prominent American official to the CSCE talks, U.S. Ambassador Kenneth Blackwell, to tell the CSCE meeting that "our delegation has sensed a substantial fear of the return of *pogroms,* as Jews here witnessed daily expressions of irrational hate, and opponents of [Gorbachev's] reform have not hesitated to attempt to tar individuals, groups or programs by labeling them as Zionist, Jewish or pro-Jewish."[33]

It was Mikhail Gorbachev who finally hurdled the barrier of silence around antisemitism at a series of commemorative ceremonies for the martyrdom of Jews at Babi Yar, planned by the then virtually independent Ukrainian government. Scheduled to begin on September 29, the unprecedented ceremonies—a major breakthrough in the USSR with

---

[32] The author was present on this occasion, while attending the Moscow meeting to gather information for his book, *The Promises We Keep: Human Rights, the Helsinki Process and American Foreign Policy* (New York: St. Martin's, 1993).

[33] *Statement by J. Kenneth Blackwell of the U.S. Delegation to the Moscow CSCE Meeting,* 27 September 1991.

respect to the Holocaust—would culminate on October 6 with special religious and educational programs organized in cooperation with Israel and world Jewry. (While the actual anniversary of the Babi Yar murders was September 29–30, 1941, the important Jewish holiday of Sukkoth fell on those days in 1991 and, therefore, October 6 was set for special Jewish observances.)

The Babi Yar fiftieth anniversary ceremonies coincided with the closing days of the Moscow CSCE meeting of the Conference on the Human Dimension. Antisemitic developments in the USSR and throughout Eastern Europe were very much on the minds of the CSCE delegates at the time. Shoshana Cardin, a prominent American Jewish leader, who was serving as a "public member" of the U.S. delegation to the Helsinki talks, sought to utilize the circumstances to press Gorbachev to end his silence.

She met with him on October 2 and pleaded with him to publicly denounce antisemitism in the Soviet Union. Gorbachev's initial response was negative. He told Mrs. Cardin that "personally, I don't think it represents a disease that is deeply rooted in our society." Moreover, in his view, it was not politically astute to focus exclusively upon antisemitism and neglect other issues. Gorbachev was quoted as saying that "it would be a mistake to single out one problem when we have so many here."[34]

Despite this negative response, Mrs. Cardin was encouraged when Gorbachev informed her that his close confidante, Aleksandr Yakovlev, would represent him at the Babi Yar ceremony on October 6. It was the first time that the Kremlin was according formal recognition to the historic Nazi massacre of Jews. What may have prompted this Gorbachev initiative was the fact that President George Bush, had deliberately visited Babi Yar on August 1 and delivered a powerful message denouncing racism and antisemitism. In addition, the CSCE meeting in Moscow had adopted even stronger measures against antisemitism.

The Gorbachev address to the Jews and to the world, as read by Yakovlev at Babi Yar, was extraordinarily moving and effective. It expressed profound sympathy for the martyred dead at Babi Yar, and it strongly condemned all manifestations of antisemitism in the USSR. The forthright character of the unexpected denunciation enormously stirred the

---

[34] Jewish Telegraphic Agency, *Daily News Bulletin*, 3 October 1991.

largely Jewish assemblage in Kiev.[35] Tragically, Gorbachev's days as a political leader were already numbered and his popularity had greatly slumped. Only six more weeks would elapse before a triumphant Yeltsin would dissolve the USSR and with it the Gorbachev presidency. The originator of glasnost would now be nothing more than a private citizen whose political influence was negligible. Earlier, in 1990, a similar tough statement on antisemitism by Gorbachev could have significantly influenced Soviet public opinion, but at that time he chose to remain silent. When Gorbachev finally spoke out on bigotry a year later, hardly anyone in Russia was listening.

State-sponsored antisemitism may have ended but shrill, vulgar and vitriolic Judeophobia was being massively promoted and distributed in a great variety of newspapers and journals. According to the Jewish monthly periodical, *Yevreiskaia gazeta,* no less than fifty-six Russian newspapers and journals published anti-Jewish material during the period August 1991–July 1992, including such sizable newspapers and journals as *Sovetskaia Rossiia* with a million readers, and *Nash sovremennik* with 164,000 readers.[36]

Other sources tended to confirm the disturbing Jewish documentation. The Anti-Fascist Center of the Russian Federation, in August 1992, charged that thirty-six newspapers and journals in Moscow alone carried antisemitic articles. *Nezavisimaia gazeta* reported on August 12 that racism was produced in thirty-five "national-patriotic" newspapers in Moscow, fourteen in St. Petersburg, and thirteen in other cities of Russia and Belarus. The Moscow daily, *Vecherniaia Moskva,* contended that there were about forty antisemitic newspapers and periodicals in Russia.[37]

In the view of the writer in *Vecherniaia Moskva,* Article 74 of the Russian Criminal Code was too imprecise for bringing legal indictments that would halt the rampaging racist propaganda. Besides the standard publications, bigots peddled all kinds of leaflets, books and booklets that focussed upon Zionist-Masonic conspiracies in the center of Moscow and in front of major hotels in St. Petersburg. Many were crudely printed broadsheets costing about one penny each, laid out by vendors on the

---

[35] *New York Times,* 7 October 1991.
[36] Institute of Jewish Affairs, *Intelligence Report,* 17 (December, 1992).
[37] *Nezavisimaia gazeta,* 12 August 1992; *Vecherniaia Moskva,* 18 September 1992.

pavements of major thoroughfares. The blight on Russia's major cities could not have gone unnoticed. Jews, democrats and tourists may have been dismayed, but the chairman of the Moscow City Council's Human Rights Committee, Valery Fadeyev, was not surprised. "In the present chaotic environment," he observed, "anything can be printed."[38]

That hate initiatives in the media might trigger destructive acts would not be surprising. A host of desecrations of Jewish graves and cemeteries were reported during 1992–93 culminating in mid-June in the swastika daubing of Moscow's main synagogue and the smashing of its windows. Chief Rabbi of Russia Adolf Shayevich complained bitterly that the police delayed responding for several days.[39]

A particularly flagrant example of Pamyat "Jew-baiting" activism was a late morning raid upon the offices of the liberal Moscow newspaper, *Moskovskii komsomolets* on October 13, 1992. Some 30 militants terrorizing the journalists read an ultimatum demanding that the editors reveal the names of all reporters who had written articles against "patriotic powers," and that the newspaper apologize to the "Russian people." As they stormed out, they left behind pamphlets which used the newspaper's masthead but replaced it with the words *Masonskii komzhidovets,* which implied that Masonic Jews ran the journal.[40] Several days later, Pamyat leader Dmitri Vasiliev, who was thought to have planned the raid, commented that the liberal organ should be prosecuted for advocating "prostitution, homosexuality and Zionism."

Russian officialdom was not unaware of the growing phenomenon of Jew-baiting. The director of the human rights department of the Foreign Ministry, Viacheslav Bakhmin, in testimony at a Washington forum of the U.S. Congressional Human Rights Caucus on March 11, 1993, observed that the "danger" of the spreading antisemitism should not be "underestimated." The "ulcer of anti-Semitism," he warned, is difficult to treat in view of the prevailing hard economic circumstances, and "especially in the absence of strong democratic institutions and the lack

---

[38] Jewish Telegraphic Agency, *Daily News Bulletin,* 19 November 1992.
[39] *Associated Press,* 15 June 1993.
[40] Union of Councils for Soviet Jews, *Anti-Semitism, Persecution of Jews, and Renewed Fear in the New Independent States of the Former Soviet Union* (Washington, DC: Union of Councils, 1992), 4.

of a legal conscience in the society."[41]

The extraordinarily frank testimony was compelling. If the organizations peddling antisemitism were "noisy and garish," Bakhmin acknowledged that the "official response" had been "rather hesitant and inconsequential." Even more incriminating were his comments on the Russian judicial system in coping with hate and hate crimes. Its "slowness... is a result of secret sympathies from some officials towards nationalists and anti-Semites."

At the historical moment when objective circumstances pointed to a growing political instability, the Russian Center for Public Opinion and Market Research (formerly the Soviet Center) once again surveyed public opinion on the Jewish question. Some four thousand persons from seven states of the Commonwealth of Independent States and three Baltic states were interviewed during March–April 1992.[42]

An especially significant finding emerged from a particular question: Whether the respondent believed that "some kind of mysterious organization... secretly controls the course of events in this country and in the entire world?" A remarkably large percentage of Russians—47 percent—said they did believe it and 27 percent were uncertain.

A leading British analyst, writing in the winter 1992, found that conspiracy theories "have always abounded in Russia, but in recent months have gained even greater currency." In his view, the profound economic and social problems in Russia produced a "national disorientation" that results in "Russians increasingly believ[ing] that 'dark'—even 'satanic'—forces are responsible for their national distress."[43] Not surprisingly, Pamyat and other antisemitic forces could exploit such perceptions. Still, the results of the survey did not indicate a deepening of antisemitism in the population.

If the 1992 public opinion survey revealed a strong, firmly-held belief in a conspiracy theory that bordered on the *Protocols* perception, it also indicated a surprising, not inconsequential, sympathetic attitude toward

---

[41] "Witnesses Warn End to Anti-Semitism Will Take A Long Time, *Radio Liberty Wire*, 11 March 1993.

[42] American Jewish Committee, *Attitudes Toward Jews in the Former Soviet Union: Public Opinion in Ten States* (New York: American Jewish Committee, 1992).

[43] John Dunn, "Hard Times in Russia Foster Conspiracy Theories," *RFE/RL Research Report*, 1, no. 46 (November 1992), 24–9.

Pamyat; 19 percent of the respondents said that they "sympathize" with Pamyat. More than twice that percentage were uncertain; 43 percent said they "don't know" or that it was "difficult to say" whether they were sympathetic. The response suggested that, at a minimum, many could fairly easily be encouraged to be sympathetic to Pamyat.

That a "secret organization" which engages in conspiracy might mean a Zionist group is suggested by responses to other survey questions; 25 percent of the respondents said that they had heard about a "world Zionist conspiracy." In answer to the query whether "such a conspiracy really exists?" only 9 percent said "yes." But a whopping 65 percent responded that it was "difficult to say." Another question elicited the extent of popular distortion and general ignorance about what Zionism meant: 17 percent thought the word meant "a policy of establishing the world supremacy of Jews." That percentage was far greater than for any other definition. Only 7 percent correctly defined it as "a movement of Jews for return to their historic homeland." Strikingly, ignorance was more prevailing than distortion: 59 percent answered with "can't say definitely."

As antisemitic activism increased and racist bigotry in the media proliferated, the far more significant development was the emergence of a strong, unifying body of communists and nationalists—the "Red-Brown" alliance. Called the National Salvation Front, it brought together under one roof a myriad of right wing and chauvinist groups. The founding congress of the Front, held in Moscow on October 24–25, 1992 brought together some 1400 delegates from over one hundred cities with an additional 1600 observers from many of the former Soviet republics.[44]

Initially, the National Salvation Front sought an image of right wing respectability. Pamyat types or those reflecting extremist lunacy, like Vladimir Zhirinovsky, were not invited or offered significant leadership roles. Still, the Front's leadership read like a "who's who" of the ultra-conservative key military officers, and prominent writers, like Valentin Rasputin and Igor Shafarevich. A co-chairman was Gennadi Zyuganov, formerly ideology secretary of the Russian Communist Party, chosen in February 1993 as the resurrected Party's new leader.

From the perspective of the Yeltsin regime, faced as it was by severe

---

[44] Wendy Slater, "Russian Communists Seek Salvation in Nationalist Alliance," *RFE/RL Research Report*, 2, no. 13 (March 26, 1993), 8–13.

economic difficulties and a powerful parliamentary revolt, the Front was perceived as the vanguard of an insurrection to return the pre-Gorbachev order. Its first appeal carried a demagogic chauvinist echo: "Our Motherland is being subjected to unprecedented destruction and desecration." The Russian president ordered that the Front be banned. But the Constitutional Court, on February 12, 1993 re-legalized the organization. It was destined to exert a potent influence on political life.

If not overtly antisemitic, the Front's opening congress set the tone of what would follow. The principal speeches reverberated with condemnation of the "Zionist/Western conspiracy" to destroy Russia. Leaflets and a brochure entitled "Lenin's Jewish Forefather" further stirred embers of hate. Once the Front began holding public demonstrations, the Judeophobia of its supporters which, inevitably, included many Pamyat members, quickly surfaced. At one demonstration it organized on March 21 outside the Yeltsin "White House," placards bearing the following were seen: "Down with Kikes and Jews!" and "Jews out of the Government!"[45] Numerous placards at various marches proclaimed a variation of the old Black Hundreds slogan: "Beat the Jews! Save the Constitution!" Others read: "Down with Zionist-Masonic Democracy!" and "Zionists: You destroyed the USSR; You will not destroy Russia!"

The intention of the demonstrators might have been to stimulate opposition to Yeltsin and his proposed referendum for a constitutional change that would augment his power. If so, the strategy backfired. The referendum in April ran very much in his favor, but the Front refused to retreat. On May 1, it took to the street in a march which turned violent as the demonstrators assaulted the riot police. Scores were injured.[46] A week later, to commemorate the victory over Nazi Germany on May 9, fifteen thousand marchers from the "Red-Brown" alliance joined by army veterans paraded onto Red Square (which had been declared off limits for the May 1 demonstration and which probably helped spark the subsequent violence). Typical of the placards were: "Save Russia from International Capitalism!" and "Yeltsin Reforms are a Zionist Diversion!"[47]

---

[45] *Jerusalem Report,* 22 April 1993, citing the Moscow weekly, *Kuranty;* National Conference on Soviet Jewry, *Newswatch,* 22 March 1993.
[46] *New York Times,* 2 May 1993.
[47] *New York Times,* 10 May 1993.

In the organization of marches and demonstrations, a key affiliate of the Front no doubt played a prominent role—the Officer's Union, comprising reactionary military officers who combined extremist nationalism with neo-Communism. Claiming a membership of 30,000, the Union, under the chairmanship of Stanislav Terekhov, was expected to become the military arm of the Front. Absorption of the traditional antisemitism of the armed forces prior to the coup would hardly prove difficult.[48]

The ideological affinity of Pamyat with the National Salvation Front was demonstrated by an appeal published in *Pravda* on January 21, 1993 on behalf of Serbia. The focus of the appeal was upon Bosnia where Western humanitarian assistance was perceived as intervention into the Slavic world which should be counterbalanced by Russian volunteers who would fight on the side of the Serbs. Along with signatures of prominent Russian nationalists and Communists associated with the Front, there was the name of Pamyat leader Dmitri Vasiliev.[49] Clearly, the National Salvation Front offered no serious objection to the inclusion of Pamyat.

The year 1993 marked historic anniversaries of major turning points of Russian antisemitism. It was exactly eighty years since the *Protocols of the Elders of Zion* were first published by the extremist tsarist, Pavel Krushevan; and ninety years since the blood libel trial of Mendel Beiliss in Kiev. Forty years previously, Stalin had unveiled the Doctors' Plot, a kind of modern variation of the *Protocols* interwoven with a certain Beiliss theme in which poison was substituted for blood.

Stunningly, the two extraordinary tsarist hoaxes experienced an almost miraculous, mind-boggling revival in contemporary Russia, on the eve— it should be noted—of the twenty-first century. In February 1993, *Sovetskaia Rossiia,* with one million readers, carried an article by the second highest-ranking clergyman of the Russian Orthodox Church, Metropolitan Ioann of St. Petersburg, which sought to demonstrate the current validity of the *Protocols*. Excerpts from that forged document were juxtaposed with published descriptions of existing dire social and economic situations in Russia.[50]

Metropolitan Ioann was not alone in these crackpot views. The same

---

[48] Stephen Foye, "Russia's Fragmented Army Drawn into the Political Fray," *RFE/RL Research Report,* 2, no. 15, 9 April 1993, 4–5.

[49] *Pravda,* 21 January 1993; *RFE/RL News Briefs,* 25–29 January 1993, 11.

[50] *Sovetskaia Rossiia,* 27 February 1993; see also *New York Times,* 22 June 1993.

perspective was held by at least two prominent editors—Stanislav Kunyayev and General Viktor Filatov. Particularly intriguing was an unfolding court case in Moscow where the central issue turned on whether the *Protocols* were authentic. It will be recalled that in 1935, almost sixty years earlier, a presiding judge in a Swiss courtroom had ruled that the *Protocols* were "nothing but ridiculous nonsense," and speculated that, in the future, no jury or courtroom would give even the slightest credence to them. In Moscow in 1993, a court demonstrated that the Swiss judge had been excessively optimistic.

The case before the court was a libel suit brought by Pamyat in May 1992 against the editor of a Jewish journal, Tankred Golenpolsky. He had earlier published in his journal a list of antisemitic newspapers in Russia which included a Pamyat organ that had carried extracts of the *Protocols*. The alleged grounds for the Pamyat suit was that the *Protocols* were authentic and, therefore, could not be antisemitic. The Moscow court actually took seriously what anywhere else would have been considered frivolous. Lengthy arguments were advanced by lawyers in the courtroom over the course of several months; clearly, the Russian judicial system and society as a whole had failed as yet to recognize and thoroughly repudiate a forgery which had only been "ridiculous nonsense."[51]

Besides, it could hardly be said that the *Protocols* were in any way harshly treated by the Russian judicial system. One case stands out in mid-1993. A Pamyat militant activist was on trial for leading a raid on the liberal Moscow youth newspaper, *Moskovskii komsomolets,* in which the journal's staff was brutally terrorized thereby holding up its printing schedule. While the Pamyat member was found guilty of interfering with press freedom, the judge—instead of imposing a tough sentence that might discourage others—merely put him on probation.[52] Pamyat members in the court responded with enthusiasm.

More disturbing than the tolerance shown the *Protocols* at high levels of society was a stunning endorsement in important political circles of the medieval myth of the blood libel. On May 5, *Pravda,* with a readership of one-half million, carried a long article entitled "The Satanic Tribe?" While examining a recent case of the murder of three Russian Orthodox

---

[51] *Forward,* 2 July, 9 July, and 16 July 1993; Alexander Lesser, "Whose Trial Is It Anyway?" *Jerusalem Report,* 12 August 1993, 36–7.
[52] *Forward,* 7 May 1993.

monks, the article speculated that "behind the murder" was a Jewish ritual of the killing "of the goyim by the Levites with the support of the rabbis...." Added to the charge was the archaic notion associated with medieval religious life: "The sacrifice of a non-Jew on the day of his [the Jew's] religious holiday was considered by the Levites as a sign of their national and religious might...."[53]

The *Pravda* essay contended that ritual murders were systematically practiced by the hasidim, a branch of Orthodox Jewry. Presumably, this wild and benighted allegation was based upon "super-secret classified data" of the KGB which had recorded the deaths annually of some fifty persons whose bodies bore "the marks of ritual torture."

None of the major Soviet press organs had previously printed articles about the blood libel hoax, even in their most virulent antisemitic period. The *Pravda* story must have brought a shock in various quarters. *Izvestiia,* on May 7, treated the article with a certain contempt, headlining its article "Satanic Games in *Pravda.*" The Russian Foreign Ministry, no doubt with an eye to American aid, on May 14, expressed "astonishment and dismay." But neither it nor the government newspaper called for legal action or, at a minimum, an investigation of how such a malignant and incitatory article could be published. On the contrary, the Foreign Ministry, even while recognizing that the essay was overtly inflammatory and "destructive," went on to stress that "one should not exaggerate the significance of this unpleasant incident."[54]

That even this belated and mild official rebuke was a result not of Moscow's moral and legal concern about slanderous Judeophobia but rather of formal U.S. pressure is suggested by a State Department press briefing on May 20. The Department spokesman, referring to the *Pravda* article as "virulently anti-Semitic," emphasized: "We have indeed talked to the Russians about this, both in Washington and in Moscow."[55]

The pressure no doubt continued and was probably augmented by urgings of those left wing *Pravda* readers who still clung to humanist aspects of Marxism. On June 17, the editors formally "offered their apologies to the readers" and blamed the author of the article for

---

[53] "The Satanic Tribe," *Pravda,* 5 May 1993.
[54] *Izvestiia,* 7 May 1993; Russian Foreign Ministry, press briefing, 14 May 1993.
[55] *State Department Press Briefing,* 20 May 1993.

"untested, unjustified statements."[56] But the editors did not explain how they had allowed such a piece to be printed in the first place.

The apology followed the publication of a letter to the editor written by Leonid Goldin, who complained that the May 5 article "discredits the socialist movement" and "provoke[s] suspicions and witch hunts." While admitting that "L. Goldin is right," *Pravda* carefully avoided saying against whom the suspicions and witch hunts would be directed. Not once were Jews mentioned; nor antisemitism.[57]

From the office of President Yeltsin not a single word of condemnation emerged despite Russia's commitment to the Helsinki denunciation of overt racism and antisemitism. In Yeltsin's historic address to the U.S. Congress in 1992, he pledged "no more lies" would be tolerated or perpetrated by the Russian government. Here was an opportunity to nail a particularly obscene and provocatory lie, that of blood libel. Instead, a studied silence engulfed the Kremlin.

The silence was scarcely surprising. As late as April 20, 1993 (only a few weeks before the episode broke in the media), President Yeltsin, at a meeting with religious leaders, was asked by Russian Chief Rabbi Adolf Shayevich, to take a clear position against an increasingly "organized and open" antisemitism.[58] As in the past, the president chose to avoid a direct response; instead, he simply asserted that antisemitism did not exist on a *state* level. But Rabbi Shayevich was not talking about the state level at all. It was on a public, social level that antisemitism flourished. To this potent danger, the Kremlin's response remained a deafening silence.

Shortly after the *Protocols* and blood libel issues traumatized Russian Jewry and its allies in the democratic community, two major hearings on antisemitism, followed by published official reports, illuminated both the depth of the problem and the limitation of the authorities in grappling with it. The reports also indicated what kind of response was essential to deal with the escalating moral crisis.

The first set of hearings was held on May 26 by the Human Rights Committee of the Supreme Soviet, chaired by the distinguished democratic activist, Sergei Kovalev. After four hours of testimony, the

---

[56] *Pravda*, 17 June 1993.
[57] Ibid.
[58] *RFE/RL News Briefs*, 2, no. 18 (19–23 April 1993) 4.

important parliamentary committee formally concluded that "alarming signs" of antisemitism "are spreading in the political and social life of Russia." The form being taken was the creation of an "internal enemy"—Jews—to provoke "national intolerance and xenophobia."[59]

The parliamentary committee statement on "alarming signs" was specific. It noted: 1) antisemitic campaigns conducted in various media organs; 2) publication of books that contain slander against Jews and that distort Jewish history; 3) antisemitic slogans at meetings and gatherings of various public organizations, including some that were officially registered; 4) desecration of Jewish cemeteries; and 5) open threats of violence against Jews.

It was the committee's view that the spreading of antisemitism was a product of "the intensification of economic and political tensions in [Russian] society." In addition, there had remained a persistent "totalitarious consciousness" in sectors of the public which ineluctably manifests itself in "xenophobia and national intolerance."

How should the Russian government deal with the serious problem of spreading antisemitism? The "basic means of struggle," the committee said was "moral condemnation." But nothing was said as to who had the primary responsibility to undertake this initiative. President Boris Yeltsin was not mentioned at all as the focal point for fulfilling the "bully pulpit" obligation.

Special emphasis was given over the appeals to violence, insults to national dignity, and acts of discrimination. Here, the organs of law and order must act immediately, the committee contended. A key problem, was that the principal organs of law and order—police and security officials—claimed that "matters relating to racial incitement were not within their spheres of competency." This critical thesis was articulated by Deputy Procurator-General Vladimir Kirakozov. He explained in testimony that the new Russian laws limited the jurisdiction of the police and security agencies precisely so their authority would be circumscribed.

Nor was the procurator's office itself particularly active. It was the judgment of the committee that Article 74 of the Criminal Code was not

---

[59] *Report on the Parliamentary Hearings on Anti-Semitism Sponsored by the Human Rights Committee of the Russian Supreme Court, 26 May 1993*. The Report appeared in *Update on Jews in the CIS, Georgia, and the Baltic Republics*, 20 June 1993. *Update* is distributed by the Consulate-General of Israel in New York.

sufficiently precise as well as flexible to deal effectively with incitement to racist violence. Kovalev made it clear that he would seek to strengthen the law.

Particularly telling in the parliamentary committee's "statement" was the comment that there existed in Russia "an atmosphere of public tolerance of anti-Semitism." Neither the state authorities (and the organs of law and order) nor the public media had sought to shape a totally new atmosphere which would shame or hold in contempt the purveyors of Judeophobia.

The most striking feature of the hearings was the almost total indifference to them by the highest executive and legislative bodies of the state and by the media. Representatives of the key ministries of interior and security, though invited to appear, either did not show up or refused to answer any questions. The bulk of the legislative body failed to express any interest or even to make an appearance. Only five of twelve committee members showed up. Attendance was extraordinarily sparse. Media coverage of the very first hearings on antisemitism ever held in Moscow was negligible. None of the major newspapers gave them any space at all. Radio and television totally ignored the proceedings.

At the very end of May, a "seminar" with the subject of antisemitism as its main theme took place in Moscow. Entitled "Combatting Racism, Xenophobia and Anti-Semitism," the two-day event (May 31–June 1, 1993) was organized not by a Russian agency or organ but by the prestigious Council of Europe, headquartered in Strasbourg, and the European Jewish Congress.[60] Since high-level foreign dignitaries participated, and, more importantly, since the subject embraced all of Europe, far greater media coverage was assured.

The declaration adopted by the seminar was pointedly sharp and severe in dealing with Russia. On the one hand, it called attention to "overt manifestations of anti-Semitism" which not only targeted Jews but were perceived as an "effective tool" of extremist and communist forces to halt democratic progress. On the other hand, and far more significantly, it openly chastised the state leaders for failure to condemn antisemitic manifestations: "While such acts are consistently condemned in the ma-

---

[60] *Report on the Seminar on Racism, Xenophobia, and Anti-Semitism Held in Moscow, 31 May–1 June, 1993;* this report appeared in *Update,* ibid.

jority of European countries, in Russia, they remain outside the purview of authorities."

Accompanying the biting admonition was a series of concrete recommendations to the "leadership of the Russian Federation." First, it should take "all possible...measures" to remove the "evil legacy" of hate, including "publicly condemning anti-Semitism." Second, legislation should be enacted to combat discrimination and incitement. And, finally, "special educational programs in the schools and universities" should be adopted to provide "a positive image of minorities...."

Symptomatic of the response of Russian leadership was the speech of Foreign Minister Andrei Kozyrev. Notwithstanding the specific topic of the seminar, he said not a word about antisemitism; nor did he even hint that the subject was a matter of concern or interest to the state leadership. And, moreover, according to Vaad leader Mikhail Chlenov, only one member of the Russian Supreme Soviet was present in the hall during the seminar. For him, this was indicative of the indifference of Russian leadership.

The indifference to growing antisemitism stood in clear contradiction with the obligations of the Helsinki process explicitly accepted by all CSCE members of Copenhagen in June 1990 and authoritatively mandated in the Paris Charter for a New Europe the following November. That the obligations upon the Russian rulers were and are especially pronounced flow inexorably from the vicious official antisemitism imposed upon the Soviet Union by the Kremlin during the previous five decades.

Guided by an incredible demonology of Zionism, Kremlin policy-makers, notably from 1967 through 1986, unleashed upon the Soviet public a massive propaganda effort with the Jew (or rather Zionist) as target. Seeds of virulent hate were sown and nourished. From them, there blossomed a general psychopathology of Judeophobia which found expression in Pamyat and various national extremist groups, some particularly potent. Sustaining the populist organizations were the instruments of state power—the army, the security forces and the Party bureaucracy.

If official state antisemitism had ended, popular Jew-baiting had significantly increased, warranting official state action to combat the dangerous evil for it ultimately threatened democracy and civil society itself. The Helsinki process set forth what has to be done on three levels: 1) authoritative moral and public condemnation; 2) application of legal measures where appropriate; and 3) embarking upon an educational program both in and out of schools to counteract racism.

Fulfillment of CSCE obligations by Moscow had yet to be meaningfully undertaken. Traditions associated with the notorious tsarist Black Hundreds and their usage of the *Protocols of the Elders of Zion* and the blood libel myth were deepening. A vigorous positive response by the state was still urgently needed. Tomorrow could be too late.

# Epilogue

An initial denouement came in October 1993. Exploiting a ferocious struggle for power by the Supreme Soviet against President Yeltsin, who had declared the parliamentary body no longer functional and had set December 12 as the date for new elections, the "Red-Brown" alliance took to the streets. By the end of September, the alliance was able to muster some ten thousand supporters to defend the Russian White House in which hundreds of the now-banned parliament stubbornly rejected the Yeltsin decision.

On Sunday, October 3, the "Red-Brown" militants, inevitably including Pamyat activists, transformed themselves into an insurrectionary force to challenge the Kremlin.[1] Supported by the Union of Officers, resurrected Cossacks, and several dismissed rightist generals like Albert Makashov, extremist nationalist and communist vanguard elements stormed police barricades in Moscow and marched on the city's major television station. The violence turned ugly.

Just as ugly were the antisemitic cries of the demonstrators: "Save Russia: Beat the Jews"—the old slogan of the Black Hundreds was carried on placards and voiced in vulgar shouts. Many of the White House defenders openly revealed to reporters their belief that an international Zionist conspiracy had seized control of the Kremlin, and was manipulating Yeltsin (often dubbed "Baruch" rather than "Boris"). Virulent antisemitic literature was put on display in front of the White House, including Hitler's *Mein Kampf* as well as neo-Nazi flags.

The putschist attempt to seize the vital central television studios turned into a fierce, bloody battle accompanied by numerous antisemitic slogans.

---

[1] *New York Times,* 4 October 1993. Additional information was provided by observers from the Moscow Jewish community.

A day earlier, on Saturday, twenty armed hatemongers had entered Moscow's Choral Synagogue and screamed antisemitic epithets. The invective became more vehement on Sunday to match the fury of the assault. For Moscow Jews, it was a moment of deep fear and anxiety.

Confronted by this dangerous offensive, President Yeltsin had no alternative but to use determined and overwhelming military power to smash the insurrection. With most of Moscow and the rest of Russia remaining on the sidelines, the Kremlin crushed the resistance. A moment of decision had been reached; for Yeltsin, the threat of a fascist counterrevolution must finally be ended.

The steps taken by the Russian president were not unexpected. Key elements of the insurrection, the National Salvation Front and Pamyat, were outlawed. Banned, too, although only for a limited time, were organs that earlier during the year had promoted xenophobia, racism, and antisemitism—*Sovetskaia Rossiia, Pravda,* and *Den.* Whether the malady of hate and bigotry had now been permanently halted and reversed remained an open question. The heavy weight of an antisemitic tradition in attitudes and in powerful institutions had yet to be seriously confronted, and of course, overcome, by the political leadership of Moscow.

The answer came quickly with the party-preference vote for the Russian parliament on December 12, 1993.[2] The results startled and shocked the West. Chauvinism emerged triumphant. The Liberal Democratic Party of hatemonger Vladimir Zhirinovsky won nearly a quarter of the total ballots cast, significantly larger than any other political party, including the party associated with Yeltsin, Russia's Choice, which rereceived sixteen percent of the total. A significant percentage of the votes went to the disgraced Communist Party and groups associated with it. All in all, two-thirds of the voting public cast ballots for parties with explicitly neo-imperialist designs. Not surprisingly, one of the first acts of the new parliament (the Duma) was the release of those who had participated in the attempted October insurrection, as well as those Communist Party leaders incarcerated for involvement in the aborted putsch of August 1991.

Zhirinovsky had borrowed a fundamental Pamyat notion about the

---

[2] *New York Times,* 13 and 14 December 1993; *Washington Post,* 13 and 14 December 1993.

Bolshevik Revolution being a Jewish plot. In his view, Jews "went for the socialist idea...tried to make a world revolution" so that they could then "dominate the world."[3] As with the fabricators of the *Protocols,* Zhirinovsky perceived the Jews as predominant in the media and in finances. He contended (without offering any documentation) that seventy percent of all persons employed in the Russian media—newspapers, magazines, television, and radio—were Jews. "Wherever you point," he exclaimed with reference to the media, "there's a Jew." Holding control of the channels of communication, the Jews "are simply infecting the country," according to Zhirinovsky.[4]

In the same way, Jews were seen as wealthy or universally well-to-do. Israel, he held, was the "richest country in the world." The statement was made without the slightest hesitancy, and, of course, without any qualifications. Nor was it expressed in jest.

The most disturbing feature of Jews, in the intensely chauvinist view of Zhirinovsky, was their supposed lack of patriotism, their utter indifference to the disintegration of the Soviet empire. He faulted Jewish writers, satirists, commentators, even comedians, for this failing. Precisely because of this alleged unpatriotic character, Zhirinovsky anticipated pogroms against Jews expressing popular wrath against those who contributed "to the destruction of the [Soviet] state." Asked by Israeli journalists how pogroms could be avoided, he placed the burden upon the would-be victims. Jews, he said, "should keep silent," by which he meant, they should not challenge Russian chauvinism.[5]

Zionist demonology stood at the core of the Zhirinovsky outlook. While vigorously denying in every interview that he was antisemitic, he had no hesitancy in declaring himself an anti-Zionist. Indeed, the ideology of his Liberal Democratic Party was articulated in anti-Zionist terms. The Party's chief ideologist, Igor Minin, asserted that "Zionism has as its final goal the establishment of the economic and political supremacy of Jewry in all the leading countries of the world...."[6] In

---

[3] *Jerusalem Report,* 13 February 1992. The comments were made in the course of an interview with Israeli journalists for the *Report.*

[4] Ibid.

[5] Ibid.

[6] Jacob W. Kipp, "The Zhirinovsky Threat," *Foreign Affairs,* May–June 1995, 82. Kipp is a specialist on military and security affairs.

consequence, Zionism was seen as the chief source of anti-Russian maneuvers by the West.

Minin was remarkably frank in linking Zionism with Jewry and attributing to the latter a dangerous genetic feature. The supposed Zionist aspiration for domination, he wrote, "is a direct result of the basic features of the national character of the Jewish people." Indeed, the governments of the United States, Great Britain, and France were seen as but tools of international Zionism. Illustrative of this perspective were Zhirinovsky's stunning public comments when he arrived at the Paris airport in April 1994 while on his way to Strasbourg to participate in the parliamentary assembly of the Council of Europe. "It's all over for you once you're Americanized and Zionized."[7] He went on with a sarcastic comment about the growing Arab population of France: "I salute Paris as the city of Arabs in 10, 20 years." The French government warned that his statements were "unacceptable."

That Zhirinovsky resonated a Hitlerian outlook was certainly startling. Russia, after all, had been almost decimated by Hitler's legions, who were stirred by a virulent anti-Slav racism. But, in Zhirinovsky's opinion, Hitler's "ideology does not contain anything negative in itself."[8] The assertion carried an "in general" qualification with a notation that some of Hitler's "extreme" measures did harm Germans. As early as 1991, Zhirinovsky even embraced a direct linkage with the Nazi ruler.[9] "I'll act as Hitler did in 1932," he told a Lithuanian interviewer. Another interviewer at the time was told that "when I come to power, there will be a dictatorship. Russia needs a dictator now."[10]

Minin went further, linking the Liberal Democratic Party to Nazism. National Socialism was seen as a "third force" rejecting both Communism and democracy. "The true carrier of the ideals of national socialism," he emphasized, "is the national-patriotic movement."[11] He did not hesitate to spell out the need to adopt some Nazi organizational features: the Russian national patriotic movement would require its own

---

[7] *International Herald Tribune* (Paris), 13 April 1994.
[8] Kipp, "Zhirinovsky Threat," 82.
[9] William Korey, "Zhirinovsky and the 1996 Election," *Star* (New York), Spring 1994, 34.
[10] Ibid.
[11] Kipp, "Zhirinovsky Threat," 82–83.

*Epilogue*

paramilitary formations—the *druzhina*. The latter were to be organized into "agitation and propaganda groups" for street operations during electoral campaigns. The echoes of the Hitlerian SA and SS rang loud and clear.

The parallels with Hitler did not go unnoticed. President Yeltsin, in his published memoirs, observed that "Russia is not immune to fascism."[12] But his caution in targeting Zhirinovsky was apparent. After the latter's electoral success in December 1993, the shocked president would only comment that "primitive nationalism, outright lies and even dangerous provocations" produced the Liberal Democratic Party achievement.[13]

Far less reluctant was Yeltsin's former liberal prime minister, Yegor Gaidar. He wrote in *Izvestiia* that during the 1993 election campaign, Zhirinovsky "reminded me of Hitler in 1929." That judgment, said the liberal economist, "was mistaken" for Zhirinovsky's vote exceeded that of Hitler in 1929, and had "achieved the result that the Nazis got in the Reichstag elections of 1930."[14]

Jews or Zionists were not the only enemies of the Russian Hitler, as the German press had dubbed Zhirinovsky. The Nazi dictator, with his chauvinistic trumpeting of the Aryan race, had expressed contempt for all ethnic groups not part of his favored Germans or somehow associated with them. The multi-national Soviet empire offered a rich melange of ethnic targets. Zhirinovsky treated the Lithuanians, together with Latvians and Estonians, with utter genocidal derision. "I'll destroy you," he warned the Balts as he threatened to bury nuclear waste along their borders. For their resistance to Moscow, the Balts "will die from diseases and radiation."[15]

Equally intolerable were the Armenians. He promised to "strangle your independence with a famine." The other major nationalities of the Caucasus, notably Georgians and Azeris, as well as those of the various central Asian republics, were perceived as unproductive and cheating elements who, as refugees, were pouring into Moscow, dangerously

---

[12] Quoted in Michael Specter, "Zhirinovsky and the Motherland," *New York Times Magazine,* 19 June 1994, 33.

[13] *New York Times,* 14 October 1994.

[14] Quoted in Specter, "Zhirinovsky and the Motherland," 33.

[15] Korey, "Zhirinovsky and 1996 Election," 34; Elizabeth Teague, "Is Russia Likely to Turn to Authoritarian Rule?," *RFE/RL Research Report,* 24 January 1992, 3–4.

subverting its population pattern as well as ruining the Russian economy. As for blacks from the United States or from Africa, Zhirinovsky had nothing but contempt. Africans were seen as carriers of the AIDS virus. Therefore, he advocated the closing down of Patrice Lumumba University in Moscow, which had for decades been a major educational institute for visiting African students.

The pronounced bigotry of Zhirinovsky and his party extended to foreign contacts. Strikingly, he maintained a strong relationship with the German People's Union, an extreme rightist group. He attended, as an honored guest, its last two conventions.[16] A particularly intimate relationship had been established with the notorious extremist Munich newspaper, *Die Deutsche National-Zeitung,* published by Dr. Gerhard Frey. After the Moscow election, Zhirinovsky traveled to Munich to meet Dr. Frey and be interviewed by his newspaper. From Munich, Zhirinovsky proceeded to Vienna, where he was hosted by a close friend, Edwin Neuwirth, who had served in Hitler's elite Waffen SS. When Neuwirth was later interviewed by reporters, he vigorously denied that the Germans had built and utilized gas chambers during the Holocaust.

In interviews with the German extremist media, Zhirinovsky displayed an unusually warm feeling toward the German state which he saw as a natural "partner" to a revitalized Russia.[17] He envisaged an "eternal alliance" and "close military cooperation" with Russia's primary enemy of World War II. Clearly, Zhirinovsky would welcome a restoration of the Ribbentrop-Molotov agreement of 1939, although, on his visit to Germany, he warned that he would rain nuclear bombs upon the country if it stepped out of line.

A remarkably explicit European map actually drafted and signed by Zhirinovsky in December 1993 highlighted the Russo-German centrality of his world perception.[18] It was given to Rolf Gauffin, the former Swedish ambassador to Russia. Two great powers were to dominate Central and Eastern Europe. On the one hand, the Russian empire would be revived, incorporating the Ukraine, Belarus, and the Baltic states, to which Slovakia would be added. Elsewhere, he talked of restoring Russia

---

[16] Amy C. Solnin, "Vladimir Zhirinovsky: The Record of a Russian Extremist," *International Notes* (New York: Anti-Defamation League, October 1994).
[17] William Korey, "Zhirinovsky and 1996 Election," 32.
[18] Kipp, "Zhirinovsky Threat," 83–84.

to its tsarist imperial frontiers of 1900, including parts of Poland and Finland. On the other hand, a Greater Germany would be established including Austria, Bohemia-Moravia, Western Polish territories (with Poland being compensated by receiving the Lvov region of the Ukraine), and the Kaliningrad area.

In southeast Europe, according to the Zhirinovsky map, the nationality principle would to some extent prevail, though it would be guided by Slavic interests in keeping with the Russian "Big Brother" orientation. Yugoslavia would be partitioned between Croats and Serbs, thereby eliminating any Muslim authority. A Greater Bulgaria would include Macedonia and Thrace. Romania would be enlarged to include significant parts of Moldavia.

Beyond Europe, Zhirinovsky's geographical aspirations focussed, upon southwestern and south central Asia in the direction of the Bosphorus and the Indian Ocean. These areas and their people were the source of "all of Russia's ills," he wrote in his autobiography, *The Final Thrust South*.[19] A commentator spelled them out: corruption, instability, warfare, hatred and ethnic hostility. Turkey, for whose culture Zhirinovsky had a boundless disdain, along with Iran, Afghanistan, and probably Pakistan, were to be conquered. Russian soldiers, he eagerly anticipated, "will wash their boots in the warm waters of the Indian Ocean...."[20]

On another occasion, Zhirinovsky dealt with Israel in terms befitting his anti-Zionist posture. A Jewish state, he said, should never have been created in an area surrounded by a hundred million Arabs. Instead, Jews should have created their isolated state on an island surrounded by water. He mentioned Mauritius, Cyprus, and Madagascar. The last, now called Malagasy, had been the choice of various Hitlerites before the decision on the "Final Solution" was taken.

To achieve his extraordinarily ambitious imperial and geopolitical objectives, Zhirinovsky inevitably indulged in the traditional fascist glorification of war. In his view, "war is the natural state of man. Either they get us or we get them."[21] This purpose required an extreme centralization of state power. Thus, he welcomed Yeltsin's appeal for

---

[19] Heritage Foundation, *Zhirinovsky in His Own Words: Excerpts from "The Final Thrust South"* (Washington, DC: Heritage Foundation, 4 February 1994), 1–11.
[20] Solnin, "Zhirinovsky," 2.
[21] Specter, "Zhirinovsky and the Motherland," 56.

enhanced presidential authority. At the same time, Zhirinovsky would do away with the autonomy of the various eighty-eight regions of the Russian Federation based upon ethnic rights.[22] Russia, the Russian language, and the Russian Orthodox Church would hold, in his militant chauvinist view, a monopoly of influence. Other ethnic and religious groups would either have to accommodate or move out.

Militarization of power ran parallel with centralization. Intense efforts were made by Zhirinovsky to exploit the shame and embarrassment resulting from the loss of empire with the consequent collapse of prestige and status. The army would be totally rebuilt and restored to its former status. Zhirinovsky said, "I see such a Russia: she will have the most powerful army in the world, strategic rocket forces, air missiles with multiple warheads. Our space combat platforms, our spaceship... missiles—this will be the missile shield of the country."[23]

During the winter 1993 election campaign, the Liberal Democratic Party concentrated more than any other party in recruiting candidates from the military, especially from mid-level officers. The result exceeded the most optimistic expectations of Zhirinovsky's colleagues. A stunned President Yeltsin revealed that one-third of the vote in the military went to the Liberal Democratic Party, no doubt a significant source of its electoral success. Chauvinism in the ranks of the military was not altogether surprising. It will be recalled that much of the ideological indoctrination in the military as late as 1991 rested upon extremist nationalism, xenophobia, and virulent antisemitism.

This earlier ideological indoctrination was extended and reinforced by what one perceptive U.S. military analyst called a national mobilization campaign built around "a shared image of a 'foreign enemy.'" The enemy was the United States "as a power," and "Zionism as an ideology."[24] Zhirinovsky has sharply castigated U.S. policy toward Serbia and Iraq, as well as U.S. efforts to bring Russia into NATO.

Still, in the long run, Zhirinovsky anticipated that the U.S. threat might diminish. Like Hitler, he expected that America would be enervated by its expanding racial minorities. Zhirinovsky expected the black population to increase to about 100 million, and that the number of Hispanics would

---

[22] Kipp, "Zhirinovsky Threat," 76–77.

[23] Ibid., 85–85.

[24] Ibid., 85.

also increase. He predicted that eventually one-half of America would be colored, and reproducing at such a rapid rate (along with an increase in crime, to which colored races were prone), that "who knows, maybe America will be seeking help from Russia in the mid-21st century?"[25]

That Zhirinovsky's popularity is linked to the massive economic and social problems afflicting Russia seems clear enough. Inflation and declining productivity were and are greatly aggravated by a burgeoning crime wave, a widening chasm between rich and poor, and of course, a deepening sense of national humiliation following upon the collapse of the communist order and the disintegration of empire. An extraordinarily clever, witty, articulate, and charismatic demagogue, touching all the buttons of discontent, cannot fail to evoke a powerful public response. Since these elements are not likely to diminish significantly over the next few years, Zhirinovsky's support will hardly disappear.

He has boasted to all concerned that he intends to win the next race for president of Russia in 1996. In the last presidential vote in spring 1991, Zhirinovsky, as a veritable political novice, performed strikingly well, winning 6.8 million votes (almost eight percent of the total). In the party preference vote for the Russian parliament, the size of Zhirinovsky's Liberal Democratic Party vote suggested a potential for doubling the 1991 vote.[26]

On the eve of the 1993 balloting, a leading independent Russian journal took an opinion poll of the populace which revealed that Zhirinovsky's approval rating was twenty-five percent, while Boris Yeltsin's reached thirty-eight percent. Yet the party backing Yeltsin lagged far behind, and given Zhirinovsky's strong showing in the race, it may very well be that his personal popularity may increase.

A survey of public opinion in late March 1994 by the respected Russian Center for Public Opinion and Market Research showed that sixty-three percent said that they did not trust Zhirinovsky at all.[27] Still, in the course of the time leading up to the election, public attitudes could change, especially if current social and economic conditions do not

---

[25] Heritage Foundation, *Zhirinovsky,* 8–9.

[26] Alexander J. Motyl, "Vladimir Zhirinovsky: A Man of His Times," Harriman Review, May–June 1994, 14.

[27] Cited in Celestine Bohlen, "Zhirinovsky Cult Grows: All Power to the Leader," *New York Times,* 5 April 1994.

significantly improve. Besides, public attitudes do not always translate into votes.

A victory for Zhirinovsky in spring 1996 cannot be ruled out. As a top specialist at Columbia University's Harriman Institute, Professor Alexander Motyl noted in mid-1994 that Zhirinovsky's "schemes" are dangerous, not because they represent marginal thinking, but rather "because they are so mainstream."[28]

For Russian Jews, a Zhirinovsky electoral victory would no doubt prove cataclysmic. His beliefs resonate with Pamyat ideology and anti-Zionist demonology. It makes no difference whatsoever that Zhirinovsky is part Jewish, having been born in Alma-Ata, Kazakhstan of a Russian mother and Jewish father with the name of Eidelshtein, according to public records accessed by journalists.[29] The same records indicate that the young Zhirinovsky applied for and received permission to change his name in June 1964. He has vigorously denied that he is part Jewish and his spokesman told the Associated Press that "the documents clearly have been forged."

Yet, Zhirinovsky retained the patronymic Volfovich, a characteristically Jewish middle name. Moreover, in 1983 he took steps to seek an invitation from Israel in order to emigrate; this initiative, which required some indication of Jewish origin was not pursued. Later still, in 1990, he was known to have participated in the Jewish organization Shalom, a newly-formed group which sought to challenge the major Jewish community group, the Vaad. Zhirinovsky has almost violently rejected any intimations of his Jewish origins and connections. Even if the evidence proved overwhelming, Zhirinovsky was certain not to modify his anti-Zionism and Jew-baiting. Self-hate, psychoanalysts have shown, can be a powerful motivating factor in a person's outlook and ideology.

Jews are not alone in being frightened of a possible Zhirinovsky victory, or of what Motyl has called the "truly frightening phenomenon" of "Zhirinovskyism" in Russia, yet not until mid-1994 did major American serious and academic journals express profound concern over this threat.[30] When Israeli Prime Minister Yitzchak Rabin, on an unprecedented visit to Moscow on April 25, 1994 raised the Zhirinovsky

---

[28] Motyl, "Zhirinovsky," 14.
[29] *Washington Post*, 4 April 1994.
[30] Motyl, "Zhirinovsky," 18.

question with Russian Prime Minister Viktor S. Chernomyrdin, the latter said that "no Zhirinovsky will be able to incite" a serious upsurge of antisemitism in Russia.[31]

Chernomyrdin continued with a determined commitment: "I can tell you unequivocally that this [Zhirinovsky incitement of antisemitism] will not happen." The Russian hatemonger and others like him may have sought "to agitate the whole country" thereby provoking Judeophobia, but, promised the prime minister, the Jews "in the world, in our country and in Israel have nothing to worry about."

Two months later, on June 21, Chernomyrdin met with American Jewish leaders in Washington and offered similar assurances. He told the group that the overwhelming majority of Russians do not share the feelings of Zhirinovsky and, indeed, manifest a general antipathy toward chauvinists.[32]

The evidence, however, is not always encouraging. Indeed, Rabin was told by the speaker of the parliament, Ivan S. Rybkin, that antisemitism was endemic in Russia, even if only a small minority in rural areas expressed the kind of "exotic views" articulated by Zhirinovsky.[33]

What remains missing, as was the case throughout the last half-dozen years, is a strong and consistent effort by the Kremlin to speak out against hate and to undertake a vigorous campaign on behalf of tolerance and understanding. President Yeltsin's long-time hesitancy to use his office as a "bully pulpit" was scarcely abridged. At a press conference on December 22, 1993, just ten days after the Zhirinovsky electoral success, he promised to deliver a speech sometime in the future against antisemitism and every form of chauvinism.[34] He has yet to fulfill that commitment.

The only forceful reference made by President Yeltsin toward bigotry took the form of a joint statement in Moscow on January 14, 1994 by U.S. President Bill Clinton and himself, largely the product of American

---

[31] Stephen Erlanger, "No Big Danger of Anti-Semitism, Russian Premier Tells Rabin," *New York Times,* 26 April 1994.

[32] A detailed summary of the meeting was prepared by the National Conference on Soviet Jewry in Washington, 21 June 1994.

[33] Erlanger, "No Big Danger."

[34] A transcript of Yeltsin's press conference was transmitted to Israeli officials by Dr. Baruch Gur of the Jewish Agency.

pressure. For the first time, Yeltsin participated in a statement on human rights which pledged both presidents "to work for the elimination of...xenophobia and anti-Semitism."[35] Most significantly, no mention of the statement was made in the Russian media. Moscow human rights activists have bitterly complained that no one in Russia has any idea that such a condemnation was ever made.

Whether Russian democratic leadership is able to cope with the Zhirinovsky threat before 1996 is rather unpredictable. Reformer Yegor Gaidar has warned that "Zhirinovsky must be seen as a symbol of something...very powerful."[36] He recalled that "we have already seen what it means to ignore this threat." Only a short time remains for Russia to be put to a critical test.

---

[35] Statement released by the Russian White House, 14 January 1994.
[36] Spector, "Zhirinovsky and the Motherland," 44.

# Index

Abalkin, Leonid, 157
Academy of Sciences, 135, 146, 167
   *International Zionism: History and Politics*, 56–59
   *Zionism in the Chain of Imperialism*, 79
Afanasyev, Viktor, 168
Afanasyev, Yuri, 169, 173, 185
"Afghantsi", 139
*Against Zionism and Israeli Aggression*, 39–40
*Agitator*, 17–18, 24, 38
Aleichem, Sholem, 106
Aleksandrov, A., 108
Aleksandrovsky, B., 66–67
All-Russian Society for the Preservation of Historical and Cultural Monuments, 131
All-Union Central Council of Trade Unions, 91
All-Union Council of Trade Unions, 172
"Alliance of Victims of Political Reprisals of 1985–90's, Slavic Assembly", 203–04
Alliluyeva, Svetlana (Stalin's daughter), 9, 10
Alpernas, Gregory, 161
America. *See* United States
*America–A Zionist Colony* (S. Dasuki), 17
American Jewish Committee, 146
American Jewish Joint Distribution Committee ("Joint"), 16, 83–84
Ananev, Anatoly, 165
Andizhan, 123
Andreyev, Kim, 136, 140
Andreyeva, Nina, 166, 167–68, 169, 172
Anti-Fascist Center of the Russian Federation, 206

Antisemitism. *See also* Official policy
   denied, 75, 77, 88, 120, 176, 182
   denounced, 75, 76–77, 179
   equated with Zionism, 44, 83, 85
   justified, 28–29
   political uses, 167–68, 169, 170, 171, 172, 183
Antisemitism law, 163
Anti-Zionist Committee, 86–114, 193
Antonov, Mikhail, 164–65
Apartheid, 50, 55
*Aprel*, 143–44, 184
Architecture, 128, 130, 198
Arendt, Hannah, 10
*Argumenty i fakty*, 113
Armed forces, 51, 195–96, 197–98, 211, 226
Arms dumping, 50
Article 36. *See* Russian Criminal Code
Article 74. *See* Russian Criminal Code
Association of Russian Artists, 164
Association of Soviet Lawyers, 110, 111
Astafiev, Viktor, 152
Astakhov, S., 43, 55
*At The Outer Limit* (V. Pikul), 154
*August 1, 1914* (N. Yakovlev), 69

Babel, Isaac, 158
Babi Yar ceremonies: antisemitism address, 204–06
Bakatin, Vadim, 200–201
Bakhmin, Viacheslav, 207–08
Baku, 123
Banking system: control of, 2, 4, 12, 38, 56–57
Barabashev, Dmitri, 172
Barruel Memoirs, 61
Beglov, I. I.: *The USA–Property and Power*, 58

Begun, Vladimir, 27, 83, 84, 126, 133, 149–50
  *The Creeping Counter-revolution*, 27–29, 35, 36, 37
  *Invasion Without Arms*, 29
  *Tales of a "Widow's Children"*, 68
*Behind the Screens of the Masons* (V. V. Malyshev), 68
Beiliss case, 3, 6, 75, 148–49
Belayev, Igor, 91, 95
Belov, Vasily, 153
  *Everything Lies Ahead*, 153
Benfrand, Aleksandr, 145
Bent, Silas, 43
Bertrand, Abbé: *Freemasonry, Jewish Sect*, 62
*Beware: Zionism!* (Y. Ivanov), 20–21, 58
Bilderburg Club, 66
Billington, James, 200
*Black Book* (Ehrenburg and Grossman), 187
*Black Hundred and the Red Hundred, The* (V. Ostretsov), 196–98
Black Hundreds, 3, 5, 74, 152–53, 158
Blackwell, Kenneth, 204
Blood libel, 212–14. *See also* Beiliss case
B'nai B'rith, 26, 49, 52, 65, 66, 69, 110
Bolshakov, Vladimir, 22, 23, 58, 99
Bolshevik (October) Revolution, 2, 139, 140, 141, 153, 158–59
Bondarev, Yuri, 157, 199
Bondarevsky, Gregory, 90, 107
Bonner, Yelena, 189–90
Book of Joshua, 50
Brazil, 32
Brezhnev, Leonid, 44, 75–76, 77, 78, 83
Briusova, Vera, 164
Brown, George, 38
Buivolov, Anatoly, 159
Bund, 15, 16
Burliaev, Nikolai: *Lermontov*, 150
Bush, George, 205
Byelorussia, 123, 192

Cairo, 17
Capitalism, 12, 38, 164, 169, 170
Cardin, Shoshona, 205
Carter administration, 25–26, 66
Cartoons, 12, 65, 203–04
*Catechism of a Jew in the USSR*, 161
Catherine II, Tsarina "the Great", 5, 70
Central Committee, 8–9, 79, 80, 81
Central Intelligence Agency (CIA), 47, 53
Chauvinism, 9–10, 80, 125, 179, 180, 220
Chebrikov, Vladimir, 189
Chelyabinsk, 161
*Chelyabinsk Worker*, 161–62
Chernenko, Konstantin, 44, 85
Chernichenko, Yuri, 185
Chernomyrdin, Viktor S., 229
Chlenov, Mikhail, 217
"Chosen people" concept, 4, 34, 36, 42, 44, 54, 58, 64, 83, 100
Christian Patriotic Union, 139
Chuyev, Feliks, 199
CIA (Central Intelligence Agency), 47, 53
Clannishness, Jewish, 36, 57
*Class Essence of Zionism* (L. Korneyev), 96
Clinton, Bill, (U.S. President), 229–30
Cohn, Norman: *Warrant for Genocide*, 15
"Combatting Racism, Xenophobia and Anti-Semitism" seminar, 216–17
Commission on Security and Cooperation in Europe (CSCE), 201, 202–04, 205, 217–18
*Communist of the Armed Forces*, 51
Concentration camps, 158, 163
Conference on Security and Cooperation in Europe, 77
Congress of Jewish Organizations, 124, 142, 145, 176, 187–88
Congress of People's Deputies, 169, 170, 172, 174–75, 193–94, 199

Conspiracy theories, 12, 208. *See also* Freemasonry
  Masonic-Jewish, 2, 4, 170
  Masonic-Zionist, 25–26, 120, 133, 150, 155, 160
Cooperatives, 122, 170
Cosmopolitanism, 9, 19, 131, 160, 164
  "anti-cosmopolitan" campaign, 8, 178
Council of Europe, 77, 216
Council of People's Commissars, 160
*Creeping Counter-revolution, The* (V. Begun), 27–29, 35, 36, 37
"Crimes" of Zionism, 55–56
CSCE. *See* Commission on Security and Cooperation in Europe
Cuba, 31–32
Culture
  destruction of, 36–37
  Jewish, 47, 98, 101, 182
  Russian, 164
  western, 156
*Curtain Rises, The* (Y. Kolesnikov), 103–06
Czechoslovakia, 19, 20, 28, 37

Dadiani, L., 39
Dahomey (Benin), 32
Dasuki, Saleh: *America–A Zionist Colony*, 17
Decembrists, 70
Defense, Ministry of, 19–20, 195–96, 198
Degtyar, Yelena, 128
Demonstrations, 173, 210, 219
  Pamyat, 129–30, 135, 136, 141–44, 174
*Den*, 196, 220
*Der Spiegel*: opinion poll, 137–38
Desecration of Jewish cemetaries, 141, 207
Deutscher, Isaac, 8
*Dezionization* (V. Yemelyanov), 26
*Dialogue aux Enfers entre Montesquieu et Machiavel* (M. Joly), 72–73
*Die Deutsche Nationale-Zeitung*, 224

Discrimination against Jews, 5, 9, 88. *See also* Employment; Higher education
Djilas, Milovan, 8
*Dnipro*, 39
Doctors' Plot, 8, 16, 84, 178
Domination. *See also* Banking system; Press
  of key posts, 2, 4, 35, 36, 60, 139, 151
  of the world, 4, 24, 28, 36, 58
Doroshenko, Nikolai, 172
Dragunsky, David Abramovich, 87, 100, 103
  Anti-Zionist Committee, 90, 91–92, 93, 97, 98–99, 100, 107
  *A Soldier's Memoirs*, 112–13
Dreyfus case, 62
Drumont, Edouard, 61–62
*Druzhina*, 222–23
Dual citizenship, 19–20
Dubcek, Alexander, 19, 25, 37, 169
Dubrovin, A. I., 3
Dyskin, Semyon, 187

Ebla tablets, 52
Economic equality, 122
Economic situation
  and antisemitism, 121–22, 208, 215
  and Nazism, 124
  and Zhirinovsky, 227
Education, higher. *See* Higher education
Educational campaign, 186–88
Efremov, Oleg, 133
Ehrenburg, Ilya, 8, 87
  *Black Book*, 187
Elections, 170–72, 199, 219, 220, 227
Elizaveta, Tsarina, 5
Elizavetgrad, 5
Elon, Amos, 72
Emigration, Jewish, 144, 159, 182
  campaigns to reduce, 81, 88, 89, 90, 93–95, 101–03
  refuseniks, 94

Emigration, Jewish–*cont'd*
  triggers for, 6, 81–82, 121, 145,
    172–73, 183–84
Employment: and Jews, 9, 11, 116, 118,
  179
*Energetica*, 145
England, 49
Ethiopia, 45
Ethnic groups, 76
Ethnic rights, 3
Ethnic tensions, 122
European Jewish Congress, 216
European map, 224–25
*Everything Lies Ahead* (V. Belov), 153
Exclusivity, Jewish, 36
Expulsion of Jews, 3, 84, 87

Fadeyev, Valery, 207
Fascism, 2, 162, 185, 200, 201
  Zionism linked with, 33–34, 36, 38,
    83, 108, 159
*Fascism Under the Blue Star*
  (Y. Yevseev), 27
Feinstein, Oleg, 184
Fifth columns, 58, 66, 133
Filatov, S., 134–35
Filatov, Viktor, 195–96, 212
*Final Thrust South, The*
  (V. Zhirinovsky), 225
Finkel, Yevgeniia, 108
Fishman, Yakov, 90–91
Ford, Henry, 42, 43
Foreign Ministry, 213
Foundation for Slavic Writing and Slavic
  Culture, 163–64
France, 222
Freemasonry, 25, 60–73, 132, 140,
  150
*Freemasonry, Jewish Sect*
  (Abbé Bertrand), 62
*French Masonry-Synagogue of Satan*
  (L. Meurin), 62
Frey, Gerhard, 224
Frumkin, Semyon, 173

Gafurov, B. G., 89
Gaidar, Yegor, 223, 230
Garrard, John and Carol, 158, 159
Gauffin, Rolf, 224
Gazenko, Oleg, 174
Genocide, 27, 163, 203
Geremek, Bronislaw, 67, 151
German People's Union, 224
Germany, 62–63, 224, 225
Ginzburg, Moisei Yakovlevich, 128
Ginzburg, Vitaly, 174
Gitelman, Zvi, 115
Glasnost, 12, 119, 120–21
Glazer, Nathan, 111–12
Gluskova, Tatiana, 159
Goebbels, Joseph Paul, 64
Gofman, Genrikh, 90
Goldanskii, Vitalii I., 124, 125, 156–57,
  177–78
Goldin, Leonid, 214
Golenpolsky, Tankred, 212
*Golos rodiny*, 66, 67
Gorbachev, Mikhail, 113, 140, 153, 179,
  186, 187, 189–90, 200, 201
  antisemitism, 120, 176, 177, 179,
    180–81, 190, 202, 204–06
  glasnost policy, 12, 119, 120–21
  *Perestroika*, 177, 190
  resistance to, 151, 152, 166–69, 170,
    171, 177, 178
Gorbachov, Vyacheslav, 150
Gorky, Maxim, 148–49
Great Britain, 222
Great Purge, 161
Greinemann, Friar, 61
Grindberg, Nataliya, 101
Grossman, Vasily, 158, 165
  *Black Book*, 187
Gulbinsky, Nikolai, 154
Gutionov, Pavel, 194–95

Haiser, Franz, 63
Helsinki conferences, 77, 86, 93,
  181–82, 202–03, 217–18

## Index

Herzl, Theodor, 72, 73, 100
Higher education: and Jews, 9, 11, 101, 116–18, 145, 179
Himmler, Heinrich, 64
Historiography
  Israeli, 108–09
  Jewish, 12, 187–88
Hitler, Adolf, 8, 36, 37, 63, 100, 222
  *Mein Kampf*, 5, 63, 195, 198
Holocaust, 109, 158, 163
  suppression of texts, 12, 165, 187, 192
Honeywell Corporation, 68
"House of Friendship": press conference, 88
Human Rights Committee, 214–16
Hungarian Radio, 140
Hussein, Saddam, 195

Identity, Jewish, 47, 98
Ideological Commission, 12
Ignatyev, Count Nikolai P., 6
Ilyaev, Gavriel, 102
Immigration: Jewish, 5
Imperialism, 22–23, 42, 68, 90
*Imperialism, the Highest Stage of Capitalism* (V. I. Lenin), 74
*In the Name of the Father and the Son* (I. Shevtsov), 21–22
*In the Service of Aggression* (V. A. Stefankin), 68
Intellectual antisemitism, 125
Intelligentsia, 147–59, 183. *See also* Writers' Union
Interfronts, 172
International Conference on the Problems of Israel and Zionism, 58
*International Zionism: History and Politics*, 56–59
*Invasion Without Arms* (V. Begun), 29
Investment firms, 57
Ioann, Metropolitan, 211
Islamic fundamentalism, 123

Israel
  assault on USSR, 95
  de-legitimization of, 31
  Jewish state, 225
  Lebanon policy, 97, 108
  life in, 40, 101–02
  military forces, 48, 88
  and South Africa, 50
  spiritual connection, 19–20, 47
  wealth, 221
  Zionism, 20, 38, 40, 43–44, 51–52, 58
Ivanov, K., 19, 20n
Ivanov, Yuri, 14n, 42–43, 71–72
  *Beware: Zionism!*, 20–21, 58
*Izvestiia*
  Anti-Zionist Committee, 93
  blood libel, 213
  Jewish activists, 53
  KGB chief, 201
  Pamyat, 120, 194–95
  Pogroms, 178
  Zhirinovsky, 223
  Zionism, 41–42, 46–47, 108

Javits, Jacob, 26
Jew-baiting, 207, 217
Jewish Cultural Association, 161
Jewish-Masonic conspiracy theory. *See* Conspiracy theories
*Jewish-Masonic Peril, The* (A. Tilloy), 62
Jewish state, 225
Jews
  descriptions of, 147, 221
  linked with racism, 47, 64
  prominent, 87, 89
Joint. *See* American Jewish Joint Distribution Committee
Joint Council of Russia, 170
Joly, Maurice, 72
  *Dialogue aux Enfers entre Montesquieu et Machiavel*, 72–73
Judaism: linked with Zionism, 12, 120, 193, 222

*Judaism and Zionism* (T. K. Kichko), 18–19
*Judaism Without Embellishment* (T. K. Kichko), 11–12, 18
Judeo-Masonic conspiracy theory. *See* Conspiracy theories

Kabachnik, Martin, 90
Kabanov, Mark, 184
Kaganovich, Lazar Moiseevich, 128, 154, 158, 160
Kahane, Rabbi Meir, 108
Kamenev, Lev, 154, 160
Kanovich, Grigory, 145, 174
Kazantsev, Aleksandr, 132–33
Kedrov, B., 79
Kerensky, Aleksandr, 25
Key positions: Jews in, 2, 4, 8–9, 11, 35, 36, 60, 139, 151
Keyes, Alan L., 45
KGB, 69, 174, 178, 194, 195, 201
Khatyushin, V., 154
Khrushchev, Nikita, 84
Kichko, Trofim K., 18, 39
　*Judaism and Zionism*, 18–19
　*Judaism Without Embellishment*, 11–12, 18
*Kino*, 37
Kirakozov, Vladimir, 215
Kirilenko, A. P., 78
Kiselev, V., 57
Kogan, Leonid, 175
Kolesnikov, Yuri, 90, 91, 93, 96, 106, 109
　*The Curtain Rises*, 103–06
*Komissar*, 173
*Kommunist*, 43, 157
*Komsomolskaia pravda*, 119
　B'nai B'rith, 52
　freemasons, 65–66
　Pamyat, 159
　pogroms, 145
　*Protocols*, 71–72
　UN resolution, 42
　Zionism, 16–17, 20, 54, 108

Konstantinov, Yuri, 17–18
Koretskii, Viktor, 124–25
Koretskoy, D., 39
Korneyev, Lev, 50–52, 67, 74, 82–83, 109, 162
　*Class Essence of Zionism*, 96
Korolenko, Vladimir G., 149
　*Yom Kippur*, 149
Korolev, Valentin, 195
Korotich, Vitaly, 120, 136, 171
Kosygin, Aleksei, 75, 78
Kovalev, Sergei, 214, 216
Kozyrev, Andrei, 217
Krall, Hanna, 151
*Krasnaia zvezda*, 20, 114
Kronstadt uprising, 7
Krupin, Vladimir, 157
Krupkin, Mark, 91, 97, 108
Krushchev, Nikita, 8, 11
Krushevan, Pavel. *See Protocols of the Elders of Zion*
Kryuchkov, Vladimir, 194, 196
Kudyukin, Pavel, 160
Kulakov, Aleksandr, 1, 139, 184–85
Kunyayev, Stanislav, 155–56, 157, 172, 212
Kuznetsov, Gennadi, 151–52

Lansky, Meyer, 51
Latsis, Otto, 157
Latvia, 123
Lebanon, 97, 100
Lecht, Yefim, 101–02
Leers, Johannes von (Omar Amin), 17
Lenin, Vladimir Ilyich, 7, 15–16, 63, 75, 174
　*Imperialism, the Highest Stage of Capitalism*, 74
Leningrad, 141, 173, 178, 199
Leo XIII, Pope, 62
*Lermontov* (N. Burliaev), 150
Lesota, Yelena, 157
Levitsky, Theodosius, 71

# Index

Liberal Democratic Party, 220, 221, 222, 223, 226, 227
Ligachev, Yegor, 164, 167, 168, 169
Likhachev, Dmitri, 133
Lilienthal, Alfred, 113
Lipavsky, Sanya, 53
*Literaturnaia gazeta*, 54, 89, 100, 178–79
*Literaturnaia Rossiia*, 39–40, 149, 162
Lithuania, 123
Litvinova, Salina, 172
*Love and Hate* (I. Shevtsov), 21
Ludendorff, Erich, 63
Lukyanov, Anatoly, 193–94

Makarov, Andrei, 185
Makashov, Albert, 219
Malik, Yakov, 33–34
Malmi, Valentina, 103–04
Malyshev, V. V.: *Behind the Screens of the Masons*, 68
Masonic societies, 2, 4. *See also* Freemasonry
Massacres, 123, 178. *See also* Pogroms
Massara, Massimo, 108
Media, 199–200, 230. *See also* Press
  antisemitism in, 81–82, 206
  official anti-Zionism campaign, 13–24, 34–35, 38–43, 60, 88
Medvedev, Roy, 81–82, 118
*Mein Kampf* (A. Hitler), 63, 195, 198
Meurin, Archbishop Leon: *French Masonry-Synagogue of Satan*, 62
*Mezhdunarodnaia zhizn*, 19, 40, 55
Middle East, 88, 97
Mikhalkov, Sergei, 199
Military, the. *See* Armed forces
*Military-Historical Journal*, 195
Military-industrial complexes, 50, 51, 57, 68
Minin, Igor, 221–22
Mishin, Vladimir, 117
Mitin, Mark B., 79
Modrzhiniskaia, E. D., 111

Modzhorian, Lydia, 111
  *Zionism as a Form of Racial Discrimination*, 44
Moldavia, 123, 192
*Molodaia gvardiia*, 149, 150, 151–52, 171, 195
Moscow: subway system, 126–27
Moscow City Komsomol Committee, 172
*Moscow News*, 130, 168, 174, 179, 195
Moscow Radio, 52, 100
Moscow State University, 117, 118
*Moskovskaia pravda*, 41, 50–51
*Moskovskii komsomolets*, 207, 212
*Moskva*, 35, 149, 154
Motyl, Alexander, 228
*Muhammed–the Messenger of Allah* (film), 52
Muratov, A., 185

Nagibin, Yuri, 177
Narodnaia Volia, 6
Narovchatov, Sergei, 79
*Nash sovremennik*, 154, 155, 156, 157, 206
  anti-Zionism, 149
  criticized, 151–52
  Defense Ministry, 195, 198
  Pamyat, 150, 158
"National Policies" resolution, 180–81
National Salvation Front, 209–11, 220
Nationalism, 9, 122–23, 163–64, 179
*Nauka i religiia*, 50
Nazism, 63–64, 87, 222–23
  linked with Zionism, 37, 54, 99–100, 105, 107–09, 111
*Nedelia*, 48–49, 55, 65, 106, 150, 159, 177
"Neo-colonialism", 58
Neuwirth, Edwin, 224
*Neva*, 67
*New Times*, 69, 99
*Nezavisimaia gazeta*, 206
Nicholas II, Tsar, 152, 158–59

Non-Jews, 25, 27–28, 36, 58
Novikov, Viktor, 172
Novit, Paul, 87
*Novoe vremia*, 56
Novosibirsk, 135, 180
Novosti Press Agency, 48, 91, 94, 96, 97, 113

October (Bolshevik) Revolution, 2, 139, 140, 141, 153, 158–59
Officer's Union, 211, 219
Official policy. *See also* Soviet Public Anti-Zionist Committee; "Zionism equals racism" resolution
  acceptance of Pamyat, 132, 134–36, 141–42, 173–74, 177, 194–95, 204
  antisemitism, 8–9, 10–11, 173–82, 199, 207–08, 214–17, 229–30
  anti-Zionism campaign, 13–29, 33–34, 45, 46–47, 74–85, 119, 182–83, 217
  *Ogonek*, 119, 154, 195
  *The Curtain Rises*, 103
  Pamyat, 127, 136, 171
  Zionism, 49–50, 54, 55, 120
Oil companies, 50
Okuneva, Ruth, 80–81
*On the Class Essence of Zionism* (A. Romanenko), 119–20
"Open Letter", 99
Opinion polls, 115–16, 122, 137, 145–46, 190–93, 208–09, 227
Organizations, antisemitic: and glasnost, 121
Organized crime, 51
Osipiyan, Yuri, 12
Ostretsov, Viktor: *The Black Hundred and the Red Hundred*, 196–98
*Otechestvo*, 121, 134

Pachtler, G. M., 61
Palestine Research Center, 58
Pamyat, 1, 121, 183, 197, 208–09, 211, 219
  activism, 125–45
  Article 74 trials, 184–86
  *The Black Hundred and the Red Hundred*, 196–98
  *Catechism of a Jew in the USSR*, 161
  criminal investigations, 178–79, 180
  criticized, 120
  CSCE parallel conference, 203–04
  demonstrations, 129–30, 135, 136, 141–44, 174
  elections, 170–72
  libel trial, 212
  *Moskovskii komsomolets* raid, 207
  official acceptance, 132, 134–36, 141–42, 173–74, 177, 194–95, 204
  "Proclamation", 136–37
  "quiet seizure of power" meeting, 172
  *Sobesednik* article, 160–61
  splinter groups, 138–39
  supporting writers, 13, 26, 126, 147, 150, 152–53, 157–58
  Yeltsin, 135–36, 202, 220
Pamyat II, 138
Panis, René, 77
Pashkin, Yevgeny, 128
Pashnin, Yevgeny, 139
Pasqually, Martinez de, 71
Pasternak, Boris, 158
Patrice Lumumba University, 224
"Patriot", 138
Patriotic Front, 173
Pavlov, S.: *Vendetta: American-Style*, 68
Pavlov, Valentin, 196
People's Russian Orthodox Movement, 1, 144
Perestroika, 124
  anti-perestroika forces, 164, 166–69, 170, 171, 179, 183, 196
*Perestroika* (M. Gorbachev), 177, 190
Peysner, S., 161–62
Pigalev, Vadim, 65, 67
Pikul, Valentin, 154
  *At The Outer Limit*, 154

*Pionerskaia pravda*, 82–83
"Plan of Measures to Strengthen Anti-Zionist Propaganda", 23
Pobedinsky, Aleksandr, 139
*Pochvenniki* (nativists), 156
Podgorny, Nikolai, 78
*Pogranichnik*, 195
Pogroms
  denounced, 147–48
  fear of, 145, 146, 178, 204
  Jews and, 44, 196–97, 221
  justified, 44
  triggers, 48, 75, 143
  Ukraine, 4–5, 197
  Uzbekistan, 123
  Zionists and, 141, 163
Poland, 28, 67, 116, 151
Polezhaev, V., 65–66
Policy, governmental. *See* Official policy
Popov, Gavril, 157
Popular antisemitism, 6–7, 49, 121, 124, 216
"Popular Orthodox Movement of Russia Pamyat", 139
*Pravda*, 40, 88, 168, 177, 211, 220
  antisemitism, 3, 75, 182
  anti-Zionist campaign, 182–84
  anti-Zionist Committee, 89, 91, 114, 193
  blood libel, 212–14
  Pamyat, 3, 120, 183
  writers, 74, 147, 183
  Zionism, 21, 22–23, 27, 99, 193
*Pravda Ukrainy*, 41, 42
Pre-Hitler era: parallels with, 123–24, 159
Press. *See also* Media
  control of, 2, 4, 13–14, 18, 20–21, 35, 50, 221
Printing equipment, 3, 78–79, 198
Prokhanov, Aleksandr, 196
Prokofev, Yuri, 142
Prostitution, 55, 120

*Protocols of the Elders of Zion* (P. Krushevan), 42, 63, 198, 211
  authenticity, 15, 155, 195–96, 212
  influence, 4, 5, 15, 56, 62–63, 71–73
  origin, 4
  Pamyat, 126, 129, 132, 133, 139
  themes in, 4, 55, 63
Pseudonyms, 155–56
Psychological pressure: and Nazism, 124
Pugacheva, Alla, 133
Purishkevich, V. M., 2, 3, 197

*Questions of CPSU History*, 119
Quota systems, 8, 9, 11, 116–18, 145

Rabin, Yitzchak, 228–29
Racial incitement, 215–16
Racism. *See also* "Zionism equals racism" resolution
  Jews linked with, 47, 64
  open propagation of, 173
  Zionism linked with, 33, 38, 43–44, 162
Radio Moscow, 113, 120
Raevsky, Vadim, 65
Rasputin, G. E., 28
Rasputin, Valentin, 152–53, 158, 179, 209
Reagan, Ronald, 95, 101, 113
"Red-Brown" alliance, 209, 210, 219
Rees, Goronwy, 30–31
Religion: campaign against, 11
Reshetov, Yuri, 142
Ribbentrop, Joachim von, 8
Riverov, Yuri, 138
Rogers, William P., 32
Rogov, Sergei, 77–78, 147, 182–84
*Roman-gazeta*, 103
Romanenko, Aleksandr, 126, 138, 203
  *On the Class Essence of Zionism*, 119–20
Romanov, Grigory, 78
Rosenberg, Alfred, 63

RSFSR Writers' Union. *See* Writers' Union
*Rukh*, 122–23
"Rus", 138
Russian Center for Public Opinion and Market Research, 208, 227
Russian Criminal Code
　Article 36, 176
　Article 74, 176, 206, 215–16
　Article 74 trials, 179–80, 184–86
Russian Liberation Movement, 139
Russian Liberation Organization, 78
Russian Orthodox Church, 5
Russian Orthodox National Patriotic Front Pamyat, 139
Russian Popular Party, 139
Russian Republic's Writers' Union. *See* Writers' Union
Russophobia, 152, 170, 180, 181
*Russophobia* (I. Shafarevich), 156
Ryazanov, Vasily, 80
Rybkin, Ivan S., 229

Safonov, Ernst, 162, 172
Saint-Martin, Henri de, 71
Sakharov, Andrei D., 31, 91, 118, 189–90
Salm-Horstmar, Prince Otto von, 63
Sazanov, Anatoly Aleksandrovich, 81
Scapegoats
　Jews, 10, 122
　Zionism, 14
Schary, Dore, 72
Scientific Center of Palestinian Research, 58
*Secret and the Overt* (film), 37–38
*Secret Societies and Subversive Movements* (H. H. Webster), 43
Security, Ministry of, 201, 202
*Selskaia zhizn*, 41
Serbia, 211
Sereda, Anatoly, 179–80
Shafarevich, Igor, 209
　*Russophobia*, 156
Shalom, 228

Shayevich, Chief Rabbi Adolf, 207, 214
Shazar, Zalman, 112–13
Shcharansky, Anatoly, 47, 75
Sheinin, Boris, 90
Sheremet, N., 161–62
Shevardnadze, Eduard, 178, 196
Shevtsov, Ivan, 21
　*In the Name of the Father and the Son*, 21–22
　*Love and Hate*, 21
Shkolnik, Leonid, 101, 107
Shmakov, Aleksei, 74–75
Shmelev, Nikolai, 157
Shmukler, Aleksandr, 122
Shtilmark, Aleksandr, 160, 161
Shulmeister, Yulian, 107–08
Sidoruk, K., 139
Simanovich, Aron, 28
Simon Wiesenthal Documentation Center, 65
Skurlatov, Valery Ivanovich, 64n
　*Zionism and Apartheid*, 64
Slansky, Rudolf, 16
Slepak, Vladimir, 48
Smirnov-Ostashvili, Konstantin, 139, 184, 185, 186, 195
Smolyanin, German, 193
*Sobesednik*, 160
Socialism: and Zionism, 46
Sokol, Yuri, 201, 202
*Soldier's Memoirs, A* (D. A. Dragunsky), 112–13
Solidarity, 67
Solodar, Tsezar, 53n, 55, 92
　*Wild Wormwood*, 53–55
Solomon, King, 26
Soloviev, Vladimir S., 148
Solzhenitsyn, Aleksandr, 25
Somalia, 31
*Sotsialisticheskaia industriia*, 50
South Africa, 50
*Sovetskaia Byelorussiia*, 68, 83
*Sovetskaia kultura*, 48, 119, 127–28, 149–50

*Sovetskaia kultura–cont'd*
  Pamyat, 134
  Theodor Herzl, 72, 73
  UN resolution, 43
  Zionism, 49, 54–55
*Sovetskaia Rossiia*, 206, 220
  anti-perestroika appeals, 166–68, 196, 199–200
  *Protocols*, 211
  Zionism, 41, 193
*Sovetskii voin*, 67
Soviet Academy of Sciences, 47, 88–89, 118, 132
Soviet Center for Public Opinion and Market Research, 190
*Soviet Circus*, 125
Soviet Committee for Solidarity with the Peoples of Asia and Africa, 91
Soviet Public Anti-Zionist Committee, 86–114, 193
Spain, 119
Stalin, Josef, 8–9, 10, 75, 84, 87, 154, 155, 167, 169
Stefankin, V. A.: *In the Service of Aggression*, 68
Stereotypes, negative, 6, 7, 12, 13–14, 104, 160
Stolypin, Peter, 131
Subversive activity, 49–50, 51–52, 55–56, 90
Surnames, Russian: taken by Jews, 155–56
Surveys. *See* Opinion polls
Suslov, Mikhail, 78
Sverdlov, Yakov, 141, 160
Sverdlovsk, 134
Sveshnikov, Aleksandr, 139
Sychev, Igor, 138, 195
Symbols, 127–28, 141
Synagogues, 28
Syria, 97

*Tales of a "Widow's Children"* (V. Begun), 68

Talmud, 28
TASS, 21, 48, 56, 59, 91, 120, 167, 178, 179
  Anti-Zionist Committee, 89, 100, 109, 111, 114, 193
Tekoah, Mr., 33
Television: "Traders of Souls", 47–49, 50
Terekhov, Stanislav, 211
Thule Society, 63
Tilloy, Monsignor Anselme: *The Jewish-Masonic Peril*, 62
Tolmassky, Ilya, 102
Tolstoy, Count Ilya, 149
Tolstoy, Lev. N., 147–48
*Top Secret*, 56
Torah, 25, 27, 28, 29
Totalitarianism, 9, 10
"Traders of Souls" documentary, 47–49, 50
Tree, Marietta, 32
Trotsky, Lev, 22, 63, 154–55, 160
*Trud*, 40–41
Tsarism, 70, 140
Tsypin, L., 53

Ukraine, 4–5, 122–23, 192, 204
UN. *See* United Nations
Unemployment, 124
Union for the Revival of the Motherland, 164
Union for the Spiritual Revival of the Fatherland, 164
Union of Officers, 211, 219
Union of Proportional Representation-Pamyat, 139
Union of Russian People, 1–4
Union of Russian Workers, 168–69
Union of the Russian People, 196, 197
United Front of Workers of Russia, 170, 171
United Nations (UN), 32–33, 45. *See also* "Zionism equals racism" resolution

United States, 32, 100, 113, 155, 226–27
  American imperialism, 22, 68
  antisemitism, 109–10
  blood libel, 213
  Carter administration, 25–26, 66
  Zionism, 17, 38, 42, 49, 50, 95, 100–101, 222
University admission. *See* Higher education
Urban, Jerzy, 36
*USA–Property and Power, The* (I. I. Beglov), 58
Uspensky, Inna Joffe, 172–73
Uzbekistan, 123

Vaad, 193
Vasiliev, Dmitri, 131–32, 135, 138, 174, 195, 207, 211
  speeches, 126–27, 128–29, 130, 132, 134, 140–41
*Vechernaia Moskva*, 48, 53, 56, 206
*Vendetta: American-Style* (S. Pavlov), 68
"Verbitsky, Soloman" (L. Korneyev), 67
Verevkin, Dmitri, 174
Vergelis, Aron, 90, 101, 107
*Vestnik yevreiskoi sovetskoi kultury*, 175
Vikulov, Sergei, 150, 158
Violence against Jews, 3–4, 144, 207, 215. *See also* Pogroms
Vladimirsky, V., 40
*Voprosy istorii*, 39
Voznesensky, Andrei, 133

Waldheim, Kurt, 186
*Warrant for Genocide* (N. Cohn), 15
Webster, Hesta H.: *Secret Societies and Subversive Movements*, 43, 72
Weishaupt, Adam, 62
Werblan, Andrzej, 116
West, the: and Soviet antisemitism, 77, 86, 101, 109
Western culture, 156, 164, 170

*White Book* (1979), 110–11
*White Book* (1985), 110, 111–12
*Wild Wormwood* (T. Solodar), 53–55
Witte, Count Sergei, 2
Woll, Josephine, 153–54
World domination, 4, 24, 28, 36, 58
World Jewish Congress, 38
World Zionist Organization, 38
Writers' Union, 152, 157–59, 162–63, 165, 198–99

Yakovlev, Aleksandr, 134, 144, 151, 166, 168, 173, 181, 205
Yakovlev, Nikolai, 69
  *August 1, 1914*, 69
Yakovlev, Yegor, 130
Yakushev, Vladimir, 171
Yarim, Veniamin, 179
Yaroslavsky, Yemelian (Yemelyan), 128, 154, 160
Yazov, Dmitri, 166, 195, 196, 198
Yedinstvo, 172
Yeltsin, Boris, 200, 203, 206, 210, 219, 220, 223, 227
  antisemitism, 180, 201–02, 214, 229–30
  Pamyat, 135–36, 202, 220
Yemelyanov, Valery, 24–26, 52–53, 66, 126, 127, 130, 135, 138, 195
  *Dezionization*, 26
*Yevreiskaia gazeta*, 206
Yevseev, Yevgeny (Yevgenii), 38, 41, 48, 52, 58, 126
  *Fascism Under the Blue Star*, 27
  *Zionism in the Chain of Imperialism*, 79
Yevtushenko, Yevgeny, 8, 121, 157, 175
*Yom Kippur* (V. G. Korolenko), 149
Young people: and Zionism, 39

*Za rubezhom*, 43
Zakharov, Dmitri, 142
*Zapadniki* (Westernizers), 156

Zaslavskaia, Tatiana, 133, 157, 162–63, 175
Zhirinovsky, Vladimir, 200, 204, 220–21, 222, 223–30
*The Final Thrust South*, 225
Zhukov, Dmitri, 35–37
Zimanas, Genrikhas, 90
Zinoviev, Grigory, 154, 160
Zionism. *See also* Official policy
  "crimes" of, 55–56
  denounced, 76, 99
  descriptions of, 13–15, 16–20, 23, 25, 28, 35–37, 46–47
  equated with antisemitism, 44, 83, 85
  linked with fascism. *See* Fascism
  linked with Judaism. *See* Judaism
  linked with Nazism. *See* Nazism
  linked with racism. *See* Racism
  Pamyat's "Proclamation", 136–37
*Zionism and Apartheid* (V. I. Skurlatov), 64
*Zionism as a Form of Racial Discrimination* (L. Modzhorian), 44
"Zionism equals racism" resolution, 30–35, 40, 41–42, 43–45, 56, 86, 162, 186
*Zionism in the Chain of Imperialism* (Y. Yevseev), 79
Zionist-Masonic conspiracy theory. *See* Conspiracy theories
Zionist Union, 114
Zionists: descriptions of, 78, 89, 221–22
Zivs, Samuil
  and antisemitic books, 95–96
  Anti-Zionist Committee, 90, 91, 92, 93, 98, 111
  Jewish emigration, 94, 102
  Zionism, 95, 107
Znanie Society, 23, 24
Zyuganov, Gennadi, 209